Transport and the

Economic Integration of South America

Transport and

the Economic Integration

of South America

Robert T. Brown

The Brookings Institution

TRANSPORT RESEARCH PROGRAM

Washington, D.C.

THE BROOKINGS INSTITUTION is an independent organization devoted to nonpartisan research, education, and publication in economics, government, foreign policy, and the social sciences generally. Its principal purposes are to aid in the development of sound public policies and to promote public understanding of issues of national importance.

The Institution was founded December 8, 1927, to merge the activities of the Institute for Government Research, founded in 1916, the Institute of Economics, founded in 1922, and the Robert Brookings Graduate School of Economics and Government, founded in 1924.

The general administration of the Institution is the responsibility of a self-perpetuating Board of Trustees. The trustees are likewise charged with maintaining the independence of the staff and fostering the most favorable conditions for creative research and education. The immediate direction of the policies, program, and staff of the Institution is vested in the President, assisted by the division directors and an advisory council, chosen from the professional staff of the Institution.

In publishing a study, the Institution presents it as a competent treatment of a subject worthy of public consideration. The interpretations and conclusions in such publications are those of the author or authors and do not purport to represent the views of the other staff members, officers, or trustees of the Brookings Institution.

Foreword

Economic development efforts in Latin America have been focused primarily on the problems and potentials of individual countries in isolation. This study attempts to present in broad outline a transportation strategy for the whole continent.

The basic assumption is that Latin American economic progress requires larger export markets, a wider geographic distribution of industrial activity, and a greatly improved international transport network to support a common market approach. The purpose of the research was to inquire into what specific transportation policies and programs are required to overcome the physical barriers that stand in the way.

This report is one of a series of studies of the Transport Research Program at Brookings, financed by a grant from the United States Agency for International Development. The author, Robert T. Brown, came to Brookings on leave from the Institute of Economic Research at the University of Chile. Following his project here, he returned to Santiago as a staff member of the AID-sponsored Chile-California Program.

The reading committee included Joseph Grunwald, John R. Meyer, and Harvey S. Perloff. Daniel Marx, Jr. served on an earlier committee to review the maritime aspects of the study. The author wishes to extend his thanks to Antonio Casas and Margery S. Coen, who served as research assistants, and to Edwin T. Haefele and George W. Wilson for their helpful suggestions. Evelyn Breck edited the manuscript and Adele Garrett prepared the index. Valuable research materials, ideas, and criticisms were obtained from many people connected with the governments of the United States and of several South American countries as well as from representatives of the maritime transport industry in both North and South America.

The Transport Research Program, under Wilfred Owen, is part of the Economic Studies Division, which is directed by Joseph A. Pechman.

Opinions expressed by the author do not purport to represent the views of the Agency for International Development, or the trustees, officers, or other staff members of the Brookings Institution.

Robert D. Calkins
President

April 1966
Washington, D.C.

Contents

CHAPTER I

A Regional Approach to Transport Planning in South America

WHAT IS THE RELATIONSHIP of transport to the economic integration of South America? Interest in this question has increased greatly in recent years, largely as a result of the formation of the Latin American Free Trade Association (LAFTA) in 1961. It has been stimulated, too, by the growing belief that South American nations must expand their exports if they are to develop, and that new export markets may well be found more easily among their South American neighbors than outside this area.

This study presents an analysis of the role of transport in economic development based on the assumption that economic integration is desirable as one part of South America's effort to increase the per capita income of its people. It also assumes that the benefits of greater industrialization should be distributed geographically as widely as possible. The concentration of industrial activities in a few urban islands throughout South America and the divergence of standards of living between these islands and the vast rural areas are already notorious. The danger exists that the spread between urban and rural living standards might well be widened even if LAFTA is successful. For this reason, it is explicitly assumed that transport policy should be used to assure that all of the people of South America have an opportunity to share in increases in regional income.

Any study of transport must recognize that individual countries have two further noneconomic objectives in relation to their own transport policy: national political integration and national defense. Border wars have been frequent in South America's history, and disputes over the location of national frontiers continue to the present day. All South American nations desire to integrate their countries politically by providing access to remote areas, thus lessening the danger that isolated communities might look to a neighboring country for the assistance they do not receive from their own national governments. At the same time, defense in South America has traditionally been focused on the danger of invasion by a bordering country. For this reason, many countries have been reluctant to improve international land communications for fear that they might be providing an easy pathway for an invading army. Obviously enough, the dual objectives of national defense and political integration are at times in conflict when isolated communities are located near an international border.

The Task of the Transport Planner

The planner charged with programming transport investments, whether for a region within a country, a country as a whole, or for a group of countries, should ideally have available a detailed economic development plan covering all of the productive sectors. This plan should identify both the location of new productive facilities and the precise time when they should begin operating. The plan should not, for example, indicate merely that national steel output will reach one million tons ten years in the future, but should rather state explicitly both the location of the new plants to be established as well as the year-to-year tonnage output. Sectoral targets, such as wheat production and coal production, are wholly inadequate unless accompanied by information on location and timing.

The importance of space and time to the transport planner is far greater than to planners of other sectors. This is because little is gained from talking of transport in the abstract. Slight use can be made of a transport plan composed solely of national targets of gross ton-miles, for example. A transport plan must deal with specific transport media—highways, railroads, pipelines—and must determine the capacity required in specific geographic areas. Thus the transport program must identify which railroad should be built or abandoned, where a highway should be constructed, and how much capacity is required in a specific port.

The transport planner is concerned with time because serious economic losses can occur if the relative priorities to be given to different transport projects are not determined. If transport is not to be an obstacle to growth, transport facilities must be available when they are needed. At the same time, the scarcity of capital in underdeveloped countries makes it undesirable to anticipate transport needs by too great a margin.

Even this sketch of the task of the transport planner is far too simplified because it has cast transport into an exclusively passive role. Here, it has been assumed that production and consumption centers are given, that traffic volumes among these points can be determined, and that the sole problem is to assure that transport capacity exists when needed. The real task of the transport planner, however, is complicated further by the fact that investments in transport affect both the pattern and the sequence of growth. Transport plays a dynamic role in the real world, and decisions in this sector affect all other sectors. It is impossible to specify the location and timing of all investments in other sectors unless transport considerations are explicitly introduced throughout the entire planning process.

Most development programs are aggregate programs, and too often it has been left to the transport planner to specify the probable location and timing of investments in other sectors of the economy. Furthermore, no development program of any sort exists for South America taken as a whole. Because the national plans that exist in a number of South American countries have given almost no consideration to the possible implications of successful economic integration, it would be impossible to prepare a useful continental plan by aggregating the separate national plans.

The various forces that contribute to the development of a particular region may be classified into three groups, namely, internal forces within the region, the impetus from exports to nearby adjoining regions, and exports to far distant regions. If the experience of the United States is observed, it is evident that the development of individual states has been due primarily to the second factor. Although both the first and third factors have been important, it is clear that the predominant force has been the opportunity which each state has had to develop exports to the others.[1] Yet in South America, the presently available development plans for individual countries focus nearly exclusively on the first factor, internal bootstrap development, and on the third factor, exports to far distant nations. No consideration is given to the growth potential of integrating the various nations into a continental economy.

Furthermore, the economic studies presently available have either examined the South American countries as separate and independent units or have treated all of Latin America as a macro unit with no spatial dimension. It is not possible to find a spatial projection—or even a vision—of a rational or desirable pattern of continental development for South America that relates the separate countries as parts of a whole.

There are a number of important restraints that limit the alternative development paths which South America as a whole can follow.

First, both the pattern and sequence of development are affected by the geographical distribution of resources, that is, by the accessibility of resources in an economic sense. The spatial distribution of minerals and of agricultural land, of power sources, and of waterways fixes margins to possible patterns of development.

Second, the future pattern of development will be influenced by the present distribution of population, the present transport networks, present economic specialization, and present trade patterns.

Third, the transport of a limited number of commodities represents a great proportion of all transport. In any economy, products such as grains, coal, oil, and minerals are the backbone

---

[1] Harvey S. Perloff and Lowdon Wingo, Jr., "Natural Resource Endowment and Regional Economic Growth," in Joseph J. Spengler, ed., *Natural Resources and Economic Growth* (Resources for the Future, Inc., 1961), pp. 192-99.

of traffic movements. If projections can be made of future traffic flows of these commodities and rational transport investments are made so as to assure their efficient movement, the transport economist will have completed a major part of his responsibility.

Fourth, it is possible to plan future development and its spatial distribution. Projections can be made of what will occur if present tendencies of population distribution continue and if present tendencies of the location of economic activities follow their past tendencies. These projections can then be examined and accepted or rejected. Their rejection implies the necessity of adopting policies that would tend to bring about a different state of affairs from that which would result from a continuance into the future of what has occurred in the past. The formation of the Latin American Free Trade Association represents such a rejection of the past and an explicit desire to change present tendencies in the economies of the member countries.

The Latin American Free Trade Association

On February 18, 1960, in Montevideo, Uruguay, seven Latin American republics signed a historic treaty which pledged greater economic cooperation among the signatory nations and established a mechanism designed to increase international trade in this area. By June 1, 1961, the treaty had been ratified by the governments of Argentina, Brazil, Chile, Mexico, Paraguay, Peru, and Uruguay, and the Latin American Free Trade Association (LAFTA) formally came into existence. By the end of 1961, the original seven members had been joined by Colombia and Ecuador, so that LAFTA included all the republics of South America except Bolivia and Venezuela. Venezuela has announced that it will also become a member.

The establishment of LAFTA was largely due to the economic studies and promotional efforts of the United Nations Economic Commission for Latin America (ECLA) during the 1950's. ECLA had pointed out since its earliest publications the difficulties that the Latin American nations were encountering and would encounter in their efforts to develop economically because of an inadequate capacity to import. ECLA argued that the Latin American countries, whose exports are concentrated primarily on a few raw materials or basic foodstuffs, would be unable to find adequate markets in the industrial nations to produce quantities of foreign exchange sufficient to finance their import needs.

The ECLA thesis both justified and encouraged the process of import substitution which was occurring to a greater or lesser extent in all the Latin American countries. Beginning with the depression of the 1930's, when these countries saw their export markets disintegrate, and continuing during World War II, when traditional suppliers of Latin American imports were dedicating their economies to the production of war goods, Latin America had sought to produce internally as many different products as was possible. By the early 1950's, however, it was becoming evident that in several countries, notably in Chile and Argentina, and to a lesser extent in Brazil, limited national markets prevented a continuation of the process of import substitution at the same rate as had previously been experienced. The great impulse which had been given to these economies during the days of easy import substitution had now diminished. Development was leveling off, and these nations appeared destined to a rate of growth hardly adequate to maintain present low living standards in the face of rapid population increases.

Regional economic integration was a logical attempt to extend to a wider area the process of import substitution that had been taking place in each nation individually. In the LAFTA area could be found, it was believed, the wide markets necessary for the establishment of new industries which could not be supported by a single nation alone. As Victor Urquidi has stated:

> The integration of Latin American industrial markets offers, therefore, ample opportunities for existing industries to increase their trade in manufactured goods. But it is in fact aimed principally at developing industrial activities that must operate on a very large scale; these cover the broad range of iron and steel processing and engineering industries, metal products and domestic appliances, and automobile and machinery manufacturing, all of which are barely beginning to be developed in Latin America. These ac-

tivities must be entered into not only because they represent a logical succession of stages in industrial development, but because exports of goods and services to the rest of the world will not be sufficient—even assuming more intensive use of foreign loans—to pay for the volume of imported machinery and intermediate products that will be demanded by a constant increase in internal investment. And unless Latin America's productivity and output capacity are expanded through internal investment, the increase in real income will not keep up with population growth, which means it will not be possible to raise appreciably the per capita income level and, in turn, the living standard.[2]

Regional integration could also be useful in correcting some of the economic distortions which have resulted from import substitution on a national scale behind high tariff barriers. In the words of the United Nations, "Customs protection has been carried to excess and, by limiting or completely preventing competition from abroad, has frequently given rise to internal restrictive practices or monopolistic combines which weaken the incentive to attain satisfactory levels of productivity."[3] With the progressive lowering of customs duties among the LAFTA members, monopolistic producers in one country would be exposed to competition from other countries with a similar level of development without the area as a whole losing scarce foreign exchange.

These are among the reasons the Montevideo Treaty is designed primarily to encourage commerce in industrial products among the member nations. Little attempt is made to stimulate greater trade in agricultural commodities, where it would be expected that the gains from specialization on the basis of comparative advantage might be great. Although the Latin American nations realize the importance of increasing agricultural productivity, they are convinced that new productive employment for their growing populations can best be found through greater cooperative efforts at industrialization.

[2] Victor L. Urquidi, *The Challenge of Development in Latin America* (Frederick A. Praeger, 1964), p. 128.

[3] United Nations, *Towards a Dynamic Development Policy for Latin America*, E/CN.12/680/Rev. 1 (1963), p. 92.

Organization of this Volume

In order to make the task of studying transport and integration more manageable, South America has been divided into nine regions described in detail in Chapter II. The delimitation necessarily reflects in part the author's vision of the pattern of a developed South American economy, and also reflects an implicit strategy of development for the continent. For this reason, it is quite possible that this or a similar classification of regions might well be useful for studying aspects other than transport.

Chapter III examines the pattern of intra-South American trade, Chapter IV the resources, and Chapter V the population and income of South America—all in order to see how past and present tendencies might influence their future development. Against this background, policies can then be formulated to foster the contribution of transport projects to integration.

Chapter VI examines in detail the development of Latin American ocean shipping policies. Since maritime transport is the single most important mode of transport in the area, policies affecting it will necessarily play an important role in the goal of increasing intra-Latin American trade.

Chapters VII and VIII analyze the way various transport media can contribute to economic integration, and Chapter IX summarizes the study with the author's suggestions for a transport policy directed at economic integration.

CHAPTER II

Geographic Description of the Regions of South America[1]

REGIONAL ANALYSIS IS FREQUENTLY a fruitful approach to understanding problems in such diverse fields as education, forestry, nutrition, land reform, philology, taxation, and transport. When this approach is used, geographical areas are delineated in such a way that the space included within a given region is homogeneous with respect to certain variables and heterogeneous in comparison to other regions with respect to the same variables. The regions chosen can be useful or not in leading to insights into the nature of the problem studied, but they cannot be termed "right" or "wrong." Although a given regional classification may often be useful for several purposes, it will not be useful for all purposes.

A regional approach is used in this study of transport and the economic integration of South America because the nature of the transport problems can be understood more readily by looking at regions and the relationships among them than by focusing solely on separate countries. South America has been divided into nine regions. In a few instances, in the analysis of maritime transport, the delineation of the regions is changed somewhat, incorporating Mexico. Among the criteria used in defining the regions were topography, population densities, level of economic development, and the author's conception of the structure of a developed South America should economic integration be successful.

[1] This chapter was written by Margery S. Coen. Material for the chapter, unless otherwise noted, has been derived from Preston E. James, *Latin America*, 3d ed. (The Odyssey Press, 1959).

9

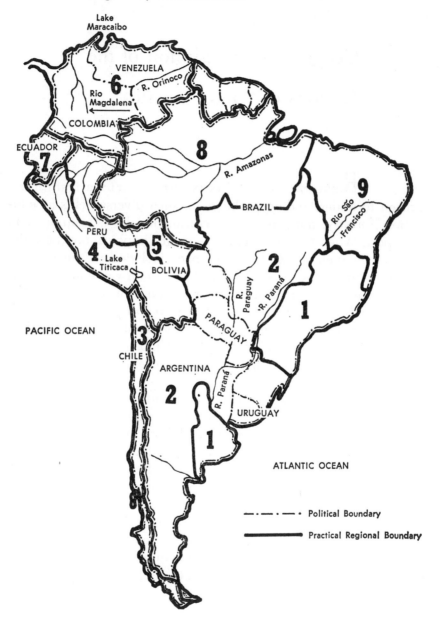

FIGURE 2-1. *Regions of South America*

Since neither national boundaries nor the lines that separate the different states or provinces within countries coincide necessarily with natural geographical divisions, an ideal set of regions is likely to encompass parts of different countries and different political units within countries. Most available data on population, international trade, or industrial output refer solely to entire countries, or at best to states and provinces of these countries, so that for practical purposes the ideal regions must be modified to make them coincide with political units. The map on page 10 shows the division of South America into nine regions that are discussed below.

Region I: The Industrial Heartland of South America

Ideally, this region would include the southern coastal part of Brazil from approximately Belo Horizonte in the north to Porto Alegre in the south. From this latter city, it narrows and includes only a thin strip along the coast of the rest of Brazil and of Uruguay, ending at Montevideo. Then it jumps the Río de la Plata and includes a portion of Argentina to the south of the Paraná River encompassing the important cities of Rosario, Buenos Aires, and Bahía Blanca. This industrial heartland is the counterpart of the region in the United States which extends from Washington, D. C., northward to Boston and then westward to include parts of Pennsylvania, Ohio, and Illinois to the southern part of the Great Lakes.

The identification of this coastal strip from Brazil to Argentina as being the key area on which future continental development should be based is not new. Roger Babson stated in 1915:

> I am a great believer in the east coast of South America, not only for our children and grandchildren, but for the present generation. The section from Bahía Blanca, Argentina, to Rio de Janeiro, Brazil (fifteen hundred miles), extending about four hundred miles westward, is a gold mine. It is a tract as large as all of our country east of the Mississippi, and is worthy of careful study.[2]

[2] *The Future of South America* (Little, Brown & Co., 1915), p. 3.

Although other centers of industrial activity will and should develop in other regions and countries, the principal industrial center should be Region I. For this reason, economic integration in South America will be significant solely if it is successful between Brazil and Argentina.

The necessity to make regional boundaries coincide with political and administrative units in order to facilitate data collection requires changes in the delineation of the boundaries of the ideal region. Thus the practical Region I includes the Brazilian provinces listed in Appendix B, Table B-4. The ideal Region I would not include parts of Minas Gerais and Espírito Santo north of the latitude of Belo Horizonte but would include a coastal strip in the State of Rio Grande do Sul. Similarly, a part of Uruguay would be included in the ideal Region I but is not included in the practical set of regions. In Argentina, the practical Region I includes the Federal District, the Province of Buenos Aires, and twelve districts of the Province of Santa Fe.[3]

Much of the population of Brazil and Argentina is concentrated in Region I, and it is here that industrialization is already the most advanced in South America. The region is blessed with a climate that permits productive agriculture, is healthful, and is sufficiently agreeable to attract people and to keep them.

Both population and economic activity are strongly concentrated in Argentina—in Buenos Aires and its associated hinterland, the Humid Pampa. The Humid Pampa is a grass-covered plain composed of a deep accumulation of loose material resting on a hilly surface of granite and crystalline rock. Much of this material has been carried in by the winds characteristic of this area.

The Río de la Plata, which flows through this area, is bordered by shallow mud flats, and continuous dredging is necessary to maintain the channel to the port of Buenos Aires from the Atlantic Ocean. To the north, the river is met by a steep hundred-foot bank known as the barranca, complicating still further the problems of transport.

The construction of railroads has been relatively easy on the Pampa because of its nearly level surface. The Junin and Mcken-

[3] See Appendix B "Methodological Note on Population Projections."

na stretch of the General San Martín Railway, for example, is the longest stretch of straight and level railroad in the world.[4] Gravel and rock are hard to find on the Pampas, however, so that maintaining adequate ballast on the rail lines is expensive. This problem also affects road construction and maintenance. Dirt roads tend to become rutted with use and because gravel is difficult to find, unpaved all-weather roads are not common.

Rainfall is sufficient over much of the area for the support of trees, although it decreases toward the southwest. Along the coast it is evenly distributed throughout the year, and to the west concentrated somewhat in the summer. It is only around Rosario and Pergamino, however, that rainfall is dependable. This region is generally one of hot summers and mild winters though frosts occur annually. Like eastern North America, the Humid Pampa has variable weather caused by the interaction of hot and cold air masses.

In Brazil, which includes almost 50 percent of the land area and people of South America, the surface of the southern coastal area is a mixture of hilly uplands, low mountains, and inner lowlands. The region is dominated by the Great Escarpment, the steep wall-like slope that fringes the coast from Salvador to Pôrto Alegre. From the border between São Paulo and Guanabara states south to the city of Santos, the Escarpment forms one unbroken slope, 2,600 to 2,900 feet above sea level from the edge of the upland to the sea—the Sierra do Mar. Elsewhere it is threaded with river valleys.

The area to the north of the state of São Paulo is dominated by an intricate pattern of hills and low mountains. The deltas of the Dôce and the Paraíba Rivers and the floodplain of the middle Paraíba are almost the only large level areas here. To the south the uplands are relieved by the lowlands of the Paraná Plateau.

Over most of the area, rainfall is from 40 to 60 inches annually with the maximum coming in the summer months. However, the highlands south of the city of São Paulo have no winter dry sea-

---

[4] *Directory of Railway Officials and Yearbook, 1962-1963* (London: Tothill Press, 1963), p. 570.

son unlike highlands found elsewhere in tropical Brazil. Scattered spots on the Great Escarpment and on the sides of mountains near the coast may receive over 80 inches a year.

The pattern of vegetation ranges from a dense tropical rain forest on the coast and rainy slopes of the Escarpment to intermingled forests and grasslands in the interior.

Topography like that just described is an important deterrent to transport development since the complex structure of mountains makes road building difficult and expensive. The Great Escarpment enhances the problems further, standing as a rugged barrier to communication between coastal areas and the interior. Despite these drawbacks, Region I already has a relatively well-developed surface transport network. Much more needs to be done, however, toward integrating the rail and highway systems of individual countries within the region.

Region II: The Supporting Hinterland

Region II is the hinterland which supports the natural industrial heartland of South America, and its development should rationally be oriented toward supplying the requirements of the vital center. This region should ideally include the whole of Paraguay, all of Uruguay except for the coastal area in Region I, that part of Argentina not in Region I, and the Brazilian state of Rio Grande do Sul south from Pôrto Alegre, the southern sections of the states of Mato Grosso and Goiás, and Brasília, the new Federal District. It would also encompass the southern part of Bolivia. The region has been modified somewhat for analytical purposes to include the whole of Paraguay and Uruguay, that part of Argentina not included in Region I, the Brazilian Federal District and provinces of Mato Grosso, Goiás and Rio Grande do Sul, and the Bolivian department of Santa Cruz.

Most of this region is part of the La Plata River System, which comprises an area estimated at between 1.2 and 1.6 million square miles drained by the Paraná, Paraguay, Alto (Upper) Paraná, and Uruguay rivers and their tributaries. The possibilities for the integration of this region through the La Plata System can be grasped somewhat when its boundaries are considered—on the north, the Brazilian plateau which marks the watershed between Brazil's north-flowing rivers, principally branches of the Amazon, and those flowing south; on the east, the low coastal ranges of Brazil and Uruguay; on the south from the confluence of the Uruguay and Paraná rivers to Córdoba, Argentina; and on the west, the Andes from around Sucre, Bolivia, to Córdoba.[5]

The topography of Region II can be roughly generalized into a western part reaching from the Andes to about 100 miles east of the Paraná-Paraguay River, which is an area of lowlands interspersed with some hilly uplands, and an eastern part largely dominated by the Paraná Plateau. Where the plateau marks its juncture with the western lowlands and hilly uplands the sharp drop in elevation causes some of the most spectacular waterfalls in the world.

East of the Andes lies the Chaco, a vast plain of sand and clay, which constitutes an extension of the Andean foothills. It encompasses the Bolivian department of Santa Cruz, Paraguay west of the Río Paraguay, and a northwest section of Argentina. Here occur the highest temperatures recorded in South America. Although summers are hot, there are occasional cool spells. Most of the area is well-drained except for the large swampy areas along the Pilcomayo River and the western side of the Paraguay. There are few surface streams on the Chaco, but the water table is only a few feet below the surface.

Patagonia, the area of Argentina lying south of the Río Colorado, is a region of high dusty winds, glaciated mountains, and an Andean piedmont with a succession of marginal lakes. Despite its relatively high altitude, it is not an area of extreme temperatures: because of its tapering land mass, southern South America is subject to the moderating influence of the ocean. No part of Patagonia receives much rainfall except the mountainous country to the west. The sparse winter rains are able to support only short grasses, but in those few places where valleys cross the cordillera, moisture-laden winds of the Pacific can penetrate to create little

[5] Economic Conference of the Organization of American States, 1957, *Transportation and Economic Growth: the La Plata River System*, Doc. 11 (Pan American Union, 1957), pp. 4-6.

islands of forest. The Patagonian desert, the only example in the world of an arid east coast in latitudes poleward of 40°, is due not only to the rain barrier of the Andes but also to the fact that cyclonic winds from the east must pass a large current of cold water before reaching Patagonia.

To the east where the hilly uplands do not intervene, Region II is mostly plateau. An elevated plateau varying from 1,000 to 2,000 feet in altitude covers the eastern third of Paraguay and extends into the Argentine Mesopotamia between the Paraná and Uruguay rivers, southern Brazil, and Uruguay. The plateau terminates in the low coastal ranges of Brazil and Uruguay. South of the Great Escarpment the coast is fringed with sand bars, lagoons, and many sand dunes.

In the north, the plateau gives way to a region of hilly uplands, all of which lie in Brazil. It is to this high country of the Brazilian interior, which is part of the thinly populated wilderness beyond the frontiers of concentrated settlement known to the Brazilians as the *sertão*, that the Brazilian leaders would like to direct a mass migration—a *marcha para oeste*. The *sertão* of the Federal District, Mato Grosso, and Goiás while containing 22 percent of Brazil's national territory is occupied by only 4 percent of its people. It is, in fact, this sparseness of population that was one of the major reasons for locating Brasília, the new national capital, here.

To the north, this area is a vast featureless plain between 3,600 and 4,200 feet above sea level surmounted by a few peaks of about 6,000 feet. In southern Mato Grosso this high surface grades gradually onto the southern plateau. Hot rainy summers and cool dry winters characterize this area. Natural vegetation is a mixture of forests and *campo cerrado*, a transition zone between woodland and grassland.

Throughout Region II, rainfall is most plentiful along the coast and diminishes to the west. Vegetation follows the same pattern, being dense in the east and thinning out to the west. The east is covered with forest, which is thickest in the valley bottoms and becomes sparser on the red sandy soils of the hills. To the west is mostly grassland. Most of the Gran Chaco is covered with deciduous scrub woodland and patches of grassland, which, westward, becomes more xerophytic, that is, drought-resistant. Temperatures range from the high 70's to the 90's in summer and in the 60's and 70's in winter, becoming more tropical from south to north.

As was pointed out above, this region is particularly fortunate in its extensive river system.[6] The Paraná-Paraguay is navigable for 1,700 of it 2,300 miles, penetrating right into the heart of the region. The Alto Paraná with its tremendous hydroelectric potential is navigable for a distance of about 500 miles from its confluence with the Paraguay and Paraná at Corrientes, Argentina to Pôrto Mendes, Brazil. Navigation is limited, however, by its shallow depths and myriad of whirlpools and waterfalls. For many hundreds of miles above the Guayra Falls the Alto Paraná and its tributaries either are presently navigable or could be made so with minor improvements. The Uruguay River is navigable from its mouth for 200 miles as far as Salto where falls and rapids interrupt navigation. Lighter commercial craft can, however, operate for several hundred miles above the falls.

The La Plata River system would be important even if it were not a potential integrating feature. For Paraguay, 1,000 miles from the Atlantic Ocean, these rivers are the only water link with the sea. They also provide it with a connection to the interior of Brazil. The Economic Commission for Latin America calls the La Plata the most important river system in Latin America.

> . . . It serves the periphery of the wheat and cotton zones of Argentina, a part of southern Brazil and western Uruguay and it is Paraguay's principal means of communication with the outside world. It has been a decisive factor in the economic development of that part of Argentina which it drains. Thus Rosario, about 400 miles from the sea, is the second largest port in Argentina. . . .[7]

Although this region is already penetrated by several railroads and highways, existing facilities are inadequate. The La Plata River system offers innumerable opportunities to improve transport facilities. It is a ready-made and far-reaching transport network, but many navigational problems must be overcome.

[6] The description of the rivers which comprise the La Plata system is taken from *ibid.*, pp. 15-27.

[7] United Nations Economic Commission for Latin America, *Economic Survey of Latin America 1948*, p. 177.

Region III: Chile

Region III coincides with the republic of Chile, in both the ideal and practical set of regions. Chile, both topographically and climatically, bears a relation to the industrial heartland of South America similar to that which California bears to the industrial heartland of the United States. Both are separated from the rest of their respective continents by high mountain ranges, but Chile is much closer to the industrial heartland of South America than is California to the east coast of the United States. Furthermore, although the Andes are considerably higher than the Rockies, they are a much narrower range. It would seem, therefore, that in the future Chile should take advantage of its fertile soils in its trade with the heartland by concentrating as does California on the production of specialized agricultural products which can bear the cost of transport to the future densely populated southeast coast. Chile will, of course, have considerable industrial development, as has California. Its industrial development will probably be more resource-oriented than that of California, as Chile has a good competitive position in the production of metal products based on its mineral resources.

The geography of Chile will be discussed in three segments—North, Middle, and South. This division is based mainly on the pattern of settlement, for although this narrow (never more than 250 miles wide) country is 2,630 miles long, almost three-fourths of its population is clustered in its center.

Northern Chile is one of the driest places on earth. Behind the coastal plateau, whose cliffed escarpment rises from the water, lies a series of dry basins, which appear to have been lake beds at one time. Here the salts contained in the lake waters were deposited. Except for one river, the Río Loa, the region is bare of surface streams. This area is almost devoid of harbors or protected anchorages.

One-third to one-half of the width of Middle Chile, the area between Coquimbo and the Río Bío-Bío near Concepción, is occupied by high snow-capped ranges of the Andes. Another third consists of a zone of coastal plateaus and terraces deeply dissected by small streams. Along most of the coast, cliffs rise from the water. Between these two areas is a structural depression known as the Central Valley which is divided by spurs of the Andes into separate basins. Its floor is not level but made of great alluvial fans built by Andean streams. Thus Chile, like the entire west coast of South America, lacks natural harbors. Also, as in the rest of western South America, the Andes form a staggering barrier to communication between the coastal areas and the interior.

The most distinctive feature of Middle Chile is its climate. Between Coquimbo at latitude 30°S. and Concepción south of latitude 36°S. a transition from northern desert to southern rainy lands occurs. This climate of mild wet winters and cool dry summers is commonly termed "mediterranean." Freezing weather, but never snow, is sometimes experienced in the Central Valley.

The three fundamental divisions of Middle Chile—high Andean ranges, coastal plateaus and terraces, and a central valley—continue into the South, although here the Andes are lower. The southern cordillera exhibits a glacial pattern of knobby hills, valley lakes, and mountains made rugged by the cutting action of ice. The dissected coastal plateaus of the South offer protected harbors at Talcahuano and Valdivia. Here the Andean border of the Central Valley, unlike the Valley's eastern border in Middle Chile, is characterized by glacial deposits and lakes. Between the rivers crossing it at right angles, mountain spurs compartmentalize it. At Puerto Montt the valley disappears, descending to sea level in a series of terraces. The southern climate is one of stormy winters and cool summers. Skies are often cloudy and violent storms with heavy rainfall are common.

South of the island of Chiloé, Southern Chile becomes a region of high winds and heavy rains. Occupying one-third of the national territory, it is occupied by only one percent of the population and remains isolated from the rest of the region since there is no land transport between Southern and Middle Chile. Its steep rocky slopes and storm-tossed waters are forbidding. Glacial activity has dug out an intricate pattern of troughs along the coast creating a labyrinth of channels and islands. Within this area is included the Strait of Magellan, long a barrier to mariners. As J.

Russell Smith described it in explaining the commercial isolation of Pacific South America: "The Strait of Magellan alone is as long as the distance from Hull to Bremen. It is crooked, narrow, rocky, and beset with snowstorms and shipwrecks, so that vessels usually tie up at night."[8]

Region IV: Coast and Highlands of Peru and Bolivia

Region IV, one of the major problem areas of South America in the future, includes the coastal and highlands parts of Peru and Bolivia. Its ideal and practical sections in Peru include all departments with the exception of Loreto and Madre de Dios. The part of Bolivia included in the ideal region includes the departments of La Paz, Oruro, Cochabamba, Potosí, and the sections of the departments of Chuquisaca and Tarija to the west of Santa Cruz. The part of Bolivia used for the practical region is identical to the ideal except that the rest of the last two departments named are also included.

The population of Peru and Bolivia is concentrated in the coastal and highland areas, and it is difficult to see how living standards of the present largely Indian population can be increased if this region must absorb the population increase which is foreseen. Although industrialization is essential, it is difficult to see how this region can be related rationally to the industrial heartland of the continent, Region I, because of the transport barrier which must be overcome.

The west coasts of all continents between 20° and 30° of latitude are characterized by a combination of cold ocean water and dry land, but on no other continent does this condition extend so far toward the equator as in South America along the coast of Peru. Most of the coastal areas are barren desert interspersed with man-made oases. In the north, there is a wide belt of lowland most of which is covered by moving sand dunes. Between the cities of Chiclayo and Pativilca, little or no coastal lowland exists with the mountains gradually pinching it out. Southward to

[8] *Industrial and Commercial Geography* (Henry Holt, 1913), p. 793.

Pisco, there is a narrow lowland irregular in width which ends with a low range of coastal mountains, a bleak rocky surface separating them from the Andes behind.

As a result of the cold water currents, air temperatures are lower than the averages for each latitude. The average in Lima, for example, is 66.7°. Most of the coast receives little, if any, rain. The average precipitation in Lima is only 1.9 inches a year. Where the clouds characteristic of the region rest against the slopes of the Coastal Range or lower Andean foothills, a heavy mist provides moisture for a dense growth of quick flowering plants and grasses—loma.

The highlands of Region IV are a complex series of discontinuous peaks. There are several active volcanoes, especially in southern Peru and western Bolivia. So little rain falls here that few streams emerge from the mountains. To the east, the Andes reach their highest summits in this region with some peaks over 21,000 feet.

Straddling the border between Peru and Bolivia is the Titicaca Basin—a population cluster severed by national boundaries—which is part of a string of intermontane basins known collectively as the Altiplano. These basins are separated by spurs extending from the western range of the Andes and thus communication among them is difficult. Along the eastern border of the Altiplano, however, the basins are connected and a level route of travel is available. One of Bolivia's main railroads now follows this route. To the east and south of the Altiplano, the structure of the eastern cordillera changes and is a high level east-facing block topped by irregularly placed ranges of high peaks. The western high part of the section, which is known as the Puna, is only slightly dissected, while the eastern lower part has been cut deeply by numerous streams.

There can be no doubt that the highland regions of Peru and Bolivia offer important barriers to the development of unified national transport systems. The steep-walled canyons and rugged mountain terrain make the construction of highways and railways difficult and costly. But these problems are not insuperable. For example, in a list of the world's railways with the greatest altitude, 18 of the first 25 are operated by Peruvian, Chilean, and Bolivian lines.[9] Bolivia's situation may be somewhat more difficult, for as a landlocked country in an area where the ocean is the main highway, it must depend on its neighbors for the use of their ports. Highway and rail transport therefore loom larger in this area than in many others.

Region V: Eastern Slope of the Andes

There are two discrepancies between the ideal Region V and the one used here for data collection. Ideally, the northeastern corner of the department of Loreto in Peru would be in Region VIII. In the region used here, however, the whole of Loreto plus the department of Madre de Dios are included. The departments of Pando and Beni comprise the Bolivian part of the practical region. However, the section of the department of Santa Cruz north of the Santa Cruz Railway should be included while sections of eastern Pando and northeastern Beni ideally belong in Region VIII.

Except for a few of the highest peaks and deepest canyons of the Andes described in Region IV, the wet eastern slopes contain the roughest surfaces of the Bolivian-Peruvian Andes. Heavy rains have created many streams and as a result these slopes are a labyrinth of narrow ridges and ravines. The Eastern Border Valleys, as they are called in Peru, and the Yungas of Bolivia also contain dense forests and are the chief barrier to transportation between Regions IV and V.

To the east, the plains are sparsely inhabited and dissected by large and partly navigable rivers flowing to the Amazon and Paraguay. Most of the isolated southeastern plain of Bolivia, which is much drier than the rest of the eastern plain, is part of the Gran Chaco described in Region II.

The plains and Andean slopes in the east present overwhelming problems for transport development. In addition to the problems associated with the ruggedness of the slopes, the selva of the rainy lowlands makes all transportation but river travel practically impossible. Moreover, the abundance of east-west flowing riv-

[9] *Directory of Railway Officials and Year Book, 1962-1963, op. cit.,* p. 563.

ers makes the construction of north-south highways costly because of the number of bridges it would require.

The northeast of Peru, located in the Amazon Basin area (Region VIII), contains an important route of access between eastern Peru and the outside world. Ocean steamers that draw less than fourteen feet are able to ascend the Amazon all the way to Iquitos. Along the mountain borders, launches and canoes can follow the streams, and these are also important landmarks for airplanes. Bolivia's section of the Amazon Basin is not so fortunate since the Rio Madeira, which gathers the streams flowing into this area, is interrupted by a long stretch of rapids as it flows northeast to the Amazon.

The advent of air travel has changed the pattern of transport in this region and brings hope for increased communication with Region IV and other parts of South America in the future. William A. Burden described the situation before the possibility of an intensive use of the airplane as follows:

> Prior to the advent of the airplane the South American continent was accessible only by sea. Its western coast, cut off from the rest of the continent by the 4,000-mile chain of the Andes, and from the Atlantic by the Isthmus of Panama, was for centuries one of the most remote inhabited areas of the world. The building of the Canal relieved its isolation but, far from integrating it with the rest of the continent, actually brought it closer to the United States or even Europe than to the east coast countries. Freight shipped from Lima to Iquitos, Peru (600 air-miles apart), for example, was often sent from Callao to Southampton, England, where it was transshipped to another steamer to recross the Atlantic and voyage up the Amazon, a total trip of some 13,000 miles.[10]

Both Peru and Bolivia hope to be able to channel their surplus population into Region V, and this migration appears desirable. What is not clear is whether Region V should be integrated economically into Region IV or whether it more rationally should be oriented toward Region II or toward regions further to the north. The transport policy that is developed for South America must reflect a strategy for the future development of Region V.

[10] *The Struggle for Airways in Latin America* (Council on Foreign Relations, 1943, p. 185.

Region VI: Colombia and Venezuela

The ideal and practical constructs of this region are almost identical. The only difference between the two is that the practical region contains all of Colombia and Venezuela while an ideal classification would exclude the southern Colombian state of Amazonas and place it with the rest of the Amazon Basin in Region VIII. That Colombia and Venezuela should be thought of together as one region stems not only from their proximity but also from their isolation from the rest of South America and their geographic homogeneity.

This area with its vast stores of oil and other natural resources could in time become the center of a large petro-chemical complex and could have a relation to the rest of South America similar to that between Texas and Louisiana and the rest of the United States. It is already tied somewhat by the beginnings of a highway and railway network. Since World War II, for example, the all-weather highway and motor truck have begun to provide low-cost transportation for the highland settlements of Colombia. The new all-weather road from Bogotá to Caracas and the expansion of Venezuelan roads into the south will lead to closer economic ties throughout the region.

This region has in the past remained largely isolated from the rest of South America by land. The Amazon Basin with its associated rain forest and mountains and the high Andean ranges make all transport except that by ocean almost impossible. The transport planner must reckon with the fact that because of the long distance between the ports of Region VI and other important Latin American ports—especially relative to the proximity of these other ports to one another—ocean transport may be costly for most items and impractical for perishable items. For example, the distance between Buenaventura and Rio de Janeiro is 6,123 nautical miles, between La Guaira and Buenos Aires 4,775 nautical miles and between Barranquilla and Valparaiso 3,181 nautical miles. Bogotá, the capital of Colombia, is about 200 miles from the nearest port.

Both countries are a mixture of plains and highlands, parts of which are common to each. The eastern two-thirds of Colombia (most of which contributes nothing to the economic support of the population) and southern Venezuela are included in the Guiana Highlands and the Orinoco Llanos. The former lie south of the Orinoco River and contain rounded hills, narrow valleys, and groups of plateaus and mesas. They are covered with coarse grasslands and semideciduous forest. The Orinoco Llanos, an almost featureless plain between the Andes and the Orinoco River, are covered with a mixture of grassland and scrub woodland. There are two sharply different seasons, a rainy season between June and October and a dry season between January and March, with transitional periods between each. With such a prolonged season of rains, all-weather roads are a necessity.

Besides these areas, Venezuela is composed of the Venezuelan Highlands and the Maracaibo Lowlands. The highlands, the most densely populated area in the country, have four subdivisions. The Central Highlands border the Caribbean between Puerto Cabello and Cape Codera. The hot dry coastline, with its scanty cover of drought-resistant plants, contrasts sharply with the rainy mountains, which rise abruptly from the coast to elevations of 7,000 to 9,000 feet. With the weather of the coastal areas so unpleasant, the capital city of Caracas grew up in a pleasant inland valley. Despite the fact that it is only six miles from its port, La Guaira, transport construction between the two has been expensive because Caracas is about 3,000 feet above sea level, requiring a myriad of bridges and tunnels to be built in lieu of climbing to 3,412 feet to reach a pass over the mountains.

The three other areas are the Northeastern Highlands, whose peaks vary in height from only about 2,600 feet on the coast to 6,700 feet in the west, the Segovia Highlands, a region of recurring droughts, deeply dissected plateaus, and a few isolated ranges of low mountains and hills, and the Cordillera de Merida in the southwest, the only place where permanent snow is found in the higher elevations. In this last area, the borders of Colombia and Venezuela cut through a population cluster, one of only three places in South America where this occurs.

The Maracaibo Lowlands are almost entirely surrounded by higher land and thus bedeviled by oppressive humidity. The heavy rainfall to the south supports a dense tropical rain forest.

Vegetation becomes sparser, however, in the north where rainfall is lighter. The mouth of the 130-mile long lake of this region has been dredged so that ocean-going tankers can carry fuel oil directly from the oil fields here to foreign markets.

The mountainous area of western Colombia boasts many peaks considerably higher than those found in Venezuela. Despite the fact that the highest peaks of the Serrania de Baudo, the westernmost range, are less than 6,000 feet above sea level, it contains the most rugged areas of Colombia created by the effects of heavy erosive rainfall. The crests of the Cordillera Occidental and Cordillera Central are unbroken by stream valleys except where the Río Cauca has made a way out to the north and the Río Patia one to the west. Otherwise, these cordilleras, both of which lack large intermontane basins, are the divides between the streams that rise on either side. The Cordillera Central, the highest of the Colombian ranges, has several peaks over 18,000 feet. These two ranges are separated south of Cartago by a deep rift valley. To the east of these ranges lie the deep (scarcely 1,000 feet above sea level) Magdalena Valley and the Cordillera Oriental. The latter is a region of rugged peaks and high basins. Little wonder with this complex terrain that Colombia had the first commercial airline to be placed in regular operation in the Western Hemisphere.

It might seem that the Magdalena Valley would offer a natural route of access to the highlands. This route has proven unsatisfactory, however, because of the many barriers to navigation—sand bars, shifting channel, fluctuation of the water level—in the Río Magdalena. The high cost of building and operating railroads in this mountainous area make it desirable to complement railroad transport with highways. No national railroad system exists in Venezuela and the difficult topography may make highway transport the primary mode for many decades.

Region VII: Ecuador

Region VII coincides with the republic of Ecuador, which has been separated out not because of its characteristics as a natural region but rather because it is not clear in which other region it should be placed. In many ways Ecuador is related naturally to Colombia. On the other hand, a good argument could be made to extend to Ecuador the Regions IV and V which are separated out in Peru. But Ecuador has an important coastal area which is quite dissimilar from any counterpart in either Peru or Bolivia. For these reasons, it seems more logical to separate Ecuador completely, for the time being, rather than to assimilate it arbitrarily into another region. As time goes on, it may appear more logical to consider Ecuador simultaneously with some other area.

The establishment of national unity in Ecuador is complicated by the division of the country into two contrasting groups of people occupying separate areas. The largely self-sufficient Indian population lives in the high intermont basins while the nationalistic, more commercially active, and largely mestizo group occupies the Pacific coastal regions.

The highland area contains some thirty active volcanoes. The loose volcanic ash of this region has been enormously dissected by streams creating rugged "bad lands" and deep canyons. The population of this region is grouped in distinct clusters in several isolated intermont basins. The rainfall, although concentrated in a season from November to May, is ample to support forests up to 10,000 feet above sea level.

Ecuador's coastal region is one of the narrowest zones of transition in South America. In a few degrees of latitude, the tropical rain forest of the north, which experiences two rainy seasons a year, changes to the desert of the south.

Region VIII: The Amazon Basin

Region VIII encompasses the great Amazon basin; like the eastern slope of the Andes it remains a land of mystery, despite the efforts of generations of men to make it productive. As William Lytle Schurz has stated:

> Generations of little men have nibbled, like mice, at the edges of the Amazonia. In terms of its magnitude, the results are almost imperceptible. Its cities are stagnant or have retrograded. The heart has gone out of them and they are full of ghosts and of mirages that will never materialize. . . . No one knows yet what

to do with it all. Its would-be conquerors generally end up shaking their heads in frustration at its impersonal challenge. Those who would solve the problem of its development must be possessed of superhuman imagination and boldness and they must have access to vast stores of capital. They must be willing to forget much that is familiar and to start anew as if on another planet.[11]

Little can be said about the future relationship of this region to the rest of South America. It remains a world unto itself.

Ideally Region VIII would contain parts of four countries: (1) the Colombian state of Amazonas; (2) the northeastern section of the Peruvian department of Loreto; (3) parts of the Bolivian departments of Pando and Beni; and (4) the Brazilian states of Rondonia, Acre, Amazonas, Rio Branco, Pará, and Amapá as well as the northern portions of the states of Mato Grosso and Goiás. In order to facilitate analysis of the region, the first six Brazilian states named above will be taken as the entire region.

The Amazon Basin of Brazil is the world's largest area of tropical rain forest. Covering nearly 42 percent of the country, it is occupied by only 4 percent of the people. This vast region is dominated by the Amazon River and its tributaries. The immensity of the Amazon River System is overwhelming. It is estimated to drain 2.7 million square miles. River steamers can travel 15,000 miles on it and ocean-going steamers frequently journey to Iquitos, Peru, some 2,300 miles from the Atlantic.[12]

Only a small part of this region can be described as a plain. Above the junction of the Rio Negro and the Rio Madeira, the plain spreads to a width of about 800 miles. But the floodplain of the main stream is less than 50 miles wide. The floodplain is bordered by sharp valley bluffs at least 150 to 200 feet above the swamps along the river. The Guiana and Brazilian Highlands, which all but join near the mouth and are widespread over much of the region, are hilly uplands with occasional low mountains.

Temperatures are high, but contrary to popular belief, not excessive. Their most disagreeable element is their monotony; the range between the averages for the warmest and coldest months

[11] *Brazil, the Infinite Country* (Dutton, 1961), p. 64.
[12] Fredein Benham and H. A. Holley, *A Short Introduction to the Economy of Latin America*, rev. ed. (London: Oxford University Press, 1961), p. 48.

is only 3.1°. Humidity is very high but decreases moving inland. Rainfall over this area is abundant, but only in the upper part of the basin and along the coast are averages more than 80 inches a year. The rain forest of the Amazon Basin is composed of many different species of trees and shrubs. On the higher surfaces of the uplands, grasslands interrupt the thick forest cover. Since the soils of the rain forest are highly leached, the river floodplains are the only areas where fertile soils are found.

The problems of transport in this area are enormous. The Amazon is a wild river and not easily navigated. Furthermore, its location makes it useless—at least in the near future—because of the problems associated with the rain forest through which it flows. Thus the area of Brazil which is richest in rivers is the area which is least habitable.

Region IX: Northeast Brazil

The region described here as Northeast Brazil encompasses a smaller area than would be ideal, as the practical region does not include the sections of the states of Minas Gerais and Espírito Santo north of Belo Horizonte. In order to aid in the collection of data, the southern boundary of the region will be taken as the southern border of the state of Bahia. A list of the ten states included in Region IX appears in Appendix Table B-4.

The Brazilian Northeast, today a region of great poverty and overpopulation, has contributed enormously to the nation in the past through its supply of intellectual, artistic, and political leaders. Because of its problem of overpopulation, it has also been a source of migrants to all sections of the nation and all sectors of the economy.

The Northeast contains five major surface features: broad coastal plains with erosive remnants, hilly uplands and low mountains, sandstone tabular uplands with their east-facing cuesta, the mesa-like *taboleiros* along the coast from Rio Grande do Norte almost to Rio de Janeiro, and the sedimentary basin of Bahia. The Northeast contains two zones, the first of which is the Zone of the Mata, the forested area where rainfall is generally more than 40 inches annually. This area runs along the coast from Natal. The other is the Zone of the Caatingas, a land with a calamitous climate of recurring droughts and disastrous floods. The natural vegetation here is a dry scrub woodland with occasional islands of trees on the wetter hill tops.

Despite the strong sentimental attachment the people of the Northeast bear to the Rio São Francisco, which flows through this region, it has proven uncooperative in efforts to tame it. Navigation is possible for shallow-draft river steamers from Juazeiro in Bahia to Pirapora in Minas Gerais, but the river is broken by the large Paulo Afonso Falls about 100 miles from the ocean. Below the falls, it passes through a deep canyon with only a few areas of floodplain near the mouth—hardly an area amenable to the establishment of river ports. The possibilities of using it for irrigation are also dim since at the places where its water would be most valuable, the topography is such that irrigation would be costly and applicable only to small areas.

CHAPTER III

Intra-South American Trade
and Transport

ONE OF THE KEY ELEMENTS that should be analyzed carefully in a study of transport and economic integration in South America is the pattern of intra-South American trade. The present level, the historical tendencies, and the commodity composition of this commerce are all useful in determining future trade flows which could develop under successful integration, in isolating instances where transport facilities and service are an obstacle to increasing commerce, and in identifying transport projects that could contribute to integration. Unfortunately, data are not easily available that would permit an analysis of trade based on the regional classifications presented in the preceding chapter, as these, in several instances, distribute a single country among several regions. For this reason, the first part of the analysis is confined to country-to-country trade flows, although later an attempt is made to relate this analysis to geographical factors.

Intra-South American Trade Patterns

Table 3-1 shows intra-South American trade in nine selected years between 1948 and 1962.[1] Each entry is based on the esti-

[1] This table and most of the others in this section are based on data presented in Donald W. Baerresen, Martin Carnoy, and Joseph Grunwald, *Latin American Trade Patterns* (Brookings Institution, 1965).

TABLE 3-1. *Intra-South American Trade, 1948–1962*

(Millions of U. S. dollars)

Trade with Other South American Countries by	1948	1952	1954	1956	1958	1959	1960	1961	1962
Argentina									
Exports[a]	165.0	96.2	181.2	123.2	129.8	147.8	169.5	111.0	153.7
Imports[a]	225.7	218.9	229.8	216.5	284.2	220.0	200.8	195.5	151.5
Brazil									
Exports	154.6	125.5	144.3	102.3	145.5	76.4	88.2	97.0	76.7
Imports	113.3	171.6	233.1	236.4	245.2	227.2	224.4	143.6	226.5
Uruguay									
Exports	16.3	29.7	39.7	27.6	13.4	2.9	3.6	6.0	8.0
Imports	52.9	58.2	69.5	49.9	61.2	43.7	66.5	46.4	43.9
Paraguay									
Exports	11.3	10.8	17.9	14.7	13.7	7.8	8.9	9.8	10.8
Imports	9.9	5.7	12.3	9.9	8.0	7.6	7.6	8.6	5.3
Chile									
Exports	30.1	66.0	57.8	44.0	34.5	40.0	31.6	37.5	41.9
Imports	74.7	67.8	95.7	60.6	46.2	53.7	80.2	99.3	87.9
Bolivia									
Exports	2.0	3.6	3.3	7.1	7.6	7.0	8.3	5.5	3.1
Imports	23.8	25.8	17.8	20.7	12.5	15.2	10.2	13.5	11.8
Peru									
Exports	61.5	73.4	45.6	51.9	41.8	49.7	36.0	32.8	50.3
Imports	38.5	17.0	20.6	22.2	20.4	20.5	28.1	34.0	46.9
Colombia									
Exports	3.2	3.1	7.3	6.2	4.1	4.3	6.1	7.2	8.3
Imports	27.9	18.0	16.2	14.5	10.1	8.7	7.4	11.1	12.4
Venezuela									
Exports	39.9	102.7	114.0	172.9	189.2	201.7	195.6	160.6	164.9
Imports	24.0	4.1	2.8	5.4	11.6	14.7	13.2	12.7	10.6
Ecuador									
Exports	10.0	7.1	12.5	7.3	10.7	9.7	8.1	7.4	6.0
Imports	3.0	2.7	3.9	4.4	2.7	4.9	2.8	2.4	4.7
Totals:									
Exports	493.9	518.1	623.6	557.2	590.3	547.3	555.9	474.8	523.7
Imports	593.7	589.8	701.7	640.5	702.1	616.2	641.2	567.1	601.5

Source: Donald W. Baerresen, Martin Carnoy, and Joseph Grunwald, *Latin American Trade Patterns* (Brookings Institution, 1965).

[a] Exports f.o.b.; imports c.i.f.

mate made by the corresponding country of its f.o.b. exports to, and c.i.f. imports from, each of the other South American republics. Before commenting on this table, it is important to note that the entries are subject to considerable error. The column totals show intra-South American f.o.b. exports and c.i.f. imports for each year, that is, the two totals should differ only by the cost of insurance and freight. So long as freight charges do not vary sharply because of either a change in the composition of trade or a general variation in ocean shipping rates, these two totals should maintain a reasonably constant relation to one another. They have, however, fluctuated widely throughout the period. The difference between total c.i.f. imports and f.o.b. exports varies as a percentage of f.o.b. exports from a low of 12.5 percent in 1954 to a high of 20.2 percent in 1948 and as a percentage of c.i.f. imports from a low of 11.1 percent in 1954 to a high of 16.8 percent in 1948. This wide variation cannot be explained only on the basis of changes in the cost of insurance and freight and must be attributed in large part to the fact that the estimate which one country makes of its exports to another country differs from the estimate of the second country of its imports from the first. For this reason, nearly all the data presented in this section are based on f.o.b. exports alone rather than on combinations of f.o.b. exports and c.i.f. imports, not because the export data are more reliable than import data, but solely so as to work with consistent figures.

Several important conclusions can immediately be drawn from Table 3-1. First, intra-South American trade has essentially stagnated since 1948. Although Venezuela's exports to the other South American nations increased dramatically, this increase was offset by reductions in the exports of other countries, most notably Brazil. Intra-South American trade has not maintained the level it reached in 1954 and 1958.

Second, despite the importance of international trade in the economies of most of the South American republics, intra-South American trade is relatively unimportant. Total intra-South American exports in 1962 amounted to only $524 million, and three of the ten nations, Venezuela, Argentina, and Brazil, supplied 75 percent of these exports. Of total intra-South American imports of $602 million, Brazil, Argentina, and Chile received 77 percent.

Both the stagnation of intra-South American trade and its relatively small importance are clear in Table 3-2. In 1962, the exports of the South American countries to one another represented only 7.5 percent of their total exports. Similarly, South American imports from South American countries represented only 10.3 percent of their total imports. Furthermore, these percentages for most countries are even lower than they were in 1948: while total trade of South America with the world increased significantly be-

TABLE 3-2. *Trade of South American Countries with One Another and with the World*[a]

(Millions of U. S. dollars and percent)

Trade with South America and the World by	1948			1954			1962		
	South America	World	South America as % of World	South America	World	South America as % of World	South America	World	South America as % of World
Argentina									
Exports	165.0	1626.7	10.1	181.2	1079.9	16.8	153.7	1215.8	12.6
Imports	225.7	1590.4	14.2	229.8	954.8	24.1	151.5	1355.8	11.2
Brazil									
Exports	154.6	1172.7	13.2	144.3	1561.8	9.2	76.7	1213.8	6.3
Imports	113.3	1134.2	10.0	233.1	1633.5	14.3	226.5	1475.5	15.4
Uruguay									
Exports	16.3	178.9	9.1	39.7	249.0	15.9	8.0	153.1	5.2
Imports	52.9	201.4	26.3	69.5	274.5	25.3	43.9	230.2	19.1
Paraguay									
Exports	11.3	28.1	40.2	17.9	34.0	52.6	10.8	33.4	32.3
Imports	9.9	24.3	40.7	12.3	32.9	37.4	5.3	34.2	15.5
Chile									
Exports	30.1	329.8	9.1	57.8	403.2	14.3	41.9	531.2	7.9
Imports	74.7	269.1	27.8	95.7	343.1	27.9	87.9	509.1	17.3
Bolivia									
Exports	2.0	112.8	1.8	3.3	111.2	3.0	3.1	76.0	4.1
Imports	23.8	68.7	34.6	17.8	65.5	27.2	11.8	79.7	14.8
Peru									
Exports	61.5	162.4	37.9	45.6	247.5	18.4	50.3	539.0	9.3
Imports	38.5	167.7	23.0	20.6	249.7	8.2	46.9	537.4	8.7
Colombia									
Exports	3.2	288.5	1.1	7.3	657.1	1.1	8.3	463.6	1.8
Imports	27.9	336.6	8.3	16.2	671.8	2.4	12.4	536.2	2.3
Venezuela									
Exports	39.9	1040.1	3.8	114.0	1689.8	6.7	164.9	2594.3	6.4
Imports	24.0	727.1	3.3	2.8	904.9	0.3	10.6	992.9	1.1
Ecuador									
Exports	10.0	48.6	20.6	12.5	100.2	12.5	6.0	116.6	5.1
Imports	3.0	49.7	6.0	3.9	86.1	4.5	4.7	95.1	4.9
Totals									
Exports	493.9	4988.6	9.9	623.6	6133.7	10.2	523.7	6936.8	7.5
Imports	593.7	4569.2	13.0	701.7	5216.8	13.5	601.5	5846.1	10.3

Source: Donald W. Baerresen, Martin Carnoy, and Joseph Grunwald, *Latin American Trade Patterns* (Brookings Institution, 1965).

[a] Exports f.o.b., imports c.i.f.

tween 1948 and 1962, intra-South American trade was practically unchanged.

The wide variation from country to country of the importance of trade with South America within total trade is also noteworthy. In 1962, 32.3 percent of Paraguay's exports went to other South American countries, but these markets received only 1.8 percent of Colombia's exports. South American countries were the source of 19.1 percent of Uruguay's imports but only 1.1 percent of Venezuela's. The variation in dollar values is even greater: while the value of Venezuela's exports to other South American countries was $164.9 million in 1962, that of Bolivia was only $3.1 million. Brazil received $226.5 million in imports from other South American countries, but Ecuador purchased imports worth only $4.7 million.

Although the trade of some countries with other South American nations is reasonably balanced, this is not generally the case. Brazil, Uruguay, and Chile consistently have heavy trade deficits within the area, as has Argentina in the past, while Venezuela has a large trade surplus. It is likely that the countries which traditionally have had deficits will be especially hopeful of increasing their exports within the Latin American free trade area.

Table 3-3 presents country-to-country trade within South America in 1962. As in Table 3-1, both f.o.b. exports and c.i.f. imports are shown. Inaccuracies in the data are evident, as in several instances (for example, Paraguay and Ecuador) imports measured in f.o.b. values exceed the c.i.f. values, while in others (for example, Chile) exports measured in f.o.b. values exceed the c.i.f. values.[2]

For the purposes of the present study, in which spatial aspects of economic integration are emphasized, it is important to determine whether geographical factors influence present intra-South American trade. This influence might be expected to show itself in two areas. First, it could be hypothesized that each South American country has relatively more commerce with those countries to which it has relatively better access. Second, it could be hypothesized that the commodity composition of each nation's

[2] For imports and exports for various years 1948-1963 among LAFTA countries, Venezuela, and Bolivia see *ibid.*, pp. 103-13.

TABLE 3-3. *Intra-South American Trade, 1962*[a]

(Millions of U. S. dollars)

From \ To	Argen-tina	Brazil	Uru-guay	Para-guay	Chile	Boli-via	Peru	Colom-bia	Vene-zuela	Ecua-dor	To-tal
Argentina											
f.o.b.	—	68.5	6.7	5.5	31.8	7.6	25.6	2.3	5.6	0.1	153.7
c.i.f.	—	85.6	8.6	5.0	42.8	7.6	30.0	2.3	6.2	1.8	189.9
Brazil											
f.o.b.	48.4	—	14.1	2.1	9.4	0.9	1.2	0.2	0.4	—	76.7
c.i.f.	62.6	—	20.5	—	7.1	0.9	1.9	0.1	0.4	—	93.5
Uruguay											
f.o.b.	1.6	3.0	—	0.2	0.9	0.1	0.1	2.0	—	0.1	8.0
c.i.f.	2.5	2.6	—	0.3	0.9	—	0.1	2.4	—	—	8.8
Paraguay											
f.o.b.	9.6	0.1	1.1	—	—	—	—	—	—	—	10.8
c.i.f.	9.5	1.0	1.8	—	—	—	—	—	0.3	—	12.6
Chile											
f.o.b.	14.9	18.5	1.1	—	—	1.7	3.1	0.7	1.4	0.5	41.9
c.i.f.	15.1	15.6	1.1	—	—	1.7	3.5	0.2	1.2	0.4	38.8
Bolivia											
f.o.b.	1.9	0.8	—	—	0.3	—	0.1	—	—	—	3.1
c.i.f.	2.0	0.5	—	—	0.2	—	0.2	—	—	—	2.9
Peru											
f.o.b.	8.3	11.1	1.4	—	23.7	1.6	—	1.0	1.7	1.5	50.3
c.i.f.	10.6	13.5	1.2	—	24.0	1.6	—	0.9	1.6	1.3	54.7
Colombia											
f.o.b.	0.7	—	0.3	—	1.0	—	3.8	—	1.0	1.5	8.3
c.i.f.	0.8	—	0.1	—	—	—	4.7	—	0.9	0.6	7.1
Venezuela											
f.o.b.	34.7	98.4	12.7	0.5	11.1	—	2.7	1.5	—	3.3	164.9
c.i.f.	48.0	107.7	10.6	—	10.4	—	3.3	1.6	—	0.6	182.2
Ecuador											
f.o.b.	0.2	—	—	—	2.2	—	0.5	3.1	—	—	6.0
c.i.f.	0.4	—	—	—	2.5	—	3.2	4.9	—	—	11.0
Totals											
f.o.b.	120.3	200.4	37.4	8.3	80.4	11.9	37.1	10.8	10.1	7.0	523.7
c.i.f.	151.5	226.5	43.9	5.3	87.9	11.8	46.9	12.4	10.6	4.7	601.5

Source: Donald W. Baerresen, Martin Carnoy, and Joseph Grunwald, *Latin American Trade Patterns* (Brookings Institution, 1965).

[a] Exports f.o.b.; imports c.i.f.

exports is affected by its own resource endowment and that of its trading partners. It is also possible that these two forces will work against each other: access is likely to be relatively better between adjoining countries, but adjoining countries are also likely to have similar resource endowments.

Economic Access and Intra-South American Trade

Access is a difficult concept to quantify empirically. Although transport costs are an important part of access, other factors—political and cultural—should not be ignored. In the following list the 45 pairs of South American countries have been classified according to whether access is relatively good between the two countries in each pair or relatively poor. The point of departure

Relatively Good Access Between Pairs of Countries	*Relatively Poor Access Between Pairs of Countries*
Argentina-Uruguay	Argentina-Peru
Argentina-Paraguay	Argentina-Colombia
Argentina-Brazil	Argentina-Ecuador
Argentina-Chile	Argentina-Venezuela
Argentina-Bolivia	Brazil-Chile
Brazil-Uruguay	Brazil-Bolivia
Brazil-Paraguay	Brazil-Peru
Uruguay-Paraguay	Brazil-Colombia
Chile-Bolivia	Brazil-Ecuador
Chile-Peru	Brazil-Venezuela
Bolivia-Peru	Uruguay-Chile
Peru-Ecuador	Uruguay-Bolivia
Colombia-Venezuela	Uruguay-Peru
Colombia-Ecuador	Uruguay-Colombia
	Uruguay-Ecuador
	Uruguay-Venezuela
	Paraguay-Chile
	Paraguay-Bolivia
	Paraguay-Peru
	Paraguay-Colombia
	Paraguay-Ecuador
	Paraguay-Venezuela
	Chile-Colombia
	Chile-Ecuador
	Chile-Venezuela
	Bolivia-Colombia
	Bolivia-Ecuador
	Bolivia-Venezuela
	Peru-Colombia
	Peru-Venezuela
	Ecuador-Venezuela

in the classification was whether the two countries adjoin. In those instances where the countries adjoin, a second criterion was added: Are there reasonably good highway, railway, or river connections between the two countries? Using these two criteria, 14 pairs of countries were classified as having relatively good access between the two nations and 31 pairs were classified as having relatively poor access. Although Brazil adjoins all the countries of South America except Chile and Ecuador, only Argentina, Uruguay, and Paraguay were classified as having relatively good access to Brazil. One exception was made in the application of the two basic criteria: although Paraguay does not adjoin Uruguay, it was classified as having relatively good access to the latter country because of the good river facilities which connect the two nations.

When commerce between countries with relatively good and relatively poor access was tabulated, it was immediately clear that Venezuela presents a special case. The importance of the resource factor, Venezuela's petroleum, overwhelmed the role of access or geographical proximity in explaining the present pattern of intra-South American trade. For this reason, two calculations were made, one covering all of intra-South American commerce and the second excluding Venezuela.

On the basis of the f.o.b. export data shown in Table 3-3 for trade in 1962, the 14 pairs of countries with relatively good access accounted for $256.7 million out of total intra-South American trade of $523.7 million. The remaining 31 pairs of countries with relatively poor access accounted for the other $267.0 million. When Venezuela is excluded, total trade drops to $348.7 million and there are only 36 pairs of countries. Now, however, the 13 pairs of nations with relatively good access account for $254.2 million, 73 percent of the new total, while the 23 pairs with relatively poor access account for only $94.5 million. Clearly access is a significant factor in explaining present trade patterns within South America. Since access was one of the elements considered in the delimitation of the nine regions of South America in the previous chapter, there appears to be tentative justification for believing that the regions chosen may well be useful.

Examination of the commerce of each South American country in 1962, after excluding trade with Venezuela, strengthens the conclusion that access has been an important determinant of the pattern of intra-South American trade. More than 75 percent of the trade of Argentina, Brazil, Uruguay, Paraguay, and Bolivia is with countries of easy access. Although both Chile and Ecuador receive more than 80 percent of their imports from countries with easy access, the smaller percentage of their exports to these same countries lowers the figure for total trade in both cases to around 68 percent. Chile exports a substantial amount of refined and smelted minerals and nitrates to Brazil, reflecting Chile's resource endowment, and Ecuador exports bananas of considerable value to Chile.

The classification of trade according to the accessibility of trading partners appears to be of less value in explaining the trade of Peru, Colombia, and Venezuela. The special case of Venezuela has already been mentioned. The relatively low percentage of Peru's trade with countries of easy access is explained primarily by its imports of more than $23 million of meat and grain from Argentina. Nevertheless, in considering the relation of access to the trading patterns of Colombia and Peru, it should be remembered that these countries have extremely difficult internal transport problems and that there is no "easy access" to them from anywhere.

In summary, it would appear that the concept of access is useful in understanding present intercountry trade in South America, as it has been found that where access is relatively easy, commerce tends to be relatively more intense. Thus it would also seem probable that if access could be improved, through improving transport, for example, commerce would be likely to increase. Although this conclusion may appear obvious, its applicability to South America is not evident a priori because of the present nearly complete dependence on ocean shipping in intercountry trade. Despite this dependence, which would be expected to diminish the importance of the geographical proximity of trading partners, access or geographical proximity appears to be significant in analyzing the pattern of intra-South American trade.

TABLE 3-4. *Exports of South American Countries to the Rest of South America Classified by Sectoral Origin and Level of Processing, 1962*[a]

(Thousands of U. S. dollars)

Category	Argentina	Brazil	Uruguay	Paraguay	Chile	Bolivia	Peru	Colombia	Venezuela	Ecuador	Total
Animal Origin											
Unprocessed	31,570.3	66.2	5,671.3	2.0	111.5	94.3	296.6	23.2	—	8.1	37,843.5
Semiprocessed	11,530.5	5.4	59.7	66.9	80.3	62.3	57.7	2.0	48.1	—	11,912.9
Processed	3,648.6	101.9	42.5	—	22.0	—	85.2	0.3	—	0.2	3,900.7
Subtotal	46,749.4	173.5	5,773.5	68.9	213.8	156.6	439.5	25.5	48.1	8.3	53,657.1
Agricultural Origin											
Unprocessed	76,537.5	4,499.7	26.0	1,334.4	3,318.7	27.3	25,995.7	572.2	0.2	2,680.6	114,992.3
Semiprocessed	6,569.3	36,384.7	270.7	2,450.5	409.0	90.3	541.7	1,468.0	2.4	2,292.4	50,479.0
Processed	3,184.3	1,279.4	76.9	94.0	826.5	0.3	462.8	900.6	3.3	0.1	6,828.2
Subtotal	86,291.1	42,163.8	373.6	3,878.9	4,554.2	117.9	27,000.2	2,940.8	5.9	4,973.1	172,299.5
Forest Origin											
Unprocessed	—	7.1	—	—	—	—	—	—	—	—	7.1
Semiprocessed	2,205.0	20,228.7	0.3	6,648.0	2,139.6	895.7	4.8	1.2	5.0	75.5	32,203.8
Processed	257.0	840.3	24.9	—	3,212.0	0.1	63.0	82.9	4.0	8.9	4,493.1
Subtotal	2,462.0	21,076.1	25.2	6,648.0	5,351.6	895.8	67.8	84.1	9.0	84.4	36,704.0
Fishing and Hunting											
Unprocessed	10.0	—	—	—	11.3	—	—	—	—	—	21.3
Semiprocessed											
Processed	21.7	0.5	4.7	—	662.2	0.1	1,537.6	—	66.3	0.9	2,294.0
Subtotal	31.7	0.5	4.7	—	673.5	0.1	1,537.6	—	66.3	0.9	2,315.3
Mineral Origin											
Unprocessed	7,742.2	2,232.1	435.3	1.6	4,477.9	1,593.5	4,657.0	6.7	129,928.4	163.1	151,237.8
Semiprocessed	2,058.7	23.4	558.5	—	16,821.3	163.0	12,112.2	3,325.5	33,028.2	0.1	68,090.9
Processed	6,480.8	9,422.0	346.4	141.7	8,829.7	108.3	2,786.1	1,415.7	923.2	915.5	31,369.4
Subtotal	16,281.7	11,677.5	1,340.2	143.3	30,128.9	1,864.8	19,555.3	4,747.9	163,879.8	1,078.7	250,698.1
Miscellaneous	1,852.0	1,502.4	670.6	150.7	863.9	12.6	1,699.6	501.7	890.9	23.5	8,167.9
Total											
Unprocessed	115,860.0	6,805.1	6,132.6	1,335.0	7,919.4	1,715.1	30,949.3	602.1	129,928.6	2,851.8	304,102.0
Semiprocessed	22,363.5	56,642.2	889.2	9,165.4	19,450.2	1,211.3	12,716.4	4,796.7	33,083.7	2,368.0	162,686.6
Processed	13,592.4	11,644.1	495.4	235.7	13,552.4	108.8	4,934.7	2,399.5	996.8	925.6	48,885.4
Miscellaneous	1,852.0	1,502.4	670.6	150.7	863.9	12.6	1,699.6	501.7	890.9	23.5	8,167.9
Grand Total	153,667.9	76,593.8	8,187.8	10,889.8	41,785.9	3,047.8	50,300.0	8,300.0	164,900.0	6,168.9	523,841.9

Source: Trade statistics of individual countries.
[a] The commodities included in each category—raw materials, semiprocessed, and processed and manufactured—are shown in App. A, Table A-l.

Resource Endowments and Intra-South American Trade

The second geographical factor which has been mentioned as likely to be significant in explaining the pattern of trade is resource endowment. Although this subject will be examined in more detail in the next chapter, it is useful at this point to comment briefly on the commodity composition of present trade. Insight into the importance of resource endowment can be attained by noting the nature of the goods that are exchanged. Furthermore, as the principal objective of current efforts at closer economic integration is to increase commerce in processed and manufactured goods, it is of interest to see the importance of these goods in existing trade.

The exports in 1962 of each South American country to the rest of South America have been classified according to whether they are of animal, agricultural, forest, fishing and hunting, mineral, or miscellaneous origin. Within each of these classifications, the exports have been grouped according to the amount of processing they have received in the country of origin. Three categories have been used: unprocessed or raw materials, semiprocessed, and processed or manufactured. It should be noted that while the miscellaneous category has not been classified according to the level of processing, a major part of these products correspond in fact to the processed or manufactured group.

Table 3-4 presents the exports of each country to the other nations of South America in 1962 classified according to these categories.[3]

In analyzing intra-South American trade on the basis of Table 3-4, it is important to remember that the absolute volume of exports of a number of countries is very small and that this commerce is dominated by Venezuela, Argentina, Brazil, Peru, and Chile. Uruguay, Paraguay, Bolivia, Colombia, and Ecuador contribute, individually, not more than 2.1 percent of total intra-South American exports.

[3] Total figures in Table 3-4 are not always equal to those in Table 3-3 because different sources were used and because of errors in both tables.

Present commerce is concentrated on raw materials and semi-processed goods, principally petroleum (crude and refined), agricultural products (chiefly grains), animals and meat, ores and refined minerals, and lumber. Processed and manufactured commodities, of which more than half are of mineral origin, represent only about 10 percent of total trade. For individual countries, however, exports of processed or manufactured products are important; more than 30 percent of Chile's exports, for example, fall in this category. Nearly 80 per cent of present processed and manufactured exports are supplied by Argentina, Chile, and Brazil.

The importance of the resource endowment of the different South American countries in the composition of trade among them is evident, as it must be when trade is concentrated on the exchange of raw materials and unprocessed or semiprocessed goods. The influence of resources is clearest in the case of petroleum exports from Venezuela, nitrate and metal exports from Chile, fishmeal exports from Chile and Peru, wheat exports from Argentina, and animal and meat exports from Argentina and Uruguay. The trade in these commodities is also representative of the composition of the exports of these countries to the rest of the world.

Undeniable, however, is the importance of access in dictating that a particular country be the source of supply even where a commodity might appear to be resource oriented. Chile receives most of its banana imports from Ecuador, while Argentina imports the same commodity from Brazil, due to the access provided by the present pattern of ocean shipping routes. There is important trade in other fresh fruits and vegetables between Argentina and Brazil, and Argentina receives most of its coffee and lumber from Brazil because of relatively easy access, despite the fact that other South American countries could also supply these products. Finally, it is probable that the percentage incidence of processed and manufactured goods within South American trade, small as it is, is greater than the incidence of these same products in the total exports of the South American countries to the world. It is also probable that the concentration of trade in these products between countries with relatively easy access is even greater

TABLE 3-5. *South American Inter-Regional Trade, 1962*

(Millions of U. S. dollars)

Exporting Regions \ Importing Regions	Argentina, Brazil, Uruguay, Paraguay	Chile	Bolivia, Peru	Colombia, Venezuela	Ecuador	Total Exports
Regions I, II, VIII, IX Argentina, Brazil, Uruguay, Paraguay	160.9	42.1	35.5	10.5	0.2	249.2
Region III Chile	34.5	—	4.8	2.1	0.5	41.9
Regions IV, V Bolivia, Peru	23.5	24.0	1.7	2.7	1.5	53.4
Region VI Colombia, Venezuela	147.3	12.1	6.5	2.5	4.8	173.2
Region VII Ecuador	0.2	2.2	0.5	3.1	—	6.0
Total Imports	366.4	80.4	49.0	20.9	7.0	523.7

Source: f.o.b. exports, Table 3–3.

than the concentration of total trade between these same countries.

As data are available only for intercountry trade, it is not possible to present a complete table showing trade among the nine regions of South America delineated in the preceding chapter. Table 3-5, however, presents an approximation of this trade. Despite the necessity for grouping together Regions I, II, VIII, and IX, it is clear from this table that present trade is concentrated on commerce within and between Regions I and II, the industrial heartland and the supporting hinterland of South America. Were information available on trade from province to province within Argentina and from state to state within Brazil, the importance of these two regions would be even more dramatic. The significance of Venezuela's exports of petroleum, especially to Regions I and II, is also clear in Table 3-5.

In summary, the influence of geographical factors, both resource endowment and access, is significant in understanding the present structure of intra-South American trade. For this reason, the attempt to promote closer integration among these countries must be based on a clear understanding of these factors if integration is to be successful. Only in this way can effort be centered on developing policies that will in fact lead to increased trade, whether the issue involved be tariff negotiations, industrial investment policy, or transport policy. A treatment of Latin American integration as chiefly a political effort ignoring the economic and spatial aspects will inevitably frustrate the entire endeavor.

International Transport Within South America

At the present time, ocean and river transport is practically the sole means by which South America moves its exports and imports.[4] In 1962, 99.3 percent of South America's foreign trade was transported by this mode. In that year, at least 96 percent of each country's exports and imports was transported by water, with two exceptions. Although 97 percent of Paraguay's exports depended on river transport, only 86 percent of its imports arrived via this mode. In the case of Colombia, 89 percent of exports and 91 percent of imports passed through the country's ports.

If information were available to break down the data showing total foreign trade carried by ocean and river transport between intra-South American trade and trade between South America and other continents, it would undoubtedly show that land and air transport is of more importance within South America than it is between South America and the rest of the world. At the same time, however, it is most probable that upwards of 95 percent of even the intra-South American commerce is moved by water. In part, this is due to the fact that more than two-thirds of trade within South America is composed of petroleum, which is transported almost exclusively in tankers.[5] Another important part of total trade within the continent is composed of grains and minerals, which again move almost entirely by water.

[4] United Nations Economic Commission for Latin America, *Estudio Económico de América Latina, 1963,* E/CN.12/696/Rev. 1, p. 97.
[5] *Ibid.,* p. 100.

Because of the overwhelming importance of maritime transport for intra-South American trade, a country-to-country breakdown of tonnage transported via this mode reflects quite accurately the pattern of total shipments. Table 3-6 presents these data for the year 1962, with total intercountry maritime transport broken down into bulk petroleum, bulk minerals and cereals, refrigerated cargo, and general cargo. The most important product from the point of view of transport is petroleum, as 9.3 million metric tons were transported in intra-South American trade in 1962, representing 70 percent of total transport of 13.4 million metric tons. General cargo is of primary interest in this study of transport and economic integration, but it represents only a relatively small part of total tonnage entering intra-South American commerce. In 1962, only 2.1 million metric tons of general cargo were transported, 15.8 percent of total tonnage. An important part of this general cargo, furthermore, was comprised of bulk products such as lumber transported from Brazil to Argentina.

When Table 3-6 is compared with Table 3-3 where the value of intra-South American commerce in 1962 was presented, it is quite clear that data on intercountry trade expressed in value terms can be misleading as an indication of the demand for transport. In Table 3-7, the South American countries have been classified into the Atlantic Coast countries (Argentina, Brazil, Uruguay, and Paraguay), the Pacific Coast countries (Chile, Peru, and Bolivia), the northern countries (Ecuador and Colombia), and Venezuela, which is separated out because of the importance of its petroleum exports. The table shows the percentage distribution of both the value of trade and the tonnage moved by water within and among these four groups of countries. In addition to the distribution of total tonnage, the distribution of the tonnages moved of general cargo is also shown.

Because of the importance of the shipments of low-valued petroleum from Venezuela, there is little relationship between the percentage distribution of the value of commerce and that of total tonnage. While Venezuela's exports represent only 31.5 percent of the total value of intra-South American trade, they account for 65.9 percent of the total tons of trade. When only general cargo is considered, the importance of the Atlantic Coast

TABLE 3-6. *Intra-South American Maritime Transport, 1962*

(Thousands of metric tons)

Exporting Countries	Importing Countries									Total
	Argentina	Brazil	Uruguay	Paraguay	Chile	Peru	Colombia	Venezuela	Ecuador	
Argentina										
Petroleum in bulk	—	116	95	3	—	—	—	—	—	214
Cereals in bulk	—	689	—	—	—	308	—	—	—	997
General cargo	—	18	68	66	122	1	4	24	—	303
Refrigerated cargo	—	150	—	—	10	8	—	20	—	188
Subtotal	—	973	163	69	132	317	4	44	—	1,702
Brazil										
Petroleum in bulk	—	—	—	2	—	—	—	—	—	2
Minerals in bulk	240	—	—	—	—	—	—	—	—	240
General cargo	497	—	82	8	22	2	—	1	—	612
Subtotal	737	—	82	10	22	2	—	1	—	854
Uruguay										
General cargo	239	10	—	2	1	—	—	—	—	252
Paraguay										
General cargo	200	9	17	—	—	—	—	—	—	226
Chile										
Minerals in bulk	172	—	—	—	—	—	—	—	—	172
General cargo	112	82	6	—	—	26	2	8	3	239
Refrigerated cargo	—	—	—	—	—	3	—	—	1	4
Subtotal	284	82	6	—	—	29	2	8	4	415
Peru										
Petroleum in bulk	27	122	—	—	6	—	—	—	—	155
Minerals in bulk	304	—	—	—	—	—	—	—	—	304
General cargo	19	38	7	—	146	—	5	9	5	229
Subtotal	350	160	7	—	152	—	5	9	5	688
Colombia										
Petroleum in bulk	—	—	—	—	17	218	—	—	—	235
General cargo	3	—	—	—	6	81	—	15	2	107
Subtotal	3	—	—	—	23	299	—	15	2	342
Venezuela										
Petroleum in bulk	1,553	5,419	692	33	621	167	13	—	191	8,689
General cargo	72	28	—	—	5	5	6	—	—	116
Subtotal	1,625	5,447	692	33	626	172	19	—	191	8,805
Ecuador										
General cargo	24	—	—	—	—	5	5	—	—	34
Refrigerated cargo	—	—	—	—	38	10	—	—	—	48
Subtotal	24	—	—	—	38	15	5	—	—	82
Total										
Petroleum in bulk	1,580	5,657	787	38	644	385	13	—	191	9,295
Cereals in bulk	—	689	—	—	—	308	—	—	—	997
Minerals in bulk	716	—	—	—	—	—	—	—	—	716
General cargo	1,166	185	180	76	302	120	22	57	10	2,118
Refrigerated cargo	—	150	—	—	48	21	—	20	1	240
Total	3,462	6,681	967	114	994	834	35	77	202	13,366

Source: United Nations Economic Commission for Latin America, *Estudio Económico de América Latina, 1963*, E/CN.12/696/Rev. 1, p. 103, Table 79.

TABLE 3-7. *Percentage Distribution of Tonnage Carried by Water and Value of Trade in Intra-South American Commerce, 1962*[a]

Exporting Countries \ Importing Countries	Argentina, Brazil, Uruguay, Paraguay	Chile, Peru, Bolivia	Ecuador, Colombia	Venezuela	Total Exports
Argentina, Brazil, Uruguay, Paraguay					
Value of trade	30.8	14.8	0.8	1.2	47.6
Tonnage:					
Total cargo	18.8	3.6	—	0.3	22.7
General cargo	57.4	7.0	0.2	1.2	65.8
Chile, Peru, Bolivia					
Value of trade	11.1	5.8	0.7	0.6	18.2
Tonnage:					
Total cargo	6.6	1.3	0.1	0.2	8.2
General cargo	12.5	8.1	0.7	0.8	22.1
Ecuador, Colombia					
Value of trade	0.1	1.5	0.9	0.2	2.7
Tonnage:					
Total cargo	0.2	2.9	—	0.1	3.2
General cargo	1.3	4.3	0.3	0.7	6.6
Venezuela					
Value of trade	28.0	2.6	0.9	—	31.5
Tonnage:					
Total cargo	58.4	5.9	1.6	—	65.9
General cargo	4.7	0.5	0.3	—	5.5
Total imports					
Value of trade	70.0	24.7	3.3	2.0	100.0
Tonnage:					
Total cargo	84.0	13.7	1.7	0.6	100.0
General cargo	75.9	19.9	1.5	2.7	100.0

Source: Tables 3–3 and 3–6.

[a] Bolivia is included in the percentage distribution of the value of intra-South American trade but is excluded in the percentage distribution of the tonnage carried by water. Although it is not known if Bolivian exports and imports which pass through Chilean and Peruvian ports are included in the tonnage figures of these countries, the error introduced is insignificant. An error is also introduced in those cases where intra-South American trade uses land transport, as occurs between Brazil and Uruguay. Again the error introduced does not change the table significantly.

countries is evident. The exports of these four countries represent 65.8 percent of the total tons of general cargo transported and their imports 75.9 percent. The trade among these four countries alone accounts for 57.4 percent of the tonnage of general cargo transported within South America by water. Table 3-7 also shows clearly the slight importance of the tonnage of exports and imports of general cargo of the northern countries, Ecuador, Colombia, and Venezuela.

In relation to the objectives of the Latin American countries in establishing the Latin American Free Trade Association, it is general cargo which is of primary interest. In this category should be included refrigerated cargo, as only with efficient transport will it be possible to increase commerce in meat and perishable foodstuffs. From the point of view of both value of trade and importance in transport, present commerce in relatively high-valued industrial goods and agricultural products is of slight importance within South America in relation to the total foreign trade of these countries. Frequent and economic transport services are essential if the South American countries are to increase production of these commodities and sell them to their neighbors.

CHAPTER IV

Resources of South America

SOUTH AMERICA'S ECONOMIC DEVELOPMENT has been and continues to be resource oriented.[1] Agricultural, mineral, and fuel exports represented more than 90 percent of the total exports of every South American country except Peru in 1959-60.[2] In those same years, agricultural exports accounted for at least 80 percent of the total exports of Uruguay, Argentina, Ecuador, Brazil, and Colombia, while mineral and fuel exports represented at least that same percentage of the exports of Chile, Bolivia, and Venezuela. Only Peru, whose agricultural exports and mineral and fuel exports represented 29 and 46 percent respectively of total exports, cannot be classified unambiguously as being an exporter of one type of raw materials. There is, furthermore, every indication that despite the attempts of these countries to diversify their exports, sales of raw materials will continue for the indefinite future to produce the great bulk of foreign exchange to finance their imports.

Resource industries also continue to contribute importantly to the gross domestic product of the South American nations. As can be seen in Table 4-1, agriculture (including forestry and fishing) and mining and smelting (including petroleum) represented at least one-third of the value added in all these countries in 1959-60

[1] For a more complete analysis on this point see Joseph Grunwald, "Resource Aspects of Latin-American Economic Development," in Marion Clawson (ed.), *Natural Resources and International Development*, Resources for the Future, Inc., (Johns Hopkins Press, 1964). Many of the ideas expressed in this section are taken from the Grunwald article.

[2] The following data are from *ibid.*, p. 335.

TABLE 4-1. *Value Added in Agriculture, Mining, and Smelting as Percent of Gross Domestic Product*

Country	Agriculture[a]		Mining and Smelting[b]		Total	
	1945–46	1959–60	1945–46	1959–60	1945–46	1959–60
Argentina	20	17	1.1	1.6	21.1	18.6
Bolivia	—	35[c]	—	13.5[c]	—	48.5[c]
Brazil	33	25	0.4	0.5	33.4	25.5
Chile	15	13	5.5	4.6	20.5	17.6
Colombia	43	36	2.2	4.1	45.2	40.1
Ecuador	31	36	3.0	2.2	34.0	38.2
Peru	33	27[c]	6.5	7.3[c]	39.5	34.3[c]
Venezuela	9	7	31.1	31.0	40.1	38.0

Source: Joseph Grunwald, "Resource Aspects of Latin-American Economic Development," in Marion Clawson (ed.), *Natural Resources and International Development*, Resources for the Future, Inc. (Johns Hopkins Press, 1964), p. 331, Tables 7 and 8.

[a] Percentages based on national currencies in constant prices. Includes forestry and fisheries.

[b] Based on national currencies in current prices. Includes petroleum.

[c] 1958–59.

except in Argentina, Brazil, and Chile.[3] This dominance of the resource industries is declining, however, except in Ecuador, among the countries included in the table. In this regard, it is interesting to note that while the agricultural, forestry, and fishing sectors contributed only 17 percent of the gross domestic product of Argentina in 1959-60, these sectors accounted for 95 percent of Argentina's exports in the same years.

Knowledge about the quality and geographical distribution of South America's resources (including agricultural land) would be of great assistance in a study of the transport requirements of that continent. The South American countries must continue to rely on resource exports to produce the foreign exchange they require, as was noted above, and these exports require efficient transport if they are to compete in world markets. Moreover, if these nations are successful in their efforts to industrialize, they will require for their own use increasing quantities of raw materials which must be produced internally or within the region, or must be imported from other continents.[4] In addition, even in highly

[3] Neither Paraguay nor Uruguay is included in Table 4-1. Nevertheless, it is believed that the assertion in this text is applicable to both countries.

[4] Grunwald, *op. cit.*, pp. 319-20.

industrialized countries, the transport of raw materials represents a large share of total transport. If the volume of some of the important industrial raw materials could be predicted in intra-South American trade, it would be possible to plan basic transport facilities adequate to meet a large part of South America's transport requirements.

At the same time, however, it is important to recognize that the means of transport that are most appropriate for the transport of iron ore and wheat could well be inappropriate for trade in industrial products. Manufactured goods account for 28 percent of rail transport and 22 percent of water transport in the United States, and if highway and air cargo transport were included, the percentages would be higher.[5] Since the principal objective sought by the South American countries in their efforts to attain greater economic integration is to increase trade in industrial products, considerable attention must be directed to the transport requirements of these goods.

Furthermore, there is likely to be some conflict between transport needs for resource exports, whether to other continents or for use within South America, and transport needs for industrialization. Port, railway, and highway investments are costly and long lived. The South American countries, whose capital resources are limited, must develop a balance between transport investments designed to facilitate raw material exports and those intended for the requirements of national and regional industrialization so that the resulting transport structure is suitable for both purposes. These countries are aware of the problem because of their experience in the past. In Uruguay, Argentina, and Brazil, and to a lesser extent in other South American countries, the existing structure of transport—especially the railroad systems—is designed almost exclusively to facilitate exports. This subject will be pursued further in the section on international transport within South America.

Despite the recognized importance of the resource industries in South America and universal interest in the economic develop-

[5] U. S. Interstate Commerce Commission *Seventy-Sixth Annual Report on Transport Statistics in the United States for the Year Ended December 31, 1962,* Pt. 1, Table 51, and Pt. 5, Table 3.

ment of that continent, little systematic research on the resource sector has been carried out on a continental scale. Such a task, furthermore, obviously extends far beyond the possibilities of the present study.

Resources are important to this study, however, only to the extent that they affect interregional transport requirements within South America. It is sufficient for this limited objective to refer briefly to the geographical distribution of some of the more important products of the resource industries (including agriculture) in relation to regional needs.[6]

Iron Ore, Iron, and Steel

Production of iron ore is distributed widely around South America, as can be seen in Table 4-2, and the ore is generally of exceptionally high grade with excellent physical and chemical characteristics. Production rose from 5.5 percent of total world iron-ore production in 1954-58 to 7.7 percent in 1962. Although production during this period increased only 19 percent in Venezuela, the largest producer in South America, it more than doubled in Peru and more than tripled in Chile. The largest absolute increase occurred in Brazil, whose production jumped from 4.1 million tons in 1954-58 to 10.6 million tons in 1962.

Most of South America's iron ore is exported. Although neither Argentina nor Colombia exports ore, Brazil, Chile, Peru, and Venezuela as a group send more than 85 percent of their production to foreign markets, nearly all to the United States, Europe, and Japan. South America's iron-ore exports represented 21 percent of total world exports in 1962, a considerably higher percentage than its proportion of total world production.[7]

Although it is difficult to measure the consumption of iron ore,

----

[6] This author was fortunate to have access to a partially completed manuscript on resources and the economic development of Latin America prepared under the direction of Joseph Grunwald with support from Resources for the Future, Inc. Unless otherwise indicated, all of the factual material which follows on minerals and forestry products is taken from that manuscript.

[7] U. S. Bureau of Mines, *Minerals Yearbook 1963*, Vol. 1, p. 620.

TABLE 4-2. *Production of Iron Ore, Iron Ore Concentrates, and Iron Ore Agglomerates*

(Thousands of long tons)

Country	1954–58 (Average)	1961	1962	1963
Argentina	69	137	119	128
Brazil	4,073	10,059	10,608	8,137[a]
Chile	2,530	6,879	7,964	8,373
Peru	2,710	8,599	5,855	6,064
Colombia	390	665	669	684
Venezuela	10,973	14,335	13,057	11,676
Total South America	20,745	40,674	38,272	35,062
World Total[b]	375,754	494,704	499,363	509,908

Source: U. S. Bureau of Mines, *Minerals Yearbook 1963*, Vol. 1, pp. 618–19.

[a] Exports.

[b] Estimate.

one useful indicator of changes in this consumption is the production of steel ingots and castings. Between 1954-58 and 1963, steel production in South America measured on this basis increased more rapidly than world production. Even in the latter year, however, it still represented only 1.2 percent of world production. Although production is distributed widely geographically around the continent, Argentina and Brazil together account for more than 75 percent of the total production of the six steel-producing countries in South America. (Chile, Peru, Colombia, and Venezuela are the others.)[8]

Argentina, the only importer of iron ore in South America, in 1962 imported 212 thousand long tons from Brazil, 125 thousand from Chile, and 309 thousand from Peru.[9] Although Argentina will have to continue to import large quantities of ore, because of the low quality and location of its own ore, there is no indication that any of the other present South American producers need recur to imports for many decades, if ever.

While intra-South American trade in steel products has some importance in the trade of a few countries, most notably Chile, it

[8] *Ibid.*, p. 649.

[9] *Ibid.*, p. 620.

is evident that for the continent as a whole great opportunities exist to increase regional production and trade. At the present time, the continent exports large quantities of iron ore and imports the greater part of the steel it requires from other continents. Consumption of finished steel in 1970 in the six countries presently producing steel has been estimated by the Latin American Iron and Steel Institute to be 2.55 million metric tons in Argentina, 4.36 million in Brazil, 0.295 million in Chile, 0.27 million in Peru, 0.61 million in Colombia, and 2.65 million in Venezuela.[10] The sum of the projected consumption in these six countries is 10.735 million metric tons, compared with production of steel ingots and castings in 1963 of 4.7 million metric tons in the same countries.

Although it is difficult to analyze future interregional trade in South America in iron ore and iron and steel on the basis of the country data presented above, a few general observations can be made. First, although Argentina must continue to import most of its iron ore, and can do so easily from other South American countries, little importance need be given to the transport requirements of this trade. The countries from which Argentina would acquire ore already have specialized installations for ore exports, and sales to Argentina would be small in relation to total exports. Transport will be by water and is not likely to be combined with the transport of other goods because of the advantages of using specialized ore carriers operating on a rigid sailing schedule. This situation might change if Argentina finds it advantageous to import ore from the Mutum and Urucúm deposits on the frontier between Bolivia and Brazil near Puerto Suarez.[11] In this case, transport would be by river barge and might well justify investments in improving navigation on the Paraguay River, which would also affect the river transport of other products.

Second, steel is presently being produced in nearly all nine

[10] Cited in Ana M. Martirena de Mantel, "Integración y Economías de Escala," *El Trimestre Económico*, Vol. XXXI (3), No. 123 (July-September 1964), pp. 414, 417. The projection is based on the regression equation $\log Y = 1.98 + 1.43 \log X$, where Y is the per capita consumption of finished steel and X is the per capita gross national product. The estimate at least for Chile appears to be unreasonably low.

[11] U. S. Bureau of Mines, *Minerals Yearbook, 1963*, p. 623.

regions of South America used in this study and decentralized steel production may well be efficient in the future. Specialization in certain types of steel and steel products, however, is probably essential for efficiency, and interregional trade in these products should be encouraged. Production in Region I, the industrial heartland, will continue to increase, and Brazil may well become a leading steel producer in the future. Argentina, which must import both iron ore and coal will probably continue to be a heavy importer of steel, perhaps from Brazil and other South American countries.

Steel production in Brazil is located near the point where Regions I, II, and IX join in that country (as well as further south within Region I). There are also plans to construct a charcoal blast furnace within Region II in Argentina on the border with Paraguay at Posadas, in the Misiones Province.[12] In general, however, it appears doubtful that Region II presents good opportunities for steel production with present technology. Should technology change and make production without coal competitive, conceivably steel could be produced within Region II near the Mutum and Urucúm desposits as petroleum deposits are located nearby and the steel would find a ready market in Paraguay, Uruguay, Brazil, and Argentina, to which there is easy access by river and by railroad.

Region III, Chile, is already an important steel producer and the only net steel exporter in South America. Because of its good access to coal, ore, and limestone, the plant at Concepción produces competitively and should be able to continue supplying Region I. It could also supply Region II near the Chilean border. Chile also exports ferroalloys and could become a major supplier for all of South America of these products.

The only production within Region IV, the coastal and highlands of Bolivia and Peru, is at Chimbote, in Peru. Because of its access to both ore and coal, the plant can produce efficiently with present technology and could supply Regions I, V, and VII in the future. Neither Region V (eastern slope of the Andes in Bolivia and Peru) nor Region VII (Ecuador) produces steel at the present

[12] U. S. Bureau of Mines, *Minerals Yearbook, 1962*, p. 705. This plant would be built with the aid of four Japanese steel firms.

time nor is it likely that it would be efficient to do so in the fore-seeable future.

Steel is produced in Region VI in both Colombia and Venezuela. Colombia's plant at Paz del Rio is located far inland near ore and coal deposits and could produce efficiently for the internal market. Except for some partial specialization and trade with Venezuela, Colombia is not likely to produce steel for export, although it could supply all its domestic needs for many types of steel. Venezuela, which has only recently begun steel production, could become an important exporter if new technology based on petroleum and natural gas instead of coal continues to improve. Because of its own need for pipe, Venezuela could well specialize in this product and supply the other regions of the continent.

Steel is not yet produced in Region VIII, the Amazon Basin, but it has been reported that the Companhia Siderurgica da Amazonia, which has ore deposits in the region, is planning the construction of a mill in Manaus. The equipment and technicians for the plant would be supplied by Krupp in exchange for iron ore from the company's mines.[13]

Should the panorama of decentralized steel production described here be realized, most of the transport of the steel products would be based on ocean shipping, as it is now. These shipping services, however, would have to be considerably improved, as regular, stable, frequent liner services would be required to permit more intensive trade in these products, especially if different countries specialize in the production of particular types of steel, depending on their neighbors for other types. Chile, for example, could not depend on Venezuela for the steel pipe it might require unless ocean services were improved between the two countries.

In several areas, land and river transport should be improved to facilitate trade in steel products, especially within and between Regions I and II. Similarly, provision of highway transport from Concepción in Chile to Argentine cities along the Andes could be the basis for increased Chilean exports of steel to these consuming centers.

[13] *Ibid.*, p. 705.

Coal

In the United States in 1962, coal and coke accounted for 28 percent of the tonnage transported by railroad and 40 percent of that by water carriers. This fantastic importance of coal, which would also be found to a greater or lesser degree in many other parts of the world, does not generally prevail in South America for several important reasons. First, despite the fact that coal is one of the most plentiful minerals in the world, little has been found in South America. The United States, Russia, and China hold nearly 90 percent of known and inferred reserves; all of Latin America has less than one percent. While coal is produced in several South American countries, there is practically no intra-South American commerce in this product, and import requirements are supplied from other continents, principally from the United States. Much of this imported coal is consumed near the ports of entry, and despite the importance of coal in the internal transport of some countries, notably Chile and Brazil, there is relatively little intraregional and interregional transport of this product.

In the second place—and extremely fortunate for Latin America—there are few areas where coal is indispensable or even where other fuels cannot be used nearly as economically. For this reason, Latin America has never depended on coal as its basic source of energy as have other parts of the world. Coal represented only 35.6 percent of total energy consumed in Latin America in 1929, and this percentage had fallen to 7.6 percent in 1958.[14] In the entire world, coal, lignite, and peat were the source of nearly 80 percent of the energy consumed commercially in 1929 and were still half that figure in 1960. To a considerable extent, Latin America has substituted hydroelectric power for electricity produced from coal, and also makes relatively far greater use of petroleum than does the rest of the world.

[14] Joseph Grunwald, manuscript on resources and the economic development of Latin America, "Coal," Table 3. Compiled from United Nations, "Energy in Latin America" (Geneva: United Nations, 1957), Table 8, p. 27, and ECLA, *Economic Bulletin for Latin America, Statistical Supplement*, Vol. VI (November 1961), Table 29, p. 67.

The importance of the transport of coal in future intraregional and interregional transport in South America will depend on several factors: (1) new discoveries of coal on that continent, (2) the success of the South American countries in meeting their energy requirements through increased production of petroleum, natural gas, and hydroelectric power, and (3) steel technology. With respect to the first factor, one can only speculate; conceivably one day immense deposits of coal will be discovered, and this commodity will take on importance in transport. Barring dramatic new coal discoveries, however, the transport of coal can largely be ignored in planning transport investments in the future, although individual countries, especially Chile and Brazil, must take it into account.

The tendency in regard to the second factor is quite clear: imports will probably remain reasonably constant in absolute terms as the South American countries slowly increase domestic coal production and rapidly increase the supply of energy from other sources. Coal imports, used primarily to convert to coke, will depend largely on what has traditionally been the single indispensable use of coal: its importance in producing iron and steel. If it becomes possible to produce steel efficiently using petroleum or natural gas, the need for coal in countries like Argentina will fall precipitously. While coal would then continue to be used in those countries where it is conveniently located in relation to iron ore, as in Colombia and Chile, it would lose its importance in other countries, such as Venezuela.

Other Minerals and Fuels

The transport requirements of other minerals and fuels can be passed over rapidly. The transport of petroleum, natural gas, and mineral ores requires specialized facilities that are generally used for only one commodity. These facilities can be planned and justified economically without concern for their use in the transport of other goods, as the basic facilities used are pipelines, specialized port loading and unloading equipment, and specialized water carriers. Only in the design of land transport facilities from mines to ports need special care be taken to assure that the investments made are consistent with the needs of various regions for a transport system adequate for increasing industrialization. This consideration affects both the route followed by and design standards of new railways and highways, as well as the choice between these two transport media.

Forestry Products

Forestry products merit considerable attention in planning a transport structure adequate for the needs of economic integration in South America. The forest resources of the continent are immense, and less than 10 percent of forest land is presently

TABLE 4-3. *Forest Resources and Use, 1958–1959*

Country	Forest Area		Roundwood Equivalent[a]			
	Total	In Use	Total Growing Stock[b,c]	Industrial Removals[d]	Fuelwood Removals	Total Removals
	(Thousands of hectares)			(Millions of cubic meters)		
Argentina	70,000	7,250	3,195	2.6	9.4	12.0
Brazil	561,660	40,000	79,150	17.6	90.0	107.6
Uruguay	550	540	98	0.2	1.0	1.2
Paraguay	20,910	5,020	1,940	0.4	1.3	1.7
Chile	20,440	4,610	3,820	2.2	3.1	5.3
Bolivia	47,000	6,000	6,960	0.5	5.4	5.9
Peru	70,000	11,050[b]	11,100	0.6	2.3	2.9
Colombia	69,400	5,900	11,800	3.1	22.0	25.1
Venezuela	45,000	1,100	5,630	0.8	4.5	5.3
Ecuador	14,850	300	2,460	0.8	2.1	2.9
Total	919,810	81,770	126,153	28.8	141.1	169.9

Source: Joseph Grunwald, manuscript on resources and the economic development of Latin America, "Forest Products," Table 1, compiled from ECLA/FAO, *Latin American Timber Trends and Prospects* (New York: United Nations, 1963), Tables 4, 5, 6.

[a] Volume of wood without bark.

[b] Estimate by FAO.

[c] Including noncommercial species.

[d] Including removals for all purposes other than fuel: construction, manufacturing, packaging materials, pulp and paper.

TABLE 4-4. *Net Trade in Forestry Products, 1960*[a]

(Millions of U. S. dollars)

Country	Logs, Sawnwood, and Similar Products[b]	Pulp and Paper[c]	Other Products	Total Forest Products, Net Balances
Argentina	−32.6	−41.1	−2.4	−76.1
Brazil	46.8	−37.0	d	9.8
Uruguay	− 6.0	− 7.8	d	−13.8
Chile	1.0	− 0.9	−0.4	− 0.3
Peru	− 3.6	− 8.9	−0.3	−12.8
Colombia	2.2	− 8.6	d	− 6.4
Venezuela	− 4.0	−15.2	−0.1	−19.3
Ecuador	1.3	− 3.4	d	− 2.1
Total	5.1	−122.9	−3.2	−121.0

Source: Joseph Grunwald, manuscript on resources and the economic development of Latin America, "Forest Products," Table 7, compiled from FAO, *Yearbook of Forest Products Statistics, 1961.*

[a] Excludes trade in secondary products, such as derivatives of quebracho, other tannery materials, natural rubber, resins, balsam, oilseeds, etc. A minus sign denotes net imports.

[b] Includes logs, poles, pilings, sleepers, plywood, veneers, particle board, and fiberboard.

[c] All pulp, paper and manufactures thereof.

[d] Less than $50,000.

being exploited. As can be seen in Table 4-3, 83 percent of the wood removed in 1958-59 was used as fuel. While the continent as a whole is nearly self-sufficient in sawnwood (see Table 4-4), imported pulp and paper still represent an important item in the balance of payments of many countries. Furthermore, as economic development continues, the demand for paper will increase rapidly. With the wider markets promised by successful integration, it will be possible to produce efficiently enough paper to meet the area's requirements.

Before relating commerce in forest products to transport, it is important to note the distinction between deciduous, or broadleaved, forests and coniferous softwoods. Deciduous forests are found throughout the continent, while the conifers are only important in the southern part of the continent, principally in Chile and the southeast of Brazil, as well as in a few parts of Argentina and Uruguay. The deciduous hardwoods are valuable for lumber and related products, and most South American countries should be able to meet their needs with their own domestic production. The conifers are also useful for lumber, but their principal importance is as the raw material for the production of pulp and paper products. Although experimental work is being carried out to permit the production of paper from hardwoods, and paper is presently produced in South America from agricultural waste products such as bagasse, the basic supply of paper in the future should continue to be produced from conifer wood pulp. Those countries where conifers thrive will find ready markets for their products within South America. In Chile, large plantations of pines planted near the coast around Concepción are already being exploited commercially, and experience has shown that the growth rate of conifers in this area is among the highest in the world.

At the present time, the principal intra-South American trade in lumber is from Brazil to Argentina, or, in terms of the regional classification used in this study, from the Brazilian part of Regions I and II to the Argentine part of Region I. After Argentina, the most important net importer of lumber in South America is Uruguay. Looking to the future, the production of lumber should increase substantially in Argentina, but Argentina and Uruguay should continue to import significant volumes, which must be considered in intraregional and interregional transport. The main supplier should continue to be the southern states of Brazil, and both land and river transport of lumber should continue to reduce the present importance of ocean transport for this commodity. Chile has also been an important supplier of lumber to Argentina in the past and could regain this position in the future. Although the transport of lumber from Chile to markets around Buenos Aires will probably continue to be by ocean for the indefinite future, land transport is practicable to Argentine markets along the Andes.

Peru and Venezuela were also net importers of lumber in 1960, but this was due primarily to inadequate internal transport, as both countries have important forest reserves. As Peru continues to improve communications between Regions IV and V, its dependence on imported lumber should diminish. Both countries may find, however, that it is advantageous to import lumber from nearby countries for their coastal markets, especially if the imported lumber has characteristics that make it especially desirable. Thus Peru could import lumber from Chile, and Venezuela could be partially supplied from Brazil. The transport in both these cases would be by ocean.

For few products is the cost of transport as significant a factor as it is in the case of lumber. Within South America, the ocean freight rate alone can easily exceed 30 percent of the f.o.b. price, so that when the cost of the transport of sawn lumber to the port and that of the logs to the sawmills is included, it is obvious that increased trade in lumber will depend primarily on improvements in transport. The high cost of transport is due basically to the difficulty of handling lumber, so that each operation of loading and unloading and transshipment is expensive. For this reason, international land transport, if it can be carried out without transshipment, is attractive. Even more desirable, however, would be a more efficient use of river transport where this is feasible, as is the case within the La Plata river system. Nevertheless, despite the advantages of substituting land and river transport for ocean transport of lumber, the greater part of the commerce in this product will continue to be based on ocean shipping. Priority should be given therefore to developing more efficient methods for handling lumber in the ports so as to reduce the cost of its transfer between ships and the land transport modes.

The production of wood pulp and newsprint in South America was confined solely to Argentina, Brazil, and Chile in 1959, with Brazil by far the greatest producer of both products. Because of the especially favorable conditions for conifers in Chile and Brazil, these two countries should logically increase their production of these products. The size of the Brazilian market is sufficiently large, however, that probably many years will pass before Brazil could begin to export to other countries, except for some specialized pulp and paper products. Only Chile is likely to become an important exporter in the near future, and, except for markets along the Argentine side of the Andes, which can efficiently be supplied by land transport, all Chilean exports to the other regions of South America would be by sea. Conceivably, air cargo transport will develop sufficiently to permit Chile to export some paper products by air in the case of products with a reasonably high unit value.

Forestry products may well prove appropriate for considerable specialization and complementarity of production among the South American countries within the framework of LAFTA. Should this develop, individual countries would then both export to and import from their neighbors, thus increasing the importance of interregional trade in these products.

Agricultural Products

Despite the fact that trade in agricultural products is already important in intra-South American trade (see Table 4-5), the potential benefits of economic integration leading to greater agricultural specialization and more intensive commerce have received surprisingly little attention. The Montevideo Treaty, in fact, assigns agriculture a minor position and includes escape clauses that reduce the possibilities of using integration to increase productivity in this sector. However, only after several years was it possible for the European Common Market to overcome the political obstacles to adopting a common agricultural policy and to set a wheat price for the entire area. It is to be hoped that South America will also make progress in this area, as agriculture is the one sector where the applicability of the concept of comparative advantage is indisputable.

The transport requirements of the agricultural sector must be given careful consideration in analyzing the adequacy of the present regional transport systems and in planning new transport investments. In the first place, the historical performance of the agricultural sector has been disappointing in South America. Production in general has barely kept pace with the growth in population, and that of specific products, such as meat, has fallen in some countries on a per capita basis. One of the factors often indicated as contributing importantly to inadequate production is the marketing process and specifically poor transport. It is commonly held that improvements in transport are essential if commercialization is to be rationalized. Furthermore, important programs in both land reform and colonization in South America can only be successfully carried out if they are coordinated with new transport investments.

In the second place, most agricultural products are perishable.

TABLE 4-5. *Intra-South American Trade in Agricultural Products, 1962*

Products	Value of Trade (Thousands of U. S. dollars)	Percent
Animal Origin		
Unprocessed:		
Live animals	29,586.6	78.2
Wool and other animal fibers	8,192.0	21.6
Products not analyzed	64.8	0.2
Subtotal	37,843.4	100.0
Semiprocessed:		
Hides and hair	2,365.7	19.9
Meat: fresh, chilled and frozen	6,024.3	50.6
Animal fat	3,315.9	27.8
Products not analyzed	206.9	1.7
Subtotal	11,912.8	100.0
Processed:		
Dairy products	3,310.9	84.9
Products not analyzed	589.8	15.1
Subtotal	3,900.7	100.0
Total, animal origin	53,656.9	
Plant Origin		
Unprocessed:		
Wheat and other grains	62,905.7	54.7
Raw and baled fibers	26,739.3	23.3
Fresh fruits	17,399.1	15.1
Legumes and vegetables	5,137.3	4.5
Nuts	2,074.1	1.8
Products not analyzed	736.7	0.6
Subtotal	114,992.2	100.0
Semiprocessed:		
Flour and other milled grains	5,230.5	10.4
Semirefined sugar	4,232.6	8.4
Dried fruits	1,844.2	3.6
Coffee, cocoa, tea, yerba mate	37,793.4	74.9
Products not analyzed	1,378.4	2.7
Subtotal	50,479.1	100.0
Processed:		
Food, including canned fruits and juices, vegetables, etc.	2,634.1	38.6
Vegetable oils, edible and otherwise	1,409.0	20.6
Products not analyzed	2,785.0	40.8
Subtotal	6,828.1	100.0
Total, plant origin	172,299.4	

Source: Export statistics of individual countries.

Markets can be opened and extended for trade in these commodities solely if transport is well organized. This problem is accentuated by the fact that production in many instances is seasonal, and transport capacity must exist to handle large volumes for a short period of time. Good organization is essential to reduce the total investments that must be made when the equipment would remain idle part of the year.

In the third place, border trade in agricultural products is now significant in a number of areas, as some sections of a country can be more easily supplied from a neighboring country than from its own principal production centers. Improved land transport across borders could lead to greatly increased trade within frontier areas of neighboring countries, benefiting considerably the inhabitants of each.

Finally, except for bulk grains and refrigerated products, agricultural products commonly use the same transport facilities used by all general cargo. Trade within each country in agricultural commodities is, of course, large, and represents a major part of total transport demand. In intercountry trade within South America, trade in products of animal and agricultural origin was 43 percent of the value of total trade in 1962. Thus in designing an adequate transport structure, agricultural products must be analyzed carefully.

In order to relate transport to agricultural products, intercountry trade in 1962 has been broken down into groups of commodities. Table 4-5 shows the 17 product groups selected for detailed analysis and the value of products traded. These products represent 98.4 percent of all trade in products of animal origin and 97.2 percent of trade in products of plant origin. The table also shows the importance of the products within each category of goods classified according to the level of processing. In all categories, the products selected represent nearly all of total trade except for processed products of plant origin. Here, the unanalyzed products reach 40.8 percent of the total because of the incidence of textiles, which are included in this category, but which were not considered to be products of the agricultural sector.

Analysis of intercountry trade in agricultural commodities in one year is not an adequate basis on which to project future transport requirements. The South American countries do not supply all their import requirements of these products from other South American nations, even though potentially they could do so. Thus Chile imported little sugar from its South American neighbors in 1962 but imported sugar from other countries. Peru, an important sugar exporter, sold little of its export surplus within Latin America. Trade in wheat shows similar tendencies, as a number of South American nations imported grain from the United States under exceptionally favorable conditions rather than from neighbors which are traditional exporters, such as Argentina. Moreover, trade in agricultural commodities can fluctuate widely from one year to the next, especially because of varying harvests in the exporting and importing countries. Data for one year, therefore, are only useful to indicate general orders of magnitude.

Finally, future trade in agricultural commodities will depend greatly on the agricultural policies adopted in the different South American countries. If countries attempt to achieve virtual self-sufficiency in all the important products, and ignore the possibilities of greater integration, the trade pattern will be quite different from that which will prevail if the philosophy of integration is extended to this sector. Land reform and colonization programs will also affect future agricultural production, not only in regard to the level of production but in relation to its composition as well.

Nevertheless, it is useful to begin with present intercountry trade, extending the analysis to intraregional and interregional trade where this is possible, in order to anticipate the type of agricultural commerce that is likely to occur in the future. A more thorough study should analyze total agricultural exports and imports rather than intra-South American trade alone and should also consider the agricultural development programs that these countries have prepared.

Products of Animal Origin

Total trade in products of animal origin amounted to $53.7 million in 1962 of which $35.6 million was composed of meat and live animals. Argentina alone accounted for 93.8 percent of the exports of these two product groups, and when Uruguay is added, the two countries' exports reach 98.7 percent of the total. Chile and Peru are the most important importers, receiving 86.1 percent of imports of meat and live animals. Brazil receives nearly all the exports of live animals of Uruguay, and when its imports are added to those of Chile and Peru, the three countries account for 92.1 percent of the imports of these products. Trade at present is almost entirely confined to the southern part of the continent; the exports and imports of meat and live animals by Ecuador, Colombia, and Venezuela are insignificant.

The present trading pattern in meat and live animals is likely to continue into the future. Despite Chile's desire to increase its meat production, it should continue to provide an important market for Argentina's surplus. Bolivia and Peru also hope to increase domestic production, especially through colonization efforts in Region V, but there is little likelihood of their becoming self-sufficient for many years. In the northern part of the continent, Colombia and Venezuela should be able to supply their own needs for meat and conceivably could become exporters in the future. Internal transport in these countries must be improved, however, because the regions that are especially appropriate for livestock are isolated from the major consumption centers. Although Brazil is an important market for Uruguay, its imports of live animals are insignificant in relation to production within Brazil itself. The geographical proximity of the two countries is likely to result in continued trade, especially if land transport facilities are improved.

The present importance of trade within South America in live animals ($29.6 million) as compared with fresh, chilled, and frozen meat ($6.0 million) is remarkable and will undoubtedly change in the future. In the case of Chile, consumers prefer freshly killed beef to either frozen or chilled meat, and to satisfy these tastes live animals are imported for slaughter within Chile. This system is inefficient, in addition to being an exception to Argentina's established policy of exporting only meat. Nevertheless, even though Chilean consumers were not willing to pay a premium for fresh beef, the present transport facilities would be inadequate to handle sizable quantities of chilled and frozen meat. Since Chile, Peru, and Bolivia will continue to import these products from Argentina and Uruguay for many years, it is important to establish an efficient transport system that meets the technological requirements of moving meat. Air transport is already being used and may well increase in importance in the future. For both air and sea transport, it is essential to have adequate reception facilities in the ports and airports as well as specialized highway and railway equipment. The possibilities of organizing an efficient transport system for these products will be greatly improved if the importing countries enter into long-term contracts with the supplying countries. At the present time, authorization for imports is given with short notice and frequently on an emergency basis to cover temporary shortages, and the transport is organized on an ad hoc basis at high cost.

The trading pattern in hides and hair ($2.4 million in 1962) is similar to that of live animals. Argentina is again by far the most important exporter, and Chile and Peru are the most important importers. The likely trading pattern in the future for meat and live animals described above is also applicable to hides and hair, so that the fact that the countries which import meat also import hides will tend to reduce the speed of a transition from trade in live animals to trade in meat.

Trade in dairy products and animal fat together amounted to $6.6 million in 1962. Argentina was the only major exporter of both products; Chile was the major importer of animal fat and Venezuela of dairy products. Dairy products traditionally have a high income elasticity of demand, and trade in these products should increase as the continent develops. As in the case of meat, the transport requirements of these products are exacting, and increased trade will require substantial improvements in present international transport.

Products of Plant Origin

Intra-South American trade in products of plant origin amounted to $172.3 million in 1962, in volume of goods transported and value of trade.

Trade in grains and milled grains will continue to be of great importance for the indefinite future in intra-South American commerce. Because of the large quantities involved, the basis for most intercounty trade in these products, especially from Argentina to Brazil, Chile, and Peru, will be bulk ocean transport using specialized port facilities. Land transport is not likely to be important in intercountry trade, although it will, of course, be the principal means of transport internally within each country. Even between Argentina and Brazil, land or river transport of wheat is not likely to become important because the southern part of Brazil, to which Argentina has the best land access, is a wheat-producing region. Thus the international transport of wheat is of less interest in planning intercountry facilities than its incidence in trade would imply. At the same time, the South American countries may desire to channel wheat cargoes to ocean liners, instead of to the more efficient bulk carriers, in order to provide a better traffic base for regular liner service. This subject will be pursued in Chapter VII.

Trade in raw and baled fibers of plant origin—primarily cotton—was also of great importance in 1962, reaching $26.7 million. Peru was the only important exporter and Chile was by far the most important importer, followed by Argentina. Land transport from Peru to other South American nations, especially from the coastal areas in Peru where cotton production is concentrated, is nearly impossible and will continue to be so, except to Bolivia. This product will therefore be of interest solely for ocean transport.

Trade in fresh fruits and legumes and vegetables was important and more widely distributed geographically in 1962 than trade in most other products. Furthermore, many countries were exporters and importers due in part to the heterogeneity of the particular products included in these categories and also to the convenience of border trade in these goods. Both product groups contain many perishable products, and increased commerce will require improvement in the organization of transport and in transport facilities. Land and river transport to facilitate trade between adjoining countries offers great opportunities for increasing the importance of this commerce. Probably air transport will also take on increasing importance in intercountry trade of the more highly valued goods in these categories.

After wheat and other grains, the most important group of ag-ricultural products in intra-South American trade in 1962 was coffee, cocoa, tea, yerba mate. Commerce in these products, al-though dominated by Brazil's exports to Argentina, Chile, and Uruguay, tended to be somewhat more dispersed than for most other products. Land transport to facilitate trade among Brazil and Paraguay as exporters and Argentina, Uruguay, and Chile as importers would seem to offer favorable possibilities as it might also be in the northern part of the continent among Ecuador, Venezuela, and Colombia.

Trade in canned and processed food and in vegetable oils barely reached $4.0 million in 1962, a small fraction of trade in fresh fruits and vegetables. Commerce was centered on the south-ern part of the continent and was mainly between adjoining countries. Improvements in transport, especially land transport to facilitate border trade, could well lead to a great increase in com-merce in these products.

CHAPTER V

Population and Income in
South America

AN ANALYSIS OF POPULATION characteristics and levels of income is essential in a study of transport requirements for several reasons. The volume of trade between two geographical units, and hence the transport demand, may be affected by changes in the population and income of each. If this is the case, the present pattern of trade can be partially explained by these variables, and their projection will be useful in predicting future volumes of trade.

Moreover, the strategy of economic development adopted will be influenced by population and income projections. If these projections indicate that in specific regions the standard of living cannot be raised significantly for the increased population which is expected, attempts will be made to encourage migration. Such a development strategy, based on migration and colonization, has obvious implications for new transport investments.

Transport can be used as a policy variable to reduce large income inequalities from region to region within a country. Regional income disparities are dangerous in an underdeveloped country and at times present a real threat to the maintenance of a government. International income divergences have also proved an important obstacle to attaining economic integration within the Latin American Free Trade Association, as the nations that are relatively less developed are reluctant to open their markets to their more advanced neighbors.

South American nations are characterized by great concentrations of population in a few disproportionately large urban centers. To bring about a greater dispersion of population geographically by encouraging the growth of medium-sized cities, either because of the expected contribution this would make to economic development or for other reasons, transport policies and investments can be used effectively.

Finally, the selection of the transport mode or modes which are appropriate for a given region will be affected by population density and levels of income. Where the density is extremely low, as in Region V, a combination of highway and air transport may be efficient, while in regions of high population density, as in Region I, railways may be suitable.

Population and Income and the Pattern of International Trade

The relation between population and income and the volume of international trade has been analyzed by Simon Kuznets.[1] His study, based on a large number of countries, showed that the volume of foreign trade, defined as the proportion of foreign trade to gross national product, varies inversely with total population. Kuznets found, however, that this association is not a direct relation but rather is the result of the relation of population to two other variables which bear a close relation to foreign trade proportions. The first of these is the size of the trading partners, measured by their gross national products, which is negatively associated with foreign trade proportions. The second is the level of development, measured by per capita product, which is positively related to foreign trade proportions. Kuznets then concludes:[2]

> If size (as measured by GNP) and foreign trade proportions are negatively associated and the latter and per capita product are

[1] Simon Kuznets, "Quantitative Aspects of the Economic Growth of Nations: IX. Level and Structure of Foreign Trade: Comparisons for Recent Years," *Economic Development and Cultural Change,* Vol. XIII, No. 1, Pt. II (October 1964). This study also lends some justification to the attempts of the members of the Latin American Free Trade Association to increase regional production of capital goods through economic integration (see pp. 66-70).

[2] *Ibid.,* p. 30.

positively associated, size of population *must* be a significant factor, negatively associated with foreign trade proportions, and accounting for much more of the variance of the latter than even GNP. . . . Population is, of course, gross national product divided by per capita product, and can thus be viewed as a combination of the size factor, taken positively and hence inversely related to foreign trade proportions, and per capita product, taken negatively and hence also inversely related to foreign trade proportions. It is, therefore, no surprise that population shows a close inverse association with foreign trade proportions—but it is not population as such that explains the relation, but rather population as a combination of size represented by total product, and level of development represented by per capita product.

Thus while population projections alone are not useful in predicting future trading patterns, these together with projections of gross national product can be used to predict the volume of trade.

Projections of Regional Population in South America

The capability of different areas within South America to provide an increasing standard of living for their population can be handled directly on the basis of the nine regions delineated previously. Table 5-1 shows estimates made in 1963 by the United Nations[3] of the population of the South American countries in 1960 together with projections to 1980. In those cases where national boundaries do not coincide with the regional boundaries defined in this study, the national population both for 1960 and in the 1980 projection has been distributed among the regions into which countries are divided. The methodology used in this distribution is described in a methodological note in Appendix B.

Table 5-2 summarizes by regions the information given in Table 5-1. As the projections to 1980 in both tables and the regional distribution are based primarily on historical tendencies in each country, they can be interpreted to represent a future state of affairs that will exist unless policies are adopted which would affect either rates of growth or migration. The projections are, of

[3] United Nations, *Provisional Report on World Population Prospects, as Assessed in 1963*, ST/SCA/Ser.R/7 (New York, 1964).

TABLE 5-1. *Population of South America by Country and Region, 1960 and 1980*

Country	1960 (In thousands)	1980 (In thousands)	Annual Rate of Growth	Percentage Distribution	
				1960	1980
Argentina:					
Region I	11,817	17,412	1.9		
Region II	9,139	11,586	1.2		
Subtotal	20,956	28,998	1.6	14.5	11.8
Bolivia:					
Region II	333	490	1.9		
Region IV	3,175	5,212	2.5		
Region V	188	298	2.3		
Subtotal	3,696	6,000	2.4	2.6	2.4
Brazil:					
Region I	37,213	72,286	3.4		
Region II	8,395	15,132	3.0		
Region VIII	2,583	4,598	2.9		
Region IX	22,268	31,700	1.8		
Subtotal	70,459	123,716	2.9	48.8	50.5
Chile:					
Region III	7,627	12,378	2.4	5.3	5.0
Colombia:					
Region VI	15,468	27,691	3.0	10.7	11.3
Ecuador:					
Region VII	4,355	7,981	3.0	3.0	3.3
Paraguay:					
Region II	1,720	2,981	2.8	1.2	1.2
Peru:					
Region IV	9,772	16,607	2.7		
Region V	427	893	3.8		
Subtotal	10,199	17,500	2.8	7.1	7.1
Uruguay:					
Region II	2,491	3,126	1.2	1.7	1.3
Venezuela:					
Region VI	7,394	14,857	3.6	5.1	6.1
Totals	144,365	245,228	2.7	100.0	100.0

Source: See methodological note in Appendix B.

TABLE 5-2. *Population of South America by Region, 1960 and 1980*

Region	1960	1980	Annual Rate of Growth	Percentage Distribution	
	(In thousands)			1960	1980
I	49,030	89,698	3.0	34.0	36.6
II	22,078	33,315	2.1	15.3	13.6
III	7,627	12,378	2.4	5.3	5.0
IV	12,947	21,819	2.6	9.0	8.9
V	615	1,191	3.4	0.4	0.5
VI	22,862	42,548	3.1	15.8	17.3
VII	4,355	7,981	3.1	3.0	3.3
VIII	2,583	4,598	2.9	1.8	1.9
IX	22,268	31,700	1.8	15.4	12.9
Totals	144,365	245,228	2.7	100.0	100.0

Source: See methodological note in Appendix B.

course, susceptible to a wide margin of error, shown by the magnitude of changes which the United Nations has made in its earlier projections (see Table B-1 in Appendix B).

The variation in the rates of growth from country to country and from region to region is remarkable. While Uruguay has a projected rate of population increase of only 1.2 percent annually, the rate for Venezuela is 3.6 percent, one of the highest in the world. The spread between the highest and lowest rates of regional growth is smaller: 3.4 percent in Region V (the eastern slope of the Andes) and 1.8 percent in Region IX (northeast Brazil). In general, however, the rates are high, and Latin America's population is growing faster than that of any other major area in the world.

Despite the fact that the South American countries will be hard put to organize their economies efficiently enough to provide productive employment for the dramatic expected increase in their populations, there should not be a general problem of excess population in relation to the resource base. There will, nevertheless, be serious problems in several specific regions should historical population tendencies continue into the future, especially in Regions IV and IX.

The importance which both Peru and Bolivia have attached to

encouraging migration out of the highlands region of their countries (Region IV) and into the unoccupied eastern areas (Regions II and V) is well founded. Should the population of Region IV reach the 22 million projected for 1980, there would be no hope of easing the already miserable lot of these people. Both Bolivia and Peru have colonization programs underway and are making large investments in highways to provide access to the new areas. Bolivia has paved the highway from Cochabamba to Santa Cruz to encourage people to move into Region II and to open a market in the highlands for sugar and rice which are grown there. Other Bolivian colonization projects have been begun further to the north in Region V. Despite the difficulties and high costs of colonization of the lowlands by highland Indians, it is clear that Bolivia has no alternative to the policy being followed. It should not be assumed automatically, however, that only links between Region IV and the lowlands are desirable. In the case of Bolivia, it might well be that migration can also be encouraged toward the lowlands by strengthening the lowlands economy through closer links between the Bolivian part of Region II and the parts of Region II in Argentina and Brazil.

The alternatives open to Peru to ease the population pressure in Region IV are somewhat wider. The coastal part of this region is very fertile if it can be irrigated, so that Peru must decide to what extent resources should be dedicated to this objective and to what extent the pay-off would be higher in colonization to the east. Peru, furthermore, has a better resource base than Bolivia, which potentially would permit a greater degree of industrialization and absorption of population in this activity. It would be difficult to argue, nevertheless, that colonization to the east, with the transport investments which this program requires, should be abandoned. It may be, however, that highways are not the best way to open remote areas when the distances are long between the settled centers and the new colonies and there is no hope of developing the space in between. In these cases, air transport may offer a more economical alternative. This possibility has been explored in studies by the Pan American Union.[4]

[4] Organization of American States, Second Meeting of Governmental Experts in Civil Aviation, "El Papel de la Aviación Civil en los Proyectos de Colonización," UP/G. 36/17 (Washington, D.C.: Pan American Union, June 1964).

The problems of the Brazilian Northeast (Region IX) have long been recognized both in Brazil and abroad. Recurrent droughts have made even life itself precarious for the impoverished inhabitants of this region and substantial investments in irrigation and other programs have been unable to change the problem significantly. Despite the fact that the rate of population increase is lower in Region IX than in any other region, the Brazilian Northeast would still have a population in 1980 of more than 40 percent above the 22 million there in 1960, if present trends continue. This clearly cannot be permitted to happen. The best policy to follow is to encourage migration from this region into Regions I and II. Transport investments that open new agricultural areas and highways between Region IX and the other regions can contribute to this migration.

Although excessive population pressure on available resources would not seem to be an immediate problem in other regions, two matters are of concern which should be considered in designing an appropriate transport system and policy: the unequal distribution of income between countries and between regions of countries, and the pattern of urbanization which is emerging in South America.

Unequal Levels of Development

In Table 5-3 is shown the wide disparity in the gross national product per capita, electric power production per capita, and the percentage of literacy among the South American countries. Venezuela had a per capita GNP in 1962 of 693 U. S. dollars, but Bolivia had only 116 dollars. Venezuela produced 715 KWH of electric power per capita in the same year while Paraguay produced only 64. Uruguay has attained a level of literacy of 88 percent of its population, while in Bolivia, only 31 percent of the population is literate.

With such sharp disparities among these nations, there are dangers to closer economic integration. The commanding lead of Argentina and Brazil in industrialization is a threat to the hopes of the smaller countries to reach the same goal because the nascent industries of these countries find it as difficult to compete

TABLE 5-3. *Gross National Product Per Capita*[a] *and Electric Power Production Per Capita, 1962, and Literacy, Latest Year Available*

Country	GNP Per Capita (U. S. dollars in prices of 1961)	Literacy Rate (Percent)	Electric Power Production Per Capita (KWH)
Venezuela	693	51	715
Chile	460	80	642
Uruguay	450[b]	88	489
Argentina	352	86	543
Colombia	291	62	275
Peru	188	50	275
Brazil	186	50	363
Ecuador	183	60	97
Paraguay	132	68	64
Bolivia	116	31	119
United States	2,820	98	5,040

Source: U. S., Agency for International Development, Statistics and Reports Division, *Latin America Trends in Production and Trade* (October 1963), pp. 14–15, Table 1.

[a] Gross national product data are necessarily crude estimates and are not directly comparable between countries.

[b] 1961.

with those in Brazil and Argentina as do these latter countries to compete with the United States and Europe. Despite the early promising start of the Latin American Free Trade Association, great difficulties were encountered in the tariff negotiations held in Bogotá in 1964. There, the solution to this problem proposed by the smaller nations was that efforts be made to further industrial complementation. Under this arrangement, several countries would share the various processes of a single industry. In this way, each would be able to participate in an industry which it could not support individually in its entirety.[5] For such schemes to be successful, with different components of a single product produced in several countries and then brought together for assembly, it is essential that well-organized transport be available. The present structure of intra-South American transport is inadequate for this purpose.

Great regional diversity in levels of economic development also exists within most of the South American countries, and there is the danger that closer international economic integration

[5] *New York Times,* Oct. 21, 1964.

would strengthen centers that are already powerful while contributing little to overcoming the disparities. In Brazil, for example, the states of São Paulo and Guanabara in 1957 contained 23 percent of the population of the country but only 4 percent of the area, and produced 45 percent of total national income and 80 percent of the nonagricultural income. In these two states, the per capita income was 520 U. S. dollars, twice the national average.[6] In Peru "more than 90 percent of the industries established since 1960 have concentrated in the Lima-Callao area mainly because of the nearby port facilities, the low cost of electricity, and the large influx of labour from the interior in the past ten years."[7] Similar examples could be cited in the other South American countries.

It is, of course, not the objective of economic development to ensure an equal and identical rate of growth for every city and farm in a country. Under dynamic growth, regional inequalities will develop as first one region and then another are better able to satisfy the demands of the rest of the economy. With a reasonable mobility of the factors of production, migration of both labor and capital will tend to reduce these inequalities. At the same time, however, it must be recognized that often the advantage which one region enjoys is a result of historical accident and that this advantage tends to be cumulative. In these circumstances, it is even possible that excessive concentration of development in a few areas, in addition to creating social and political problems, may work to the detriment of economic development for the nation. This is clearly seen in the countries where agriculture has largely been ignored, with stagnant and even decreasing incomes, and where as a result a large proportion of the national population provides no effective demand for the industrial products that the country wishes to produce.

While not wishing to enter into a discussion of the relative advantages of "balanced" and "unbalanced" growth, it seems evident that in many instances it is desirable to adopt policies to

[6] Lincoln Gordon and Engelbert L. Grommers, *United States Manufacturing Investment in Brazil* (Boston: Harvard University, Graduate School of Business Administration, 1962), p. 4.

[7] Bank of London and South America, *Fortnightly Review*, Vol. 29, No. 722 (June 13, 1964), p. 483.

stimulate the development of specific regions that have lagged behind the rest of the national economy. Among the policy tools available for this purpose are improvement of transport facilities and transport rate policies. As the Economic Commission for Latin America has stated:

> A policy of investments and transport development which is oriented excessively by criteria relating to traffic demand and the profitability of investments in the short run incurs the risk of provoking a process of cumulative worsening of the regional economic inequalities which already exist. Thus, an adequate transport development policy can constitute a decisive factor in bringing about a more equilibrated and harmonious growth, implying a maximum dispersion of economic development in as many centers as possible, compatible with maximum general economic development.[8]

Pattern of Urbanization

In 1950, more than 40 percent of the total population lived in urban localities, defined as localities with 2,000 or more inhabitants, in Argentina, Chile, Uruguay, and Venezuela. By 1975, however, it is predicted that in all the South American countries more than 40 percent of the population will live in urban centers. By that year, in fact, the proportion will be greater than 50 percent in all the countries except Bolivia (45 percent), Brazil (46 percent), Ecuador (41 percent), and Paraguay (48 percent). If past trends continue, the proportion of urban population in 1975 should reach 84 percent in Uruguay, 74 percent in Chile, 73 percent in Venezuela, 71 percent in Argentina, and 51 percent in Peru.[9]

The tendency toward greater urbanization is, of course, a world-wide phenomenon, by no means unique to South America. Even without any internal migration, sheer population increase would raise many localities to the urban category. The principal

[8] United Nations Economic Commission for Latin America, *Los Transportes en América Latina*, E/CN.12/673 (March 25, 1963), p. 62 (translation).

[9] W. Stanley Rycroft and Myrtle M. Clemmer, *A Study of Urbanization in Latin America*, rev. ed. (Commission on Ecumenical Mission and Relations, The United Presbyterian Church in the U.S.A., 1963), pp. 20-21.

force behind the rapid rates of urbanization at the present time, however, is migration.

The factors responsible for this migration vary from one South American country to another. In Colombia, the terrorism of the bandits, which only recently has been brought under control, was an important force. In Brazil, famine in the Northeast has been a key element. Elsewhere, the causes have been less dramatic, but universally they reflect the belief of rural people that their lot can be improved by moving to the cities. Whatever the problems that arise from urbanization, in terms of providing housing, water, urban transport, education, and productive employment for the urban population, there is clearly no hope of reversing the migration, and it is doubtful that colonization schemes and other policies to improve rural living will affect significantly these trends. It may be, in fact, as Lauchlin Currie has argued,[10] that no attempt should be made to stem the flow of people to the cities, because policies which effectively increase agricultural productivity will inevitably release labor from the rural areas.

Whatever might be one's (philosophical) views on urbanization per se, it is important in planning transport investments and policies to consider explicitly the pattern of urbanization, that is, the size and relationship of the different urban centers desired. While people cannot be held down on the farms once they have seen Buenos Aires, they can be guided toward migrating to particular cities or regions other than the capital city through conscious governmental policies in the fields of housing, transport, taxation, etc., so as to reduce the tendency for already large urban centers to grow more rapidly than smaller urban localities.

There would be little reason to be disturbed, perhaps, about the concentration of population in large cities in South America except that the concentration commonly is in a single large city, and the growth of that city does not reflect the productive employment of large numbers of industrial workers. South American countries are characterized by what Bruce Herrick calls "hypercephalism,"[11] the concentration in a single city, most com-

[10] Lauchlin Currie, "Operación Colombia," *La Nueva Economía*, Toma 1, No. 4 (August 1961).

[11] Bruce Hale Herrick, "Internal Migration, Unemployment, and Economic Growth in Post-War Chile," unpublished Ph.D. thesis, Massachusetts Institute of Technology, 1964, p. 35.

TABLE 5-4. *Centralization of Population in Largest City*[a]

Country	City	Year	Percent of Population in City	Year	Percent of Population in City
Argentina	Buenos Aires	1947	19	1958	19
Bolivia	La Paz	1942	11	1957	10
Brazil	São Paulo	1940	3	1960	6
Chile	Santiago	1940	19	1960	26
Colombia	Bogotá	1951	6	1959	8
Ecuador	Guayaquil	1950	8	1960	11
Paraguay	Asunción	1950	16	1960	18
Peru	Lima	1940	7	1960	12
Uruguay	Montevideo	—	—	1955	33
Venezuela	Caracas	1941	9	1959	21
Canada	Montreal	1941	10	1956	10
United States	New York	1940	7	1960	6

Source: Bruce Hale Herrick, "Internal Migration, Unemployment, and Economic Growth in Post-War Chile," unpublished Ph.D. thesis, Massachusetts Institute of Technology, 1964, p. 37, Table 3.1.

[a] Populations refer to metropolitan area rather than city proper except in the case of Buenos Aires and São Paulo. In 1955, Greater Buenos Aires contained about 60 percent more people than the city proper; São Paulo about 25 percent more.

monly the capital, of economic, educational, cultural, and diplomatic functions. This concentration of population can be seen in Table 5-4, where the tendency toward greater concentration over time is also evident. In 1960, only 6 percent of the total population of the United States lived in the single most important metropolitan area, New York. In no South American country did a smaller proportion of total population live in the largest city around that same year and only in Brazil and Colombia are the proportions nearly the same. In Uruguay in 1955, 33 percent of the total population lived in Montevideo, while in Chile in 1960, 26 percent lived in Santiago.

The dominating position of single cities is also clear in Table 5-5 where the population of both the largest and second largest cities is shown. While the second largest cities in the United States and Canada had populations equal to 63 and 84 percent respectively of the population of the largest cities in recent years, only in Brazil, Colombia, and Ecuador did the second largest city have more than half the population of the largest city. In the other South American countries, the proportions run from 34 percent (Venezuela) to 10 percent (Peru). In summary, only in Brazil

TABLE 5-5. *Population of Largest and Second Largest Cities*[a]

Country	Cities	Year	Population of Cities (In thousands)	Second Largest City as a Percent of Largest
Argentina	Buenos Aires	1958	3,768	
	Rosario	1958	562	15
Bolivia	La Paz	1957	339	
	Sucre	1957	40	12
Brazil	São Paulo	1960	3,674	
	Rio de Janeiro	1960	3,124	85
Chile	Santiago	1960	1,907	
	Valparaiso- Viña del Mar	1960	368	19
Colombia	Bogotá	1959	1,124	
	Medellín	1959	579	52
Ecuador	Guayaquil	1960	450	
	Quito	1960	314	70
Paraguay	Asunción	1960	311	
Peru	Lima	1960	1,262	
	Arequipa	1960	129	10
Uruguay	Montevideo	1955	860	
Venezuela	Caracas	1959	1,356	
	Maracaibo	1959	456	34
Canada	Montreal	1956	1,621	
	Toronto	1956	1,358	84
United States	New York	1960	10,695	
	Los Angeles	1960	6,743	63

Source: Bruce Hale Herrick, "Internal Migration, Unemployment, and Economic Growth in Post-War Chile," unpublished Ph.D. thesis, Massachusetts Institute of Technology, 1964, pp. 37a, 39, Tables 3.1 and 3.2.
[a] Populations refer to metropolitan areas with some exceptions, such as Buenos Aires and São Paulo. In 1955, Greater Buenos Aires contained about 60 percent more people than the city proper; São Paulo about 25 percent more.

and Colombia is there a clear exception to "hypercephalism" in South America, as the rank-size distribution of cities in those two countries is not greatly dissimilar to that in the United States. A partial exception is found in Ecuador, where there are two dominant cities.

Economists and others are by no means agreed that "hypercephalism" represents an important obstacle to economic development, but this lack of consensus is due primarily to the fact that little empirical work has been done in this area. That serious problems presently exist in the dominant South American cities is undeniable. It also seems true that in general people migrating to these centers do not easily find productive employment and are forced to scrape a living from performing services with little value to the community.[12] As can be seen in the following table showing the percentages of economically active population in industry and in services in several cities, it would be difficult to maintain that these cities owe their size to the needs of industry for workers.[13]

City	Census Year	Industry	Services
Buenos Aires	1947	40	56
Santiago	1957	36	61
Lima	1940	35	56
Medellín	1950	43	41
São Paulo	1950	47	51

If it were true that in the normal course of development of an emerging country, the existence of a primate city or cities is inevitable, and that a more even distribution of city sizes is a characteristic of only developed countries, there would be less need for concern with this problem. This particular question has been examined empirically by Brian J. L. Berry, who comes to the following conclusions:

There are no relationships between type of city size distribution and either relative economic development or the degree of urbanization of countries, although urbanization and economic development are highly associated. It appears that there is a scale from primate to lognormal distributions which is somehow tied to the number and complexity of forces affecting the urban structure of

[12] University of Chile, Institute of Economic Research, *La Economía de Chile en el Período 1950-1963* (Santiago, Chile, 1963), Tomo 1, pp. 15-20.
[13] Rycroft and Clemmer, *op. cit.*, p. 48.

countries, such that when few strong forces obtain primacy results, and when many forces act in many ways with none predominant a lognormal city size distribution is found.[14]

It thus seems that governments can adopt a conscious policy aimed at bringing about the pattern of urbanization the government considers to be desirable. Most likely the objective of such a policy would be to encourage migration to cities other than the primate city. Such a policy would also be consistent with the objective of encouraging a wide geographical dispersion of economic growth within countries so as to reduce regional inequalities. While such policies cannot be undertaken without a continuing reappraisal of their effects on general economic development, they are desirable to the extent that they do not conflict with this development. In planning transport investments and policies, these multiple objectives should be kept in mind.

Population Densities and the Selection of Transport Modes

The factors which must be considered in selecting the appropriate transport mode or modes for a region are many and include topography, nature and volume of goods produced, economic potential of the region, and relative factor costs, as well as population densities. Thus population densities alone cannot determine whether a railroad should be built, or whether air transport should be the principal transport mode, but they are suggestive in the early planning stages.

Figure 5-1 shows the predicted population density in 1980 in the nine regions into which South America has been divided in this study. Although the population projections on which this map has been based differ somewhat from those used earlier in this chapter, the general pattern is the same. It is immediately clear from this map that in Regions V, VIII, and parts of Region II the pop-

[14] Brian J. L. Berry, "City Size Distributions and Economic Development," *Economic Development and Cultural Change*, Vol. IX, No. 4, Pt. 1 (July 1961), p. 587.

FIGURE 5-1. *Projected Population Density in South America, 1980*

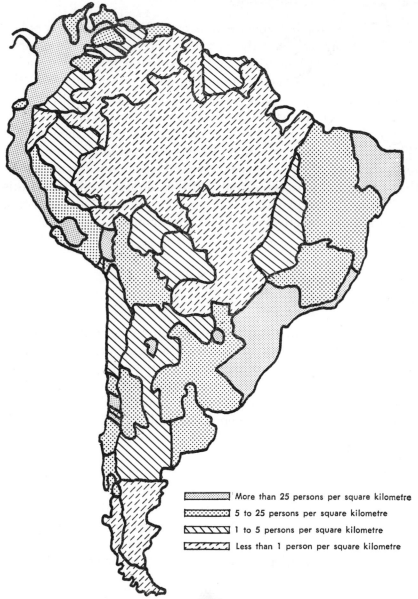

More than 25 persons per square kilometre
5 to 25 persons per square kilometre
1 to 5 persons per square kilometre
Less than 1 person per square kilometre

Source: United Nations, *The Population of South America, 1950-1980*, ST/SOA/Ser. A/21 (New York, 1955), p. 28.

ulation density will be less than five persons per square kilometer. In these areas, proposals for costly transport investments should be viewed with suspicion, as they would benefit few people. Here new railroad investments, except for short lines built for specific purposes, would not seem to be justified, and even highway investments should be made solely after river and air transport alternatives have been evaluated and discarded.

In Region I, on the other hand, and in parts of Region II which adjoin Region I, population density will be greater than 5 persons per square kilometer and frequently greater than 25 persons. Here, attention should be concentrated on the possibilities of improving land transport communications, including major railroad improvements and renovation. In other regions, the population density will also be greater than five persons per square kilometer, but other factors, principally topography, make a priori judgments more dangerous.

In summary, population projections for South America indicate that while excessive population will not be a generalized problem throughout the continent, it will be serious in some areas, especially in Regions IV (highlands of Peru and Bolivia) and IX (Northeast Brazil) unless policies are adopted that affect either rates of growth or migration. Transport investments are a critical policy variable in permitting and encouraging migration out of these regions and into areas of colonization. Although demographic pressure is restricted geographically, wide per capita income differentials exist both among countries and among regions within each country. These disparities endanger Latin American economic integration and internal political stability and may also represent an obstacle to national economic development. Transport investments and policies can contribute to reducing these differentials and to spreading development as widely as possible. Finally, the pattern of urbanization which is emerging in Latin America, with a large percentage of the total population concentrated frequently in a single primate city, is considered to be unnecessary and undesirable. Although rural to urban migration cannot be stopped, transportation policies and investments can be used to encourage migrants to locate in cities other than the primate city.

CHAPTER VI

Latin American Shipping Policies and The LAFTA Maritime Convention

Bᴇᴄᴀᴜsᴇ ᴏꜰ ᴛʜᴇ ᴏᴠᴇʀᴡʜᴇʟᴍɪɴɢ importance of maritime transport in intra-South American commerce, the establishment of the Latin American Free Trade Association stimulated interest in the extent to which present ocean shipping is adequate for economic integration and especially for increased trade in industrial products. This new interest in transport services within the South American continent, however, is not an isolated phenomenon but rather is added to the traditional concern of the Latin American countries regarding their transport connections with the rest of the world.

Latin American Shipping Policies in the Past

As far back as 1889, when the First International Conference of American States was held in Washington, the Latin American nations have searched for ways to reduce the cost of maritime transport and to improve ocean shipping services between their countries and those that buy their exports and supply their imports. Until World War II, these republics restricted their activity to passing resolutions in the occasional international conferences advocating better services, which were provided up to that time almost exclusively by foreign shipping companies, and criticizing rate levels, which were and are fixed entirely by shipping conferences. During this period, there was essential agreement between the Latin American countries and the United States on the importance of improving ocean communications.

During World War II, when the ships of the foreign companies which served Latin America were withdrawn from their traditional routes and were dedicated to the war effort, the Latin countries began to develop a new maritime policy designed to stimulate the development of their own merchant marines. These countries were now convinced, for reasons which will be detailed in the next section, that only by having their own merchant fleets would they be able to assure adequate service at a reasonable cost, without at the same time placing an undue burden on their precarious balance of payments.

Countries that adopt as a national policy the development of a national merchant fleet have open to them two major policy paths. First, they can grant direct subsidies to the maritime industry so as to reduce the cost of acquisition of new vessels and to reduce the cost of operating them. This is the policy that has been adopted by the United States, which spends more than $300 million a year on this type of subsidy. Second, they can create a protected market for domestic vessels by limiting foreign competition or by giving national carriers a competitive advantage through reserving certain cargoes for them and giving shippers an incentive to use domestic vessels. Although the United States reserves some cargoes for its own ships, it has been the Latin countries that have pioneered the use of this policy to favor national shipping companies.

Direct subsidies, principally through budgetary transfers to state-owned shipping companies, are also of some importance in Latin America, but these countries were convinced decades ago that their national treasuries could not resist a maritime development program based solely on subsidies, especially since they believed that they would be competing with the treasury of the United States. For this reason, the Latin countries have depended primarily on policies designed to assist national vessels that do not require large subsidies from the national budgets. Many measures have been adopted. Chile passed a law requiring that 50 percent of all cargo in its foreign trade be carried on national ships; Peru increased the tax on all ocean freight and turned over part of the receipts to the Peruvian state shipping line; Ecuador charged lower consular fees when goods were carried on national ships; Venezuela applied lower import duties to goods carried on national vessels than on goods transported by foreign companies; Brazil permitted importers to use a favorable rate of exchange when the goods were imported on Brazilian ships.

The United States has never opposed in principle the objective of the Latin countries to develop their own merchant fleets. Neither has it objected to these countries using direct subsidies to increase their shipping capacity, as this, after all, is the basis on which the maintenance of the U. S. fleet depends. The United States, however, despite its own insistence that part of government-financed cargoes be carried on U. S. ships, has consistently based its international shipping policy on the thesis that all commercial cargo carried between all countries should be available for carriage by any ship from any nation. The Merchant Marine Act, 1920, in fact, authorizes and directs the Federal Maritime Commission to take action whenever a foreign government adopts policies that impede equal competitive access to cargo by ships from all countries.

The policies applied by the Latin American countries to favor their national vessels thus came into direct conflict with the maritime policy of the United States, as the United States maintained that many of the measures adopted by the Latin nations discriminated against U. S. shipping companies. On four occasions, in the cases of Chile, Ecuador, Venezuela, and more recently Uruguay, the United States Federal Maritime Commission prepared rules and regulations to be applied to the vessels of these countries designed to offset the competitive advantage which they had been given by their national governments and thus to permit U. S. companies equal access to the previously favored cargoes. As yet, however, these offsetting regulations have never been applied. In the first three cases, the Latin American countries modified their own policies, and in the case of Uruguay, the regulations were postponed. Despite this success of the United States in bringing about changes in specific measures, the Latin nations continue determined to develop their own merchant fleets and also continue applying policies designed to channel cargo to national vessels.

The Latin American countries have been reasonably success-ful in building up their national fleets during the twenty-five years since World War II. Table 6-1 presents the merchant fleets of the South American countries and Mexico as of June 30, 1964. Argentina and Brazil account for two-thirds of the total, both in terms of number of ships and gross tonnage. The combined fleet of these nine countries represents only one-third of the privately owned U.S. merchant fleet in terms of gross tonnage and only one-sixth of the merchant fleet of the United Kingdom.

Table 6-2 represents a crude attempt to relate the growth of the merchant marines of some of the Latin American countries to the growth of their foreign commerce. The figures are not compara-ble from country to country because goods handled include only goods loaded and unloaded in international trade while the mer-chant fleets include ships engaged in coastwise shipping. Further-more, the United States figures are distorted by the fact that the entire government reserve fleet is included.

It is clear from Table 6-2 that among the Latin countries shown, only Argentina has a merchant fleet which, in comparison to its foreign trade, is comparable to the worldwide average. Fur-thermore, an important factor in explaining how Argentina has been able to develop its merchant marine more rapidly than its foreign commerce is the fact that the physical volume of its trade has fallen in absolute terms. While there is no reason to believe that the merchant fleet of every country should bear a constant relation to its foreign commerce, as this would imply that the law of comparative advantage does not apply to shipping, it appears clear that in general the Latin American merchant marine is far smaller than the foreign trade of this area would appear to justify, at least on the basis of a comparison with the United States, the United Kingdom, and the world average.

The increase in the size of the Latin American merchant fleets since 1938 has been substantial even though they still represent only a small percentage of total world tonnage. As Table 6-2 shows, the only country whose gross tonnage did not increase at a faster rate than world tonnage between 1938 and 1961 is Chile, principally because it is one of the few countries in Latin America among those shown in the table which has not channeled sub-stantial government resources into a national merchant fleet. To

TABLE 6-1. *Merchant Fleets of Selected Countries, June 30, 1964*ᵃ

(Tonnage in thousands)

Country	Total		Combination Passenger and Cargo		Freighters		Freighters-Refrigerated		Bulk Carriers		Tankers (Including whaling tankers)	
	Number	Gross Tons	Number	Gross Tons	Number	Gross Tons	Number	Gross Tons	Number	Gross Tons	Number	Gross Tons
Argentina	164	1,120	14	101	72	410	6	18	3	13	66	551
Brazil	238	1,142	20	101	152	558	2	7	16	62	48	414
Chile	51	273	6	25	28	116	—	—	10	55	7	77
Colombia	22	98	—	—	22	98	—	—	—	—	1	1
Ecuador	7	23	—	—	6	22	—	—	—	—	1	1
Mexico	39	239	1	15	11	31	2	5	3	10	22	178
Peru	28	128	1	6	22	97	—	—	—	—	5	25
Uruguay	16	97	1	8	11	48	—	—	—	—	4	41
Venezuela	35	283	—	—	14	47	—	—	6	30	15	206
Subtotal	600	3,403	43	256	338	1,427	10	30	38	170	168	1,493
United States												
Private	968	10,082	29	421	561	4,671	18	110	65	691	291	4,131
Government Reserve	1,554	11,741	235	2,129	1,250	8,820	23	106	1	7	75	679
United Kingdom	2,168	20,132	105	1,490	1,092	6,913	159	1,436	276	1,842	509	7,904
Norway	1,382	13,714	24	99	645	3,472	29	102	208	2,706	474	7,326
All Countries	18,072	140,288	1,097	8,836	11,087	61,095	605	3,255	1,779	16,672	3,459	49,713

Source: U. S. Maritime Administration, *Merchant Fleets of the World*, Report No. MAR-560-20, Sept. 16, 1964.

ᵃ Includes oceangoing steam and motor ships of 1,000 gross tons and over. Excludes ships operating exclusively on the Great Lakes and inland waterways and special types and merchant ships owned by military forces.

TABLE 6-2. *Growth of Merchant Fleets of Selected Countries*

	Argentina	Brazil	Chile	Colombia and Ecuador^c	Peru	Venezuela	Mexico	United States	United Kingdom	World
1938										
Goods handled[a]	19,024	8,847	5,650	4,065	2,894	28,194	3,517	89,849	116,100	940,000
Gross registered tons[b]	281	483	158	—	35	76	29	11,404	17,675	66,870
Ratio goods handled to gross registered tons	68	18	36	—	83	370	123	8	7	14
1948										
Goods handled	23,092	11,462	7,401	4,328	2,233	69,649	3,548	141,274	85,725	980,000
Gross registered tons	683	706	188	37	87	96	114	29,165	18,025	80,292
Ratio goods handled to gross registered tons	34	16	39	117	26	726	31	5	5	12
1955										
Goods handled	19,128	20,127	6,447	7,283	4,936	116,775	6,852	245,564	114,971	1,660,000
Gross registered tons	1,043	893	230	83	98	216	172	26,423	19,357	100,569
Ratio goods handled to gross registered tons	18	23	28	88	50	541	40	9	8	17
1961										
Goods handled	16,622	28,572	11,565	8,104	10,780	161,320	6,808	298,667	157,378	2,320,000
Gross registered tons	1,195	1,201	258	137	136	324	177	24,238	21,465	135,916
Ratio goods handled to gross registered tons	14	24	45	59	79	498	39	12	7	17

Source: Year 1938: United Nations, *Statistical Yearbook, 1955*, Table 136. Other years: United Nations, *Statistical Yearbook, 1962*, Tables 141 and 143. Gross registered tons for Ecuador and Colombia: Federal Maritime Administration data.

[a] Goods handled represent the weight in thousands of metric tons of goods in external trade loaded onto and unloaded from sea-going vessels of all flags at the ports of the country in question. U. S. figures include Great Lakes international traffic.

[b] Gross registered tons in thousands on June 30 of each year. Vessels of less than 100 gross tons are excluded. U. S. figures include the government reserve fleet.

[c] For Ecuador and Colombia with the exception of 1961: Gross registered tons in thousands on December 31 of each year. Vessels of less than 1000 gross tons are excluded.

93

what extent the policies other than direct government subsidies have contributed to the growth of these national fleets is impossible to ascertain. Perhaps the safest conclusion to draw is that when a national government is willing to put up the necessary capital to establish a merchant fleet and to cover operating losses, policies designed to assure this fleet a protected market are significant in reducing the operating subsidy from the government that would otherwise be required. If the national fleet is especially well administered, as in the case of the Flota Mercante Grancolombiana, owned jointly by Colombia and Ecuador, these policies can even permit the vessels to operate without an operating loss.

The Importance of National Merchant Marines

An analysis of ocean transport and the economic integration of Latin America cannot usefully be made without considering maritime transport between Latin America and the rest of the world. As will be detailed more completely in the next section, the desire of the Latin countries to develop their own merchant marines is an important factor in understanding the policies that these countries advocate within the framework of the Latin American Free Trade Association. For this reason, it is convenient at this point to review briefly the principal arguments which are given in support of national merchant fleets.

Most of the reasons expressed by the Latin countries regarding their wish to increase their shipping capacity are identical to those used in the United States to justify governmental subsidies and cargo reserves. The arguments that are most frequently encountered are: (1) national defense, specifically to ensure uninterrupted shipping services in times of emergency when the merchant ships of the traditional maritime nations are diverted for other uses; (2) to aid the balance of payments by conserving scarce foreign exchange; (3) to assure adequate and regular service; (4) to provide these countries with more leverage in the determination of freight rates which are fixed by ocean conferences; (5) to promote exports in general: "trade follows the flag."

National Defense

Latin America is almost completely dependent on ocean transport for both its intraregional and extraregional trade. This trade, furthermore, is the means by which these countries live: many are not self-sufficient in agricultural products, all must import some raw materials, and all must import the greater part of capital goods. An interruption in ocean transport has immediate and serious repercussions on the internal economies of these republics. The experience of Chile during World War II is recounted by Tomás Sepúlveda Whittle:

> . . . There was a strict rationing of gasoline and a great shortage of fuel oil. Industries, housewives, patients that went to the dentist and found that there was no electric current to run the drill, owners of automobiles, people who depended on public transportation, the entire national economy and the whole country suffered terribly because we did not have tankers and Chile at that time did not produce petroleum. The only tankers which were available were two small ones belonging to the Navy, the "Maipo" and the "Rancagua," and these, as the saying goes, "plowed the sea" to bring gasoline and fuel oil to the country. I sailed during that period to Talara on one of those ships on which depended the industry of the nation and the normality of many other activities, because the majority of the foreign-owned tankers which had served our trade before the war were now fully occupied supplying their own countries with this essential product and the remaining ships left these routes to search better opportunities within the war zone, where the freight rates on petroleum skyrocketed.[1]

A national or regional merchant fleet is a form of insurance for the LAFTA countries in that an annual premium is paid in the form of a subsidy to shipping lines or as freight rates that are higher than those prevailing in the world market, and in return these countries have the guarantee that ships will continue to be available in the event of world crises. This, of course, is essential-

[1] Tomás Sepúlveda Whittle, "Transporte Marítimo en la Asociación Latino-Americana de Libre Comercio," (Valparaíso, Chile: ICARE, Seminario sobre Mercado Común Latino-Americano, November 1961), p. 13. Free translation.

ly the same basic justification that is given for the United States shipping policy. Even when it is accepted that this type of insurance is desirable, however, both the United States and the LAFTA nations still face difficult decisions in determining the minimum size of the fleet which should be maintained in the light of the annual premium that must be paid. As is true of any form of insurance carried by an individual, the decision on the amount of coverage is not wholly an economic one but rather reflects other factors as well, such as the attitude toward risk.

It is also worth pointing out that the subsidy which is paid to the shipping companies and the shipyards in the United States comes from the budget of the Department of Commerce and not from the Department of Defense. It is quite doubtful, in fact, that the Department of Defense would consider that the contribution to national defense of an annual expenditure of $300 million for ship construction and operation is comparable to the benefits which could be obtained from a similar expenditure in other areas. Latin America, however, is faced with defense problems quite distinct from those of the United States, as in the southern continent assurance of continuity of ocean transport services is of primary importance.

Balance of Payments

One of the reasons given most frequently in defense of national merchant marines is that they either earn or save foreign exchange and hence contribute to the balance of payments. A representative of the Committee of American Steamship Lines testified before the Joint Economic Committee of the U. S. Congress that U. S. flagships earned $924 million net of foreign expenditures in 1962. This places ocean shipping as the third most important industry in the foreign trade of the United States, after aircraft, aircraft parts and accessories, and automobiles, trucks, and parts.[2] Magariños, analyzing transport problems within LAFTA, has stated: "Unless a substantial part of the intrazonal

[2] Testimony by Frank A. Nemec, *Discriminatory Ocean Freight Rates and the Balance of Payments*, Hearings before the Joint Economic Committee, 88 Cong. 1 sess. (1964), Pt. 3, p. 395.

trade is carried by means of transport belonging to the zone, a high percentage of the foreign exchange that is saved through the increase in zonal commerce and the substitution of imports from outside the zone will be lost and will again end up in foreign coffers because of payments for freight rates."[3]

Data on the importance of payments for transport and insurance in international commerce are difficult to obtain for many underdeveloped countries. Recently, the Economist Intelligence Unit, London, prepared estimates for a paper on "Ocean Shipping and Freight Rates and Developing Countries," which was submitted to the United Nations Conference on Trade and Development.[4] The figures for the LAFTA countries plus Bolivia and Venezuela have been taken from this study, which was based on information received from the International Monetary Fund, and are presented in Table 6-3.

This table, which refers to the year 1961, should be interpreted with care, because the figures are gross figures and include payments not normally included in balance of payments presentations. The orders of magnitude, however, are undoubtedly correct and are useful in indicating the incidence of transportation receipts and expenditures in the balance of payments of these countries. According to the I.M.F. estimates, the net deficit for transportation of these eleven countries in 1961 was $587 million. Both Argentina and Venezuela had deficits of over $100 million: $103 million and $140 million respectively. The total net transport deficit of $587 million corresponds to a net deficit of $465 million for freight payments, $60 million for insurance on goods shipped, and $62 million for "Other Transport," which includes passenger fares and expenditures of domestic carriers for items such as stevedoring, harbor and airport dues, and other purchases abroad.

A comparison of the debit side of "Other Transport" ($212.6 million) and the credit side of "Freight" ($196.4 million) in Table 6-3 is graphic proof that the freight earnings of domestic carriers

---

[3] Mateo J. Magariños de Mello, "El Problema del Transporte en la ALALC y sus Vinculaciones con el Desarrollo Económico General de la Zona," in Instituto de Estudios de la Marina Mercante Argentina, *La Marina Mercante Argentina, 1962* (Buenos Aires, 1962), p. 180.

[4] United Nations Conference on Trade and Development, *Ocean Shipping and Freight Rates and Developing Countries*, E/CONF. 46/27, Jan. 28, 1964.

TABLE 6-3. *Transportation in the Balance of Payments of Selected Countries, 1961*[a]

(Millions of dollars)

Country	Freight		Insurance		Other Transport		Total		
	Credit	Debit	Credit	Debit	Credit	Debit	Credit	Debit	Balance
Argentina	56.6	131.4[b]	—	14.6[b]	69.8	83.6	126.4	229.6	−103.2
Bolivia	—	9.5	—	0.9	0.1	1.6	0.1	12.0	− 11.9
Brazil	54.0	136.0	—	9.0	34.0	23.0	88.0	168.0	− 80.0
Chile	21.1	57.8[b]	—	6.1[b]	6.5	19.3	27.6	83.2	− 55.6
Colombia	55.6	47.2	—	2.4	13.2	49.4	68.8	99.0	− 30.2
Ecuador	—	13.3	—	0.5	—	2.0	—	15.8	− 15.8
Mexico	—	52.5	—	11.4[b]	0.3	6.4	0.3	70.3	− 70.0
Paraguay	0.6	5.8	—	0.7	0.5	0.9	1.1	7.4	− 6.3
Peru	6.4	60.1	1.6	2.1	6.2	5.9	14.2	68.1	− 53.9
Uruguay	0.6	18.7[b]	—	2.1[b]	1.4	0.6	2.0	21.4	− 19.4
Venezuela	1.5	129.1	—	11.7	18.8	19.9	20.3	160.7	−140.4
Total	196.4	661.4	1.6	61.5	150.8	212.6	348.8	935.5	−586.7

Source: United Nations Conference on Trade and Development, *Ocean Shipping and Freight Rates and Developing Countries*, E/CONF. 46/27 (Jan. 28, 1964), pp. 55–57, 65.

[a] Freight Credit includes all earnings of domestic carriers on exports, cross-trades *and* imports.

Freight Debit includes payments to foreign carriers for transport of compiling country's imports *and* earnings of domestic carriers for carriage of imports of country concerned.

Insurance entries are similarly inflated by the inclusion of premiums on imports received by resident insurance companies as both credits and debits.

Other Transport Debit includes (i) payments by residents of compiling country to all foreign ocean, air, etc. carriers for international passenger fares; (ii) payments by domestic enterprises to foreigners for time-charter of foreign-owned vessels, aircraft, etc.; (iii) all disbursements abroad by domestic ocean, air, etc. carriers for port fees, stevedoring, maintenance and repairs of vessels and aircraft, purchases abroad of supplies for vessels and aircraft, expenditures abroad of domestic carrier crews, etc. (iv) payments for mail fees, salvage earnings and earnings of foreign carriers in domestic coastal traffic.

[b] I. M. F. staff estimates.

while engaged in foreign trade do not all represent net foreign exchange earnings for the country concerned. The debit side of "Other Transport" includes the disbursements made abroad by the selected Latin American countries for port fees, stevedoring, maintenance and repair of vessels, etc., items that absorb a large share of the freight revenues included on the credit side of "Freight." A similar comparison of the credit side of "Other Transport" ($150.8 million) and the debit side of "Freight" ($661.4 million) shows that the payments to foreign carriers for freight charges do not all represent a loss of foreign exchange, as these carriers incur considerable costs, especially for cargo handling, in each country. These costs are included on the credit side of "Other Transport." Unfortunately, since "Other Transport" also includes air passenger fares, mail fees, and other costs associated with air transport, no numerical estimate can be made of net foreign exchange losses from ocean shipping on the basis of Table 6-3.

The extent to which a national merchant marine can contribute to the balance of payments of the country concerned varies widely from nation to nation, depending in large measure on the extent to which the country produces its own ships and fuel, where repairs are carried out, and the nationality of the crews. It has been estimated that in Argentina about 50 percent of the foreign exchange earned by Argentinian flag carriers must be spent for expenditures abroad.[5] For the United States, on the other hand, it has been estimated "on the average that when freight and passengers move on American flag ships only about 20 cents of every revenue dollar represents an outflow from the United States."[6]

These estimates tell only half the story, however. The total contribution to the balance of payments depends not only on what domestic carriers must disburse abroad but also on what foreign carriers would have disbursed domestically had they carried the cargo. Thus the net foreign exchange earnings of the Argentine merchant marine are considerably less than the 50 percent indicated above, and those of U. S. flagships are well under the 80 percent cited. Indeed, according to the draft recommendations prepared by Sweden for the United Nations Conference on Trade and Development:

> The currency gain which is expected from substitution of national carriers for those of other flags is greatly exaggerated. If taking into account the loss of foreign exchange income obtained from disbursements of foreign flag vessels in the ports of the country concerned—and the currency expenditures—operating and capital cost—of national vessels abroad, the true gain obtainable by such

[5] Instituto de Estudios de la Marina Mercante Argentina, *La Marina Mercante Argentina, 1962*, p. 18.

[6] "Statement of Wilfred J. McNeil, President, Grace Lines, Inc., and Chairman of the Committee of American Steamship Lines," *Discriminatory Ocean Freight Rates and the Balance of Payments*, Hearings, *op. cit.*, Pt. 3, pp. 338-39.

substitution is of the magnitude of 20 to 25 percent of the gross freight income in the case of cargo liners.[7]

Support for the Swedish assertion is not difficult to present. On the basis of the percentage distribution of the costs incurred by ocean carriers given by one expert,[8] the following table was prepared. The first column of Table 6-4 shows the incidence in total costs of each cost item. The second and third columns indicate the way in which these costs might be distributed between expenditures in dollars and in Latin American currency when cargo is carried between the United States and Latin America by a Latin American ship. The fourth and fifth columns show this same distribution were a foreign carrier to transport the cargo. No claim is made here for either the exactitude of the percentage distribution of costs among the different cost items or the distribution between dollar expenditures and expenditures in Latin American currency for the foreign and Latin American carriers. The incidence of port and cargo handling costs is so high that appreciable variations may be introduced without affecting significantly the conclusions that are drawn from the table.

Table 6-4 can be interpreted in the following way. Suppose that initially all the cargo that enters a Latin American country's foreign commerce is transported by foreign carriers. Then, according to column 4, of each $100 spent by the Latin American country for freight, $28 returns to the country, principally because of cargo handling and other port costs. Suppose next that a domestic carrier of the Latin American country captures all the trade and that freight continues to be paid in foreign exchange. Of each $100 in freight earned by that carrier, $47 must be spent abroad (see column 3). Only $53 returns to the country as a foreign exchange contribution. This $53 is not a net contribution, however, as $28 would have returned in any case. Thus the net contribution is the difference between these two returns, that is, $25 or 25 percent of gross freight payments.

[7] United Nations Conference on Trade and Development, "Improvement of the Invisible Trade of Developing Countries: Sweden: Draft Recommendations," E/CONF. 46/C. 3/L. 29 (May 1, 1964), p. 3.

[8] P. Garoche, "Importance of Handling Charges in a Ship's Operating Costs," United Nations, *Transport and Communications Review,* Vol. 3 (April-June 1950), pp. 15-18.

TABLE 6-4. *Expenditures in Domestic and Foreign Exchange by Domestic and Foreign Carriers*

(Percent)

Cost Item	Incidence in Total Costs	Distribution Between Latin American and Foreign Currency when Goods are Carried on			
		Latin American Ships		Foreign Ships	
		Latin American Currency	Foreign Currency	Latin American Currency	Foreign Currency
	(1)	(2)	(3)	(4)	(5)
Cargo handling, agencies and port charges	51	25.5	25.5	25.5	25.5
Fuel	6	—	6.0	—	6.0
Insurance	4	1.0	3.0	—	4.0
Depreciation	7	—	7.0	—	7.0
Supplies	2	1.0	1.0	1.0	1.0
Advertising	1	0.5	0.5	0.5	0.5
Officers and crew, pay and subsistence	13	12.0	1.0	1.0	12.0
Maintenance and repairs	4	1.0	3.0	—	4.0
Administration and other operating costs	4	4.0	—	—	4.0
Interest on capital and reserves	6	6.0	—	—	6.0
Dues and taxes	2	2.0	—	—	2.0
Total	100	53.0	47.0	28.0	72.0

Source for Incidence of Cost Items in Total Costs: P. Garoche, "The Importance of Handling Charges in a Ship's Operating Costs," United Nations, *Transport and Communications Review*, Vol. 3, (April–June 1950), p. 15.

As was pointed out above, this 25 percent is by no means invariable. Shipbuilding, for example, is already taking on importance within Latin America. On January 1, 1964, of the 710 vessels with a total of 3.6 million gross registered tons which compose the Latin American fleet, thirty ships with a total of 92,550 gross registered tons had been built in Brazil (17 ships), Argentina (10 ships), Uruguay (2 ships), and Peru (1 ship). Furthermore, of the 57 merchant ships that either had been ordered or were under construction for Latin American shipping companies on January 1, 1964, 30 had been contracted for in shipyards in Latin

America.[9] In the future, as these countries rely increasingly on vessels constructed within the region, and as they are able to handle for themselves ship maintenance and insurance, the net foreign exchange earnings or savings will rise above the present estimate of 25 percent.

Furthermore, even 25 percent is likely to appear important when total freight payments are high. From Table 6-3 it can be seen that in 1961 the LAFTA countries (plus Bolivia and Venezuela) paid $722.9 million for freight and insurance for the transport of the imports of these countries to both foreign *and* domestic carriers. Applying to this the potential net foreign exchange saving of 25 percent (some of which is already being realized) gives $180.7 million. This amount of foreign exchange is clearly significant to the economies of these countries.

Left unanswered in this analysis is the important question of who pays the freight rate. Transport costs are conceptually quite similar to import duties, and there is a complete literature on the incidence of tariffs between buying and selling nations showing the importance of supply and demand price elasticities. A treatment of this problem goes far beyond the pretensions of the present study, but it is quite clear that the conventions used in the balance of payments accounts, whereby exports are registered f.o.b. and imports c.i.f., cover up a multitude of complex theoretical issues. For this reason, the assertion of any country that it "pays out" or "receives" a certain sum of foreign exchange for freight rates should be accepted with considerable caution.

Adequate Service at Reasonable Rates: Trade Follows the Flag

It is frequently maintained both within Latin America and abroad that a national merchant fleet contributes importantly to the foreign commerce of a country. Most of the arguments used in support of this assertion fall into three categories: (1) a national fleet can provide service that is beneficial to a country but which would not be of interest commercially to foreign carriers; (2) domestic carriers can exert pressure within the freight conferences

[9] Instituto de Estudios de la Marina Mercante, *La Marina Mercante Iberoamericana, 1964* (Buenos Aires, 1964), pp. 17-18.

that set international freight rates; (3) "trade follows the flag."

Implicit in the first group of arguments is the assumption that the service concerned is uneconomic, in the sense that it requires a subsidy, and that it is preferable to pay a subsidy to a domestic carrier rather than to a foreign carrier. The service might concern the provision of shipping capacity over a route that would otherwise not have service; more frequent sailings than foreign carriers would be willing to provide; or lower rates than would otherwise prevail.

The relevance of this type of argument to intra-Latin American trade will be left to the next chapter. In relation to trade between the South American countries and other continents there are instances where a Latin shipping company has pioneered new routes, as the service which Lloyd Brasileiro opened to Japan and Africa. Furthermore, some South American companies provide service for ports which do not generate sufficient cargo to interest foreign carriers. In general, however, the Latin American shipping companies provide service over the same routes as those served by foreign carriers, and there is no indication that the resulting increase in the frequency of sailings over these routes has a significant impact on the foreign commerce of these nations.

Ocean freight rates are set by shipping conferences, associations of shipping companies that operate over a given trade route. Conferences are essentially cartels that implicitly or explicitly set prices, regulate sailings of members, and distribute cargoes. The monopoly power of the conference is based primarily on the dual-rate contract system, under which shippers who use ships belonging to the conference exclusively are quoted a lower freight rate than that accorded shippers who also patronize nonmember carriers. The dual-rate contract system also makes it difficult for a shipping company to operate outside of the conference, and as a result the Latin American shipping companies are forced to become members if they are to obtain cargo. Few shippers are willing to lose the lower conference contract rate by patronizing a nonmember carrier, and seldom is the service provided by a single Latin American company sufficiently frequent to provide a shipper with adequate service even though the Latin carrier is willing to quote a low freight rate.

Because of the key role of freight conferences in establishing both the level and structure of international freight rates, it is commonly maintained that only by the presence of domestic carriers in these conferences can pressure be exerted so as to prevent the adoption of policies which are detrimental to a country's foreign commerce and its economic development. As one Argentinian maritime expert has argued:

> By their presence in the shipping conferences, our shipping companies maintain a degree of control over the decisions which those conferences adopt in relation to the freight rates which are applied to and from our ports. Our shipping companies are able to influence these decisions in the defense of the foreign commerce of the country. If we did not have our own liner companies, the Argentine economy would be entirely at the mercy of foreign decisions in an area of the importance of freight rates. A sudden increase in these rates can automatically exclude us from foreign markets, which, on the average, are more than 5,600 miles away. The freight rate, at a given moment, can be the factor which increases or wipes out our possibilities to export. The action of our shipping companies can prevent or greatly ameliorate these effects, even to the extent of threatening to compete as an "outsider," if this were necessary, to defend our economy.[10]

At times the argument is pushed considerably further, and it is maintained that the shipping conferences consciously adopt policies on rates that are designed to assist the economies of "some" countries at the expense of "others," and presumably also at the expense of their own profits. The control of Latin America's trade routes, as a former official of the Argentine has stated, "is in hands which respond to other interests, to other economies, to other purposes, in seeking the welfare of other collectivities."[11] This argument has even been used in the United States, most recently in the investigation of the Joint Economic Committee of the U. S. Congress on Discriminatory Ocean Freight Rates and the Balance of Payments. There, it has been held that one reason

[10] Instituto de Estudios de la Marina Mercante, *La Marina Mercante Argentina, 1961* (Buenos Aires, 1961), p. 31. Free translation.

[11] Speech of Capitán de Navío Alberto San Martín, formerly National Director of the Merchant Marine and Ports of Argentina, Oct. 7, 1959, cited in Instituto de Estudios de la Marina Mercante Argentina, *La Marina Mercante Argentina, 1960* (Buenos Aires, 1960), p. 17.

freight rates on U. S. exports tend to be higher than rates on imports is because the shipping conferences that control U. S. commerce are "foreign dominated."[12]

Despite the attacks, it has never been shown that conferences use any criteria other than profit-making in setting their rates. Indeed, from any one country's point of view, conferences are always "foreign dominated," and because of the multinational composition, no conference could long survive that placed other objectives ahead of the commercial interests of the associated carriers. Undoubtedly, there are instances where within a particular conference a carrier has opposed a rate increase or a port surcharge because of anticipated repercussions within the carrier's country. It would be extremely difficult to prove, however, that over any extended period of time the level of freight rates has been significantly affected by these national considerations.[13]

Yet there might be an important grain of truth that national participation in shipping conferences is desirable even though the conferences act solely to obtain profits for their members. The reasoning that follows would also seem to be relevant to the assertion that "trade follows the flag." International commerce is a complicated matter which, besides transport, involves knowledge of markets and suppliers, banking and credit, and layers of governmental regulation of foreign exchange, and export and import permits. A change in only one of these factors, if not accompanied by simultaneous changes in the others, is not likely to lead to a significant increase in trade. Both the existing structure of freight rates and these other institutions are geared to the present pattern of international trade. The whole package tends to perpetuate what is and has been and to present a formidable obstacle to change.

Yet change is a requisite for the economic development of the Latin American countries. These nations maintain that it is essential that new exports be created, not only to other republics with-

[12] "Ocean Freight Rates," paper prepared by the staff of the Joint Economic Committee, *Discriminatory Ocean Freight Rates and the Balance of Payments,* Hearings, *op. cit.,* Pt. 3, pp. 338-39.

[13] Allen R. Ferguson and others, *The Economic Value of the United States Merchant Marine* (The Transportation Center at Northwestern University, 1961), pp. 422-430, 469.

in the LAFTA area but to other countries as well. Latin American governments now give considerable emphasis to the importance of expanding and diversifying exports, and the recent United Nations Conference on Trade and Development showed that the developed nations have also acquired a new understanding of these problems.

Among the important changes that must be made if Latin America is to export new products is a re-structuring of the ocean freight rates presently in use. The rates which would apply to the export of new products are presently only "paper rates," in that they exist in the conference tariff, but no products move under them. Simultaneously with reforms in government regulations and banking practices, these freight rates must be modified. National carriers, aware of the aspirations of their countries and knowledgeable in the workings of the conferences, can act as key agents in bringing about changes in the rate structure. They can thus make an important contribution in assuring that when concerted action is taken on all fronts to promote new exports, ocean freight rates do not act as a bottleneck because of inertia of less interested carriers.

In summary, the Latin American nations see important reasons for increasing their merchant fleets. For countries heavily dependent on foreign commerce, as is the case of these countries, national vessels provide protection for the national economy not only in time of world war but also during more limited crises such as the Korean War and the Suez crisis, when the world's vessels are diverted from their customary routes. National vessels also earn or save foreign exchange, and though this saving may not exceed 25 percent of gross freight, even this can be significant in the balance of payments of many Latin American nations. Having a voice and vote in the shipping conferences which establish freight rates to and from a country's ports is also useful, especially when a country makes a concerted effort to expand and diversify its traditional exports.

At the same time, it would be difficult to maintain that the existence of these national fleets has contributed in an important way to improving the frequency or rapidity of ocean services to Latin America or to reducing ocean freight rates. In instances where there is sufficient traffic to justify regular commercial service, there has seldom been a lack of foreign shipping lines willing to serve the trade. The national fleets of the Latin American countries, with some exceptions, have seldom maintained over any period of time service on routes that were commercially unremunerative.

Maintaining a national merchant fleet, furthermore, involves a cost, and this cost must be set off against the benefits. Ocean shipping is highly capital intensive in relation to the employment which is created, an important consideration in view of the problem of the Latin countries to provide productive employment for burgeoning populations. If the ships are acquired abroad, the foreign exchange required could be applied to alternative economic activities. This factor can be reduced in importance, however, by chartering ships instead of purchasing them. If ships are constructed within Latin America, the steel and other resources required could be used for other purposes.

If national merchant marines cannot compete with foreign traditionally maritime nations, subsidies are required that could be devoted to other objectives, or a protected market must be created that may result in poorer service or higher freight rates. The comparison of the net benefits from the expansion of Latin American merchant fleets with the associated cost is complex, but unquestionably it should be made. The issues involved are far too important either to dismiss the Latin American aspirations as economic nonsense or for these countries to push blindly ahead without an objective analysis of the economic justification of their policies.

Latin American Shipping Policies and LAFTA

Although the 1960 Montevideo Treaty, which established the Latin American Free Trade Association, does not mention transport, there was immediate recognition of the importance of improved communications if the objective of economic integration was to be achieved. In August 1960, six months after the original treaty was signed, thirty-six delegates from the signatory countries met in Montevideo to study transport problems. At this meeting, it was agreed that national commissions should be established in each country to begin the task of collecting information on intrazonal transport. It was also agreed that in the next meeting priority should be given to the simplification of ship documentation, the establishment of a common nomenclature of cargo, and the creation of a technical assistance program for port administration, operation, and labor problems.

Despite this promising start, a second meeting was not held until two years later in July 1962. At this meeting, attention shifted from a primary concern with transport as an obstacle to economic integration to a search for ways to use the Montevideo Treaty as a basis for developing the Latin American merchant fleet. Although there is considerable overlap between the development of Latin America's shipping capacity and the improvement of transport services within the LAFTA region, it is obvious that the two objectives are not identical. The first resolution of this second meeting absorbed most of the time of the delegates. When approved, it established the principle that cargo transported among the LAFTA countries should be reserved for vessels belonging to these countries. The cargo would be reserved on a bilateral basis; that is, each country would have the right to the carriage of 50 percent of the cargo transported to and from each of its trading partners. If a country did not carry its 50 percent, the first option on the cargo would be given to the trading partner, and if this country could not carry the goods, preference would be given to another country of the area.

Shortly after this meeting of the transport experts, the Second Period of Sessions of the Conference of the Contracting Parties (CCP) began in Mexico.[14] Again the transport experts were called together, this time to prepare resolutions for submission to the CCP incorporating the conclusions of the second meeting in Montevideo. Of the three resolutions approved by the CCP in October 1962, the first recommended that the Contracting Parties sign a convention establishing the principles of a maritime and river transport policy for the zone. Among these principles, it was

[14] The Conference of the Contracting Parties is the supreme governing body of LAFTA.

affirmed, should be the reservation of a "substantial" part of intra-zonal cargo for LAFTA ships while not adversely affecting maritime service and rates.

The second resolution recommended that a Transport Advisory Commission (TAC) be established on a permanent basis to improve LAFTA maritime services and also that the Latin American shipping companies form an association to promote intrazonal commerce and to set up maritime freight conferences which would fix "just and reasonable" rates. The third resolution incorporated nearly all the other recommendations of the second meeting of transport experts designed to improve port efficiency.

Although the CCP had shown a basic concern with improving shipping services and rates within the LAFTA region, the next two meetings of the Transport Advisory Commission, held in June 1963 and April 1964, were dedicated almost exclusively to the preparation of a draft maritime convention, the basic objective of which would be to stimulate the development of Latin American merchant fleets by reserving intra-LAFTA cargo for ships from the region. Working parallel to the TAC was the Latin American Shipowners Association (ALAMAR), established in July 1963, which was also primarily concerned with policies that would favor Latin American vessels. Unfortunately, during this entire period, no significant advance was made by LAFTA in regard to the many other transport problems, especially those affecting the ports.

Reaching a consensus among the state and private shipping companies and among the northern, eastern, and western countries was not easy. The principal obstacle encountered was determining the basis on which cargo reserves should be applied. Should the reserves include all the LAFTA cargo or only part of it? Should bilateral reserves be used, whereby the cargo between pairs of countries is reserved for the ships of the trading partners, or should multilateral reserves be applied, under which LAFTA cargo could be carried by any LAFTA ship? Additional questions also had to be answered: How should freight rates be set? How should freight rates and cargo reserves be enforced? What conditions should a vessel fulfill to be considered a LAFTA ship?

The draft agreement which was approved by TAC in April

1964 and by the Permanent Executive Committee of LAFTA for submission to the CCP was a compromise among the many conflicting interests and points of view. Under the draft convention, each LAFTA member has the right to transport 40 percent of the cargo which it trades with each of the other members, so that in effect 80 percent of intra-LAFTA cargo is reserved on a bilateral basis. An additional 10 percent of total cargo plus that part of the 40 percent reserved for a member which it does not wish to carry is reserved for all LAFTA ships on a multilateral basis. The final 10 percent is reserved for any LAFTA ship and for foreign ships that serve regularly a route between their country and Latin America. The convention, however, does not indicate the mechanism by which the reserves would be applied.

The draft agreement provides for freight conferences that would establish freight rates, promote the regularity of services, and aid the governments in the enforcement of cargo reserves. The convention is ambiguous, nevertheless, regarding the way in which the rates set by the conferences would be reviewed or controlled by the member governments. The convention also establishes the conditions that must be met for a vessel to be considered as a LAFTA ship and hence entitled to participate in the cargo reserves.

Although the convention was approved by the Permanent Executive Committee in ample time for submission to the Conference of the Contracting Parties held in Bogotá at the end of 1964, it was never considered at that meeting. Instead, the conference resolved solely, "That a meeting be held at the governmental level for the purpose of analyzing the different aspects of the sea and river transport policy of the Association."[15] In part, the decision to postpone a decision on the agreement reflected the lack of unity among LAFTA members. The Brazilian government, for example, is apparently skeptical regarding the desirability of bilateral reserves and the Pacific coast countries, especially Chile and Peru, which are heavily dependent on foreign shipping companies for an important part of their intrazonal trade, fear the effect on service and rates of the proposed cargo reserves.

[15] Asociación Latinoamericana de Libre Comercio, Conferencia de las Partes Contratantes, Cuarto Período de Sesiones, ALALC/C.IV/Resolución 106 (IV), Dec. 8, 1964.

Another significant factor, however, was undoubtedly the sharp opposition of the United States to the implementation of cargo reserves within Latin America, even though these would not directly affect trade between the United States and Latin America. Under strong pressure from the U. S. shipping lines which operate routes to Latin America, the Federal Maritime Commission announced that if United States ships were excluded from carrying cargo from one Latin American country to another, the United States would not permit ships of one Latin American nation to carry goods between the United States and another Latin American country. Argentina, for example, would no longer be able to participate in the coffee trade between Brazil and the United States.

The implementation of a policy of this sort would be a serious blow to the LAFTA shipping companies, as they transported 733,000 tons of cargo in 1962 as third-flag carriers in the foreign commerce of the United States with Latin America. The revenue loss to these companies would be many times the loss to U. S. companies should they be excluded from intra-LAFTA trade, because in 1962 the U. S. lines earned only $2.8 million from way-to-way cargo within Latin America.

In March 1965, one month before the meeting of governmental experts contemplated in Resolution 106 (IV) of the Bogotá Conference, the members of ALAMAR met in Montevideo. The difficulties of finding common ground among the various national interests and public-private interests represented in that organization were again clear. As a result, the document prepared by ALAMAR for submission to the Permanent Executive Committee of LAFTA[16] did not contribute to resolving the basic problem of cargo reserves and their distribution. The necessity for cargo reserves was reaffirmed, but there was no mention whether they should be bilateral or multilateral. The desirability that foreign ships that traditionally provide regular service to the area participate in intra-LAFTA transport was also explicitly recognized, but there was no mention of the percent of cargo for which they would be permitted to compete. There was, however, one innovation of importance, as the document asserts that a maritime pol-

[16] Asociación Latinoamericana de Armadores (ALAMAR), "Acta Final de la Tercera Asamblea Extraordinaria" (April 1, 1965).

icy should be adopted which would permit LAFTA ships not only to carry the goods traded within the region but also a substantial part of those traded between the region and the rest of the world. This widening of ALAMAR's horizon could become significant, especially since the principle of greater participation by LAFTA ships in the area's trade with other continents was reaffirmed in the Declaration of the Governmental Meeting on Water Transport the following month.[17]

Since the May Governmental Meeting was intended primarily to achieve a consensus among the LAFTA members regarding maritime transport policies, especially with respect to cargo reserves, the results of the discussions can only be termed a failure. The declaration of the meeting asserts that a substantial quota of the cargo traded within the region should be reserved for LAFTA ships on a multilateral basis and that the reserves should be applied gradually both with respect to time and to tonnage. While the acceptance of multilateral, rather than bilateral, reserves represented an advance, Resolution I of the meeting makes clear that there was no agreement on how the reserves should be implemented.[18] This resolution concludes with four different proposals, presented by Argentina, Brazil, Chile, and Uruguay, on how to put the reserve policy into effect, together with a recommendation that future work in the Association designed to produce a maritime convention take into account these proposals, as "no agreement had been reached on the matter." Colombia, Ecuador, and Mexico asserted that they agreed with the principle of cargo reserves but did not believe that these should be enacted at the present time. The LAFTA members appeared to be as far from their goal of elaborating a maritime policy for the Association as they had been five years earlier.

It is unfortunate that neither the LAFTA members nor the United States officials concerned with shipping policy have made a more thorough analysis of the economic effects that the different LAFTA proposals would have were they implemented,

[17] Asociación Latinoamericana de Libre Comercio, Reunión Gubernamental de Transporte Acuático, "Declaración," ALALC/RTA/I/dt 6 (May 8, 1965).

[18] Asociación Latinoamericana de Libre Comercio, Reunión Gubernamental de Transporte Acuático, "Resolución I," ALALC/RTA/I/dt 7 Rev. 1 (May 8, 1965).

as this analysis could aid considerably in reconciling the many conflicting positions. If it could be shown that cargo reserves, for example, could contribute effectively to the economic development of the LAFTA nations, this would go far in softening United States opposition. The three million dollars which could be lost by the U. S. carriers, after all, represent but a small portion of the aid given annually by the United States to the LAFTA republics. It also represents less than one percent of the annual construction and operating-differential subsidies that the United States gives to its merchant marine.

It is also unfortunate that the attention of the LAFTA members during five years has been dedicated largely to devising a draft convention designed to develop the Latin American merchant fleet instead of solving the more important problem of improving ocean transport service within the LAFTA region. The following chapter analyzes present maritime service and rates within Latin America so as to determine if inadequate transport represents a serious obstacle to economic integration and also whether the implementation of proposals such as those contained in the draft maritime convention would contribute to the objectives of LAFTA.

CHAPTER VII

Ocean Transport and

Economic Integration

FROM THE DESCRIPTION OF THE geography of South America and the present patterns of population distribution, production, and consumption presented in earlier parts of this study, it is clear that for many decades to come ocean transport must continue to provide the only transport for low- and medium-value cargo between many pairs of regions. If South America is divided into three "super regions," the Atlantic coast countries (Argentina, Brazil, Uruguay, and Paraguay), the South Pacific countries (Chile, Bolivia, and Peru), and the northern countries (Ecuador, Colombia, and Venezuela), it is obvious that there is no hope for the foreseeable future of providing an alternative to ocean transport for the cargo moved between the northern countries and the more southern Atlantic and Pacific coast countries. Similarly, despite the promising prospects of land and river transport within the southern part of the continent, ocean transport must inevitably be the basis for most transport between Brazil and Peru, Argentina and Chile, northeastern Brazil and Argentina, etc.

Ocean transport, in other words, must in South America play the role that the transcontinental railroads fulfilled in the United States nearly one hundred years ago. For this task, maritime shipping has many disadvantages that must be overcome if South America is to have the rapid, frequent, and economic transport which is essential for closer economic integration. At the same time, however, it also has some advantages compared with land transport: the initial capital cost for ports is far less than that required for transcontinental railroads or highways, and the vessels themselves can be left in the hands of foreigners or chartered from them until sufficient traffic develops to warrant ship construction or purchase. Vessels, furthermore, are mobile and can be shifted from route to route and even sold or chartered elsewhere as the demand for transport changes and as greater reliance is placed on other transport modes.

Characteristics of the Maritime Shipping Industry

Before turning to an analysis of present ocean transport within Latin America, it will be useful to describe briefly some of the principal characteristics of the maritime shipping industry. Ocean freight transport can be classified in three major categories: tramp service, liner service, and service in vessels owned by shippers. With tramp service, the shipper rents an entire ship either to make a specific voyage (voyage charter) or for a specific period of time (time charter). A time charter, furthermore, can be entered into for a period of years, in which case it does not differ essentially from transport carried out by vessels owned by the shipper. Although general purpose cargo ships are chartered on both a voyage and time basis, the greater part of the world's fleet which is under charter or which is owned by shippers is composed of specialized vessels, such as tankers and ore carriers. Charter rates are set by the forces of world supply and demand and can fluctuate widely over time.

Liner ships provide a common carrier service, as they operate over fixed routes following a previously announced schedule of port calls and charge rates according to a published tariff based on the commodity which is transported and its weight or volume. The vessels used in liner service are usually either general purpose freighters or combination passenger and cargo ships, although at times they are more specialized so as to carry refrigerated cargo or containers. In general, the liners do not carry bulk cargo, as this can be handled more cheaply by the tramps in shipload quantities of a single commodity. Interest in this study focuses on liner service within South America because rapid common carrier ocean transport is the key to successful economic integration, especially in the industrial sector.

Both the level and structure of liner costs vary from country to country and from route to route depending on the cost of ship construction, crew requirements set by law or by accord between ship-owners and unions, wage rates, taxes, ports served, and ship utilization. The cost of cargo handling in the ports, however, is the single most important cost factor. When crew wages, fuel costs, and depreciation are prorated between time spent in navigation and time spent in port, and these costs are added to cargo handling charges and other port expenses, total port expenses can reach 75 percent of total costs on many routes, as the time spent in port is commonly greater than that spent at sea.[1] The cost of transporting cargo 100 yards from a railroad car to a ship in the port of origin and another 100 yards from the ship to a truck in the port of destination is greater than the cost of transporting that cargo 5,000 miles between the two ports.

The structure of costs for liner ships has a number of important implications for intra-South American transport. First, the overwhelming incidence of terminal costs in ocean transport is a powerful force favoring the concentration of cargo in as few ports as possible so as to minimize the time which a ship must spend taking on and leaving cargo. For this reason, ocean transport works against one of the objectives of economic integration in South America which was indicated above: the geographical dispersion of economic development over as wide an area as possible. Reliance on ocean transport tends to perpetuate the present dominance of a few industrial centers and represents a powerful obstacle to the establishment of new centers outside the zone of attraction of already important ports.

Second, efforts to reduce the cost of ocean transport in South America and throughout the world must obviously begin in the

---

[1] A recent study has estimated the distribution of time spent in ports and in navigation during a year for representative classes of ships as follows: passenger liners, 225 days at sea and 135 days in port; cargo liners, 145 days at sea and 215 days in port; deep sea tramps, 205 days at sea and 155 days in port; tankers, 290 days at sea and 70 days in port. U.N. Conference on Trade and Development, *Ocean Shipping and Freight Rates and Developing Countries*, E/CONF. 46/27, Jan. 28, 1964, p. 147. See also Table 6-4 of this study, where the cost composition of a typical liner ship is presented.

ports. Unless handling charges and ship turnaround time can be reduced, there is little hope of lowering ocean freight rates. Large improvements in fuel consumption, ship construction costs, and crew requirements have a relatively small impact on total costs in comparison with even marginal changes in the ports. This lesson is even more applicable to South America where the navigation distance between many pairs of countries is relatively short.

Finally, except for the important cargo handling costs, most of the remainder of the costs associated with liner ships vary with time rather than with tons carried or ton-miles of transport. Depreciation, insurance, wages and salaries, fuel, etc., are all either annual costs or voyage costs which are affected little by the tons carried on a particular voyage. Once it has been decided to make a voyage, a major part of the total costs are immediately determined, and the only marginal cost which can be assigned to a particular shipment is its handling cost in the ports of origin and destination. Given a particular sailing schedule, the level of average costs is determined by the extent to which a ship's cargo capacity is used. In these circumstances, and considering that the size of the individual transport "vehicle," the ship, is extremely large, the marginal transport cost to the carrier can be far less than the average cost. This factor is of great importance in explaining the rise of shipping conferences and their acceptance by governments, as these are generally convinced that without the stabilizing element introduced by conferences, freight rate wars would be common and both service and rates would be subject to wide fluctuations which are considered undesirable in common carrier transport.

The Role of Freight Conferences

Generally a separate freight conference exists for each direction on each major shipping route, so that a particular carrier may belong simultaneously to a number of different conferences. The criteria used by a conference to establish freight rates are not always clear but among the factors considered are the following:[2]

[2] Inter-American Maritime Conference, *Report of Delegates of the United States* (Government Printing Office, 1941), pp. 25-28.

1. Character of the cargo
2. Volume of the cargo
3. Availability of cargo (if ready for prompt shipment without delay)
4. Susceptibility to damage
5. Susceptibility to pilferage
6. Value of goods
7. Packing
8. Stowage (including problem of odors)
9. Relationship of weight to measure
10. Heavy lifts
11. Extra lengths
12. Competition with goods from other sources of supply
13. Cargo via competitive gateways
14. Competition from other carriers
15. Direct cost of operation
16. Distance
17. Cost of handling
18. Lighterage
19. Special deliveries (receive or deliver at special docks, etc.)
20. Fixed charges
21. Insurance
22. Port facilities
23. Port regulations
24. Port charges and dues
25. Canal tolls
26. Port location
27. Possibility of securing return cargoes

This list includes cost factors, demand factors (value of service), and considerations of competition, and thus reflects the imperfect monopoly position of freight conferences. While conferences are able to apply price discrimination with respect to particular commodities, ports, and the direction of shipment, they are subject to competition from tramps and nonconference liners, which limits the extent to which their monopoly power can be exercised. Probably the best way to characterize rate setting by conferences is as full-cost pricing with some price discrimination.

The monopoly power of many conferences is sufficiently great, however, to introduce an important possibility of inefficiency in ocean transport. When rates are set by a conference and adhered to by the member carriers, the only way an individual carrier can obtain more traffic for itself is by providing a faster or more frequent service than its competitors. There is thus an incentive for the carriers to invest in more modern ships and to increase the frequency of their sailings, since they cannot individually attract more freight by offering lower freight rates. Since all carriers are likely to operate in the same fashion, and at times new carriers must be admitted to the conference, the cargo capacity offered collectively by the conference over a particular route may increase and the average use of individual vessels fall. One possible result in these circumstances will be a breakdown of the conference if carriers begin to quote lower than conference rates in order to attract more traffic.

A more probable result, however, is that the carriers will decide that their financial position can be improved by a rate increase. Since conferences rarely set rates that reflect their true monopoly position, but rather rates based on full cost, a rate increase will usually increase total revenue to the conference carriers. Under the new higher rates, however, it may now be profitable for an individual carrier to again increase the number of its sailings, so that eventually carriers' earnings will fall and a further rate increase will be required.

Obviously enough, the effect of this intraconference competition can be disastrous for shippers, as they must pay higher and higher freight rates in order to maintain in service cargo capacity and a frequency of sailings in excess of what is required. Furthermore, since each successive rate increase will reduce to at least some extent total cargo carried, the under use of the conference ships is likely to worsen, giving additional impetus to still further increases. This effect, however, may be offset to some extent by the natural growth of world trade over time.

A third course is also open to the carriers when they find their earnings eroded by intraconference competition. The carriers may be able to extend the control of the conference so that it includes not only the rates that are fixed but also the service that is offered. In other words, the carriers may be able to agree on a reduction in their sailings and in the capacity offered so as to increase the average use of their vessels and hence reduce their average costs. This can usually only be accomplished, however, if the carriers have an advantageous alternative for the use of their vessels, which for subsidized U. S. flagships is not always possible. United States subsidized carriers are not free to shift their ships from route to route because in receiving the subsidy they agree to provide service over a specific route. Thus the subsidy policy of the United States may tend to lead to overtonnaging on particular routes and rates that are higher than are essential to maintain an adequate service.

The agreements among carriers by which the liner service offered is regulated are called "pooling agreements." The description of these agreements in the report of the Celler committee in 1962 merits citing:

> There are several types of agreements between lines which masquerade under the heading of "pooling agreements." Some pooling agreements are in reality nothing more than sailing agreements whereby the parties agree to alternate sailings of their vessels periodically in a given trade. To apply the term "pooling agreement" to such arrangements is strictly a misnomer since there is no provision therein either for pooling of revenues, division of profits, or allocation of tonnages. Other so-called "pooling agreements" are in effect simply joint ventures to which each party contributes a portion of the carrying capacity for the entire operation which in turn is placed under some unified direction. A few "pooling agreements" go so far as to divide the tonnage in the trade equally or in given proportion between the participants without actually effectuating a pooling of total revenues.
>
> By far the most common type of pooling agreement is one between two lines providing for the establishment of joint sailing schedules with revenues to be divided on the basis of some stated proportion or in accordance with a formula based upon services furnished to the trade. Occasionally, the arrangement will extend to passenger as well as cargo carriage. In many cases, these arrangements more nearly resemble joint service agreements than pools.
>
> Two other types of agreements falling within the general classification of "pooling agreements" should be noted. One may be more appropriately described as a "minimum guarantee" arrangement rather than a pool in that, although revenues are distributed on the

basis of actual carryings, a minimum percentage of the trade is nonetheless assured each of the participating lines. The second is a true pool in the international cartel sense. The latter effectuates a division of the entire trade between participating lines on a previously agreed upon basis, with fixed quotas of sailings and carriage allotted to each of the participants on the one hand, or an apportionment of net revenues on a predetermined basis on the other.[3]

Although the extension of agreements among carriers to include the service offered as well as rates charged is more "monopolistic" than rate agreements alone, the shippers may obviously benefit by this extension. No one is benefited by an excessive number of sailings when the shippers must pay high rates to cover high average costs due to poor use of ship capacity. If rates are in fact reduced, or at least held from increasing, while ship sailings are "rationalized," both shippers and carriers may benefit. The problem is one of obtaining the potential benefits of better efficiency without suffering the potential dangers from a more complete monopoly.

Shipping Rates and Service as a Tool of Economic Integration

The Latin American Free Trade Association was created primarily as a means to stimulate industrial development in Latin America. Whatever other benefits might result from the Montevideo Treaty, it must be remembered that the basic objective that induced the LAFTA nations to become signatories was the desire to expand the market for industrial products, and especially for new products not produced within the member countries. For this reason, when analyzing ocean shipping services and freight rates, it is important to relate these elements to the transport requirements of industrial commodities. The type of ocean transport that might be appropriate and adequate for commerce based on a few bulk products such as petroleum, coal, iron ore, wheat,

[3] *The Ocean Freight Industry*, H. Rept. 1419, 87 Cong., 2 sess. (1962), pp. 157-58.

and lumber may well be inappropriate for trade in products such as refrigerators, trucks, railroad locomotives, and plate glass.

Ocean Transport Service

Turning first to the service side of ocean transport, it is possible to isolate a number of key variables:

1. Adequate transport capacity among the member countries. If a large industry is to be placed in one country and is to supply all or a large part of the LAFTA area with its products, it is essential that transport service exist between this country and all potential markets. Although a direct service may not be absolutely essential, there must at least be good transshipment facilities at intermediate ports.

2. Speed of service. Industrial goods have a high value per ton, and each additional day that passes between the time a product leaves the factory and the time it is acquired by the final consumer increases the amount of working capital that is necessary. In a continent where capital is one of the scarcest resources, transport time must be given great weight.

3. Frequency and reliability of service. The total time which elapses between production and consumption depends not only on the speed of the good while it is in transit but also on the delay in waiting for transport. Infrequent and unreliable service requires the maintenance of large inventories both at the sending and receiving centers, and larger inventories mean higher costs.

4. Type of ship. An important variable to be considered, both because of its importance in relation to the speed and cost of service and its relation to the quality of service, is the technical characteristics of the ships used. Unless refrigerated ships are available, there is little possibility of Argentina's expanding its exports of high quality chilled meat to other LAFTA members. Ships which draw a great deal of water may be unable to enter certain river ports, and in other ports may be forced to use lighters to transfer goods to and from shore. To reduce costly handling charges and to make theft more difficult, containers may be appropriate in some traffics and will require special ship facilities.

Freight Rates in Ocean Transport

The freight rate side of ocean transport calls for a similar list of key variables:

1. Level of rates. A basic argument favoring the Latin American Free Trade Association is based on the assumption that there are important economies of scale in the production of many industrial goods. Thus no individual South American country can afford to produce solely for its own internal market a number of products that are presently imported from outside the region. If a plant were located in one country which could serve both its own market and that of other LAFTA members, thus obtaining the cost advantages of large-scale production, it is believed that a price competitive with imports could be established. Moreover, in many instances industrial products are produced in South America for limited national markets behind high protective import barriers, and costs and prices are high. If markets could be broadened, perhaps even by eliminating the production of some goods in LAFTA countries where they are presently produced, productivity would increase and prices could be reduced.

The scope of the market, however, and the extent to which the advantages of large-scale production can be realized are limited by transport costs. Within Latin America as throughout the world, markets farther away from the center of production can be reached only by incurring higher transport costs. Thus here as elsewhere there is a playoff between economies of scale and transport costs, so that the lower the ocean freight rates, the wider is the market that can be reached, and the greater are the benefits from economic integration.

2. Variance in freight rates among products, according to the direction of shipment, and according to distance. Once it has been decided that a ship will make a particular voyage, a significant part of the total voyage costs are common costs to all the cargo that is carried. It then becomes impossible to distribute this common cost among specific products or among cargo which is transported between specific pairs of ports. Traditionally, this

common cost is distributed on the basis of the ability to pay of the products carried, and ocean freight rates have involved considerable price discrimination. It is important to assure that the particular rate structure adopted is consistent with the economic objectives of LAFTA. The relative rates for raw materials and for finished products, for example, can have a considerable impact on the location of industries.

3. Intra-LAFTA rates versus rates to and from other continents. The LAFTA nations can use import duties to fix the relative prices of goods imported from LAFTA countries as compared to goods imported from traditional suppliers. Ocean freight rates work in much the same way as import duties. If the freight rate is higher between Peru and Brazil than it is between Europe and Brazil, the effect is just the same as though transport were costless and an import duty were applied to Peruvian goods. For this reason, it is important to compare intra-LAFTA freight rates with those to and from other continents to assure that potentially efficient LAFTA suppliers are not eliminated from potential markets because of important differences in relative freight rates.

Needless to say, the different variables that have been listed here, in regard to both service and freight rates, are not independent. There are important interrelationships among them that must be kept in mind at all times. An increase in the quality of service, for example, can only be attained at a cost. Thus the LAFTA area must search for the most efficient combination of these variables if it is to attain its objectives.

Present Maritime Service Within the LAFTA Area

It is difficult to devise research techniques based on available statistics which could be used to determine whether the maritime service presently offered within the LAFTA area is adequate for the area's requirements. Suppose, for example, that information existed showing port-to-port cargo movements and the shipping capacity offered over different routes. Should it be found that the two closely approximate one another, it might well be that inadequate capacity is being provided and that potential exporters do not energetically seek new markets because of the difficulty of obtaining transport. Despite the fact that theoretically the supply of maritime transport services is elastic, shipping companies may be reluctant to establish new services because of the uncertainty of obtaining enough cargo to assure remunerative voyages. Even though a latent demand exists, it may be necessary to supply unused shipping capacity for a considerable period of time before exporters will have sufficient confidence to seek new markets actively. Although a shipping company might believe that new traffic might be developed in the future if service were expanded, it might well be unwilling to bear interim losses until traffic reaches a remunerative level. This would be especially true when there is a strong possibility that once traffic increases, a competitior will enter the trade and eliminate the developer's profits.

Even should it be found that excess capacity is offered on a particular route, there is still no indication that the maritime service is adequate for the needs of the area. If the rates are closely controlled by shipping conferences, and competition among carriers is based solely on the service offered by each, it is quite possible that rates have been set high enough to prevent carrier losses despite a poor use of their capacity. In this case, shippers are forced to pay for more service than they need, or can afford to use with present high rates. Shippers might well prefer a reduction in the frequency of sailings, if rates were lowered to reflect the lower average carrier costs brought about through better ship use.

Unfortunately, data presently available do not permit a comparison between tonnage moved and capacity offered within the LAFTA region. Insight into the nature of the problem can be obtained, nevertheless, from the pattern of present intra-LAFTA ocean transport, because generally service is reasonably adequate where transport volumes are large and inadequate where volumes are small.

In Table 7-1 the countries of South America have been divided into three areas: Area 1, the west coast of South America, includes Chile, Peru, Ecuador, and the Pacific ports of Colombia; Area 2, the east coast of South America, includes Argentina, Uruguay, Paraguay, and Brazil (the first three of these countries,

TABLE 7-1. *Cargo Transported by Sea Within South America, 1962*

(Thousands of metric tons)

Area	Cargo Transported				Percentage Distribution	
	General Cargo	Wheat in Bulk	Refrigerated Cargo	Total Cargo	General Cargo	Total Cargo
Within Area 1 (West Coast)	235.5	—	52	287.5	15	10
Within Area 2 (East Coast)	624.0	689	150	1463.0	41	53
Within Area 3 (Caribbean)	10.5	—	—	10.5	1	1
Between Areas 1 and 2	439.5	308	18	765.5	29	28
Between Areas 2 and 3	128.5	—	20	148.5	8	5
Between Areas 1 and 3	88.0	—	—	88.0	6	3
Totals	1526.0	997	240	2763.0	100	100

Source: Table 3-6.

however, have been treated as a single country and the trade among them has been excluded from the table); Area 3, the Caribbean countries, includes Venezuela and the Caribbean ports of Colombia. Ideally Area 1 should include the Pacific ports of Mexico, and Area 3 the Atlantic ports, but data were not available on tonnage flows between Mexico and South America. If information were available, however, regarding Mexico's demand for transport to and from the other countries, the basic pattern shown in Table 7-1 would be little changed.

In order to separate Colombia's trade between its Pacific and Caribbean ports, it was assumed that one-half of its trade with each trading partner goes through the ports on each coast. The table shows intra- and inter-area tonnage flows of general cargo, wheat, and refrigerated cargo. Excluded are petroleum products and mineral products in bulk.

The extent to which transport in 1962 was concentrated within and between Areas 1 and 2 is clear in Table 7-1. It is also important to note how little tonnage is transported within Area 3 and between this and the other two areas.

Service within the LAFTA region is presently provided by shipping companies from the United States, Latin America, and other continents.[4] The greatest concentration of companies is found along the east coast, where service is provided by as many as sixteen LAFTA companies and twenty-nine foreign companies. The greater part of at least the foreign companies operating in this area, however, ply between the east coast of South America and the United States and Europe, and many have little interest in traffic from one South American port to another. Perhaps as many as seventeen companies provide service along the Pacific coast from Chile to Mexico, and seven companies serve routes between the east and west coasts, of which six provide service only from Brazil around Cape Horn to Peru. Within Area 3 and between this area and Areas 1 and 2, service is offered by only a few companies.

The shipping companies that combine service among the South American ports with that to other continents provide liner service, in that sailing schedules are usually known with anticipation. The rates charged, however, are frequently not published in tariffs available to the public. Although several Latin American companies dedicate their ships to providing liner service within Latin America without extending their lines abroad, most Latin American lines operating solely within this region offer service which is somewhere between tramp service and liner service. Their vessels commonly ply over a particular route, as between Argentina and Brazil, but they do not adhere to an announced schedule of sailings. The rates, however, are frequently published and can be consulted by interested shippers.

Persons who know well the problems of ocean shipping in Latin America have indicated several areas where their own experience has shown that inadequate service is presently an obstacle to attaining the objectives of LAFTA. One such expert, Andrés Avendaño, has observed that trade between the following areas is frequently subject to the necessity of transshipment from one ship to another and that direct service would contribute to eco-

[4] Asociación Latinoamericana de Armadores, "Líneas de Navegación que Atienden la Zona Latinoamericana de Libre Comercio," Cartas Circulares a los señores Asociados Nos. 19/64, 20/64, 23/64, and 43/64.

nomic integration:[5] (1) Brazil and River Plate to Pacific ports of Mexico; (2) River Plate to Ecuador and Colombia; (3) South American Pacific ports to Caribbean ports of Colombia and Venezuela; and (4) South American Pacific ports to Pacific ports of Mexico. Avendaño does not state, however, that direct service *should* be established, because the present small volumes of traffic would make a regular and direct service costly.

Twenty-five years ago, Raul Rivera criticized the first resolution of the Inter-American Maritime Conference, which advocated direct service among all the American nations, as being unrealistic given the small trade between nations to the north and south of the equator.[6] Today the volumes traded are still small, but it appears clear that this is due in part to the inadequate maritime service. If the LAFTA effort is taken seriously, it is essential that each member be assured of regular liner service to each of the other members, that is, of the availability of direct and frequent cargo capacity according to a fixed sailing schedule at published freight rates. Low traffic volumes cannot justify the lack of adequate service because without this service new trading patterns cannot be established and new traffic cannot be generated. Maritime service alone is not sufficient to guarantee that commerce will increase; other measures in other areas are equally important. But improved service is a prerequisite, especially between the nations to the north of the equator and those to the south.

Breakdown of Tonnage Flows

The difficulties involved in providing adequate and economic shipping services for LAFTA can be seen more clearly if the data presented in Table 3-6 showing intra-South American maritime transport in 1962 is broken down into clockwise and counterclockwise movements within and among the three areas used in

[5] Andrés Avendaño Fuenzalida, "Los Transportes y la Zona de Libre Comercío," talk given on May 18, 1964, as part of a seminar sponsored by the Instituto de Organización y Racionalización de Empresas of the University of Chile on the theme, "El Empresario Chileno Frente a la ALALC," pp. 3-4.

[6] Raul Rivera Blin, *Transportes Marítimos de los Paises Latinoamericanos* (Valparaiso, Chile: Cámara Central de Comercio, 1941), p. 8.

TABLE 7-2. *Tonnage Flows of General, Refrigerated, and Bulk Cargo, 1962*
(Thousands of metric tons)

Country	Area 1	Area 2	Area 3	Areas 1–2	Areas 2–3	Areas 1–3	Total
Colombia, Caribbean to Pacific							
Clockwise	—	—	—	—	—	30.5	30.5
Counterclockwise	—	—	—	—	—	57.5	57.5
Colombia to Ecuador							
Clockwise	6.0	—	—	2.0	—	23.0	31.0
Counterclockwise	44.5	—	—	1.5	—	54.5	100.5
Ecuador to Peru							
Clockwise	12.5	—	—	2.0	—	20.5	35.0
Counterclockwise	96.5	—	—	25.5	—	53.5	175.5
Peru to Chile							
Clockwise	34.0	—	—	321.0	—	9.0	364.0
Counterclockwise	187.0	—	—	89.5	—	8.0	284.5
Chile to River Plate							
Clockwise	—	—	—	476.0	—	—	476.0
Counterclockwise	—	—	—	289.5	—	—	289.5
River Plate to Brazil							
Clockwise	—	587.0	—	24.0	73.5	—	684.5
Counterclockwise	—	876.0	—	120.0	46.0	—	1,042.0
Brazil to Venezuela							
Clockwise	—	—	—	—	101.5	—	101.5
Counterclockwise	—	—	—	—	47.0	—	47.0
Venezuela to Colombia							
Clockwise	—	—	7.5	—	1.5	24.5	33.5
Counterclockwise	—	—	3.0	—	2.0	13.0	18.0

Source: Table 3-6.

Table 7-1. Table 7-2 shows the disequilibrium in tonnage flows of the total general cargo, bulk cereals, and refrigerated cargo for intra- and inter-area trade in 1962. Table 7-3 and the tabulations on pages 132 and 133 show separately the flows for the three types of cargo. It is important to note the extent of the disequilibrium in tonnage flows because a sharp imbalance in directional trade, that is, the lack of return cargoes, usually increases the cost per ton of transport. The breakdown between intra- and inter-area traffic flows shows the extent to which inter-area transport tends to offset intra-area directional tonnage imbalances, and hence whether inter-area shipping routes would tend to bring about a fuller use of ship capacity than routes organized separately for

TABLE 7-3. *Tonnage Flows of General Cargo, 1962*
(Thousands of metric tons)

Country	Area 1	Area 2	Area 3	Areas 1–2	Areas 2–3	Areas 1–3	Total
Colombia, Caribbean to Pacific							
Clockwise	—	—	—	—	—	30.5	30.5
Counterclockwise	—	—	—	—	—	57.5	57.5
Colombia to Ecuador							
Clockwise	6.0	—	—	2.0	—	23.0	31.0
Counterclockwise	44.5	—	—	1.5	—	54.5	100.5
Ecuador to Peru							
Clockwise	11.5	—	—	2.0	—	20.5	34.0
Counterclockwise	48.5	—	—	25.5	—	53.5	127.5
Peru to Chile							
Clockwise	30.0	—	—	5.0	—	9.0	44.0
Counterclockwise	149.0	—	—	89.5	—	8.0	246.5
Chile to River Plate							
Clockwise	—	—	—	150.0	—	—	150.0
Counterclockwise	—	—	—	289.5	—	—	289.5
River Plate to Brazil							
Clockwise	—	587.0	—	24.0	73.5	—	684.5
Counterclockwise	—	37.0	—	120.0	26.0	—	183.0
Brazil to Venezuela							
Clockwise	—	—	—	—	101.5	—	101.5
Counterclockwise	—	—	—	—	27.0	—	27.0
Venezuela to Colombia							
Clockwise	—	—	7.5	—	1.5	24.5	33.5
Counterclockwise	—	—	3.0	—	2.0	13.0	18.0

Source: Table 3–6.

intra- and inter-area traffic. The breakdown between types of cargo shows whether the inclusion of bulk wheat tends to reinforce or offset the disequilibrium in general cargo and refrigerated cargo.

In constructing the tables, it was assumed that Colombia's trade with the other LAFTA nations (and Venezuela) is divided evenly between Colombia's Pacific and Caribbean ports. It was also assumed that maritime transport between Area 1 and Area 2 is via Cape Horn while that between Area 1 and Area 3 is via the Panama Canal. It should also be remembered that the tables tend to underestimate the actual tonnage flow imbalance because they are based on annual data, and hence it is implicitly assumed that all the transport takes place simultaneously. Were these tables prepared on a monthly or weekly basis, the imbalance would probably increase.

General Cargo

Since the key to the relation of maritime transport to economic integration is the establishment of regular liner service, it is appropriate to begin with an analysis of Table 7-3, "Tonnage Flows of General Cargo," as it is general cargo that liners are designed to transport. It is clear from this table that there is a sharp directional imbalance in the flow of cargo clockwise and counterclockwise within each of the three areas, although total traffic within Area 3 is insignificant (in part because no data on Mexican commerce are included). On the west coast (Area 1), the north to south flow is more than four times the south to north flow. On the east coast, between the River Plate ports and the Brazilian ports (Area 2), the disequilibrium is even greater: the flow north to south is 587,000 tons while the flow south to north is only 37,000 tons. This latter comparison is somewhat misleading, however, because a large part of the north to south traffic is composed of lumber, which could be carried in tramp ships.

Adding transport between Areas 1 and 2 to the intra-area flows increases the imbalance within Area 1 and somewhat offsets the imbalance within Area 2. On the link between the two areas, that is, between the River Plate ports and the Chilean ports, the flow of general cargo is sharply unbalanced, with nearly twice as much cargo flowing from the west coast to the east coast. Adding the transport of general cargo between Areas 2 and 3 increases the disequilibrium between the River Plate ports and the Brazilian ports and introduces a sharp disequilibrium on the link between the two areas, that is, between the Venezuelan ports and the Brazilian ports. Adding the transport between Areas 1 and 3 reinforces the disequilibrium within Area 1. The total flow of general cargo thus has sharp directional imbalances, in part because the inter-area imbalances tend generally to reinforce the already unbalanced intra-area flows.

Refrigerated Cargo

The tonnage flows of refrigerated cargo in 1962 is shown in the table below (in thousands of metric tons) and is included within total cargo shown in Table 7-2.

Country	Area 1	Area 2	Areas 1–2	Areas 2–3	Total
Ecuador to Peru					
Clockwise	1	—	—	—	1
Counterclockwise	48	—	—	—	48
Peru to Chile					
Clockwise	4	—	8	—	12
Counterclockwise	38	—	—	—	38
Chile to River Plate					
Clockwise	—	—	18	—	18
River Plate to Brazil					
Clockwise	—	150	—	—	150
Counterclockwise	—	—	—	20	20
Brazil to Venezuela					
Counterclockwise	—	—	—	20	20

Care must be used, however, in summing the flows of this traffic to those of general cargo. Refrigerated cargo can only be said to reinforce or offset the disequilibrium in the flows of general cargo if cargo space can be used for both types of cargo; that is, if general cargo can be stowed in refrigerated compartments when these are not being used for cargo specifically requiring refrigeration. With this cautionary note, it can be seen from a comparison of Table 7-3 and the tabulation above that flows of refrigerated cargo heighten the imbalance within Area 1 and reduce it within Area 2.

Bulk Cereals

Bulk cereal flows are likely to fluctuate violently from one year to the next, so that it is unrealistic to generalize on the basis of the flows which occurred in 1962, even though these did fall into a rather normal pattern for South America. In that year, the wheat shipments from River Plate ports to Peru more than offset the imbalance in the flow of general cargo between Peru and

Chile and Chile and River Plate. Had there been wheat shipments to Chile as well, as has been common in the past, the disequilibrium would have been even greater. The impact of the
wheat shipments from River Plate ports to Brazilian ports on the
imbalance of general cargo was similar. An excess of 500,000 tons
north to south over south to north in general cargo was transformed into an excess of 360,000 tons of south to north cargo over
north to south cargo when both refrigerated cargo and bulk cereals are included. The tonnage flows of bulk cereals in 1962 were
as follows (in thousands of metric tons):

Country	Area 2	Areas 1–2
Peru to Chile		
Clockwise	—	308
Chile to River Plate		
Clockwise	—	308
River Plate to Brazil		
Counterclockwise	689	—

It would thus appear that if some part of the wheat transport
were reserved for liner ships, it could aid in assuring a better use
of ships dedicated exclusively to LAFTA transport on a multilateral basis and hence would permit a more regular and economic
service. The problem that arises is that cereals are not a constant
cargo throughout the year, because generally the exporting country wishes to sell when the wheat is harvested and the importing
country wishes to buy only after its own harvest has been consumed. Thus if the transport of wheat were to be used to assure return cargoes for liners operating on regular schedules, it would be
essential to have an agreement among the countries involved to
spread out the transport over the year. These wheat shipments,
although perhaps potentially useful in balancing cargo flows
within Area 2 and between Areas 1 and 2, would not aid in correcting the sharp disequilibrium in the flows within Area 1 to the
north of Peru.

To this point, the analysis has implicitly assumed that LAFTA
cargo would be carried on ships dedicated exclusively to this service, that is, that LAFTA service would not be combined with ca-
botage within a particular country nor with service to Europe,

the United States, and other continents. In general, this is the situation at the present time within Area 2 and between Areas 1 and 2, where the disequilibrium in general cargo has made difficult regular liner service with reasonable rates. This problem was brought about in part because of past bilateral cargo reserves between Argentina and Brazil, Argentina and Chile, and Argentina and Peru. On the west coast, however, the frequent use of foreign liners as well as LAFTA liners offering service to other continents has tended to reduce the effect of the unbalanced flows.

In summary, an analysis of the transport flows in 1962 indicates that regular liner services would be difficult to provide if these services are organized separately for intra- and inter-area commerce. The provision of service on a bilateral basis between pairs of countries would be even more inefficient. Furthermore, the organization of inter-area service on a multilateral basis might be more efficient if part of the transport of bulk wheat were reserved for liner ships operating on regular schedules. Finally, difficult problems exist in the service between Mexico, Colombia, Ecuador, and Venezuela on the one hand, and the other LAFTA nations on the other hand, because of the small traffic volumes over these trade routes.

Rates Within the LAFTA Region and Compared with Rates from Abroad

An analysis of ocean freight rates, like that of custom duties, is treacherous. Global comparisons are often meaningless because of weighting problems: with extremely high freight rates, as with prohibitive duties, no goods are traded, and hence the high rates and duties are not included within the averages. Product-by-product comparisons of freight rates between different points are difficult because of the problem of defining the product and because different units are used on which to base the rates—weight, value, volume. In addition, these comparisons are often meaningless because a product is traded in only one direction and would be even though transport were costless, so that in effect a real freight rate is compared with an arbitrary paper rate. Data on ocean freight rates are also difficult to obtain, except in the United States trades, and the rates found may not represent what shippers pay, as rebates and surcharges are common and are subject to frequent changes.

Because of these many difficulties, few scholars have attempted serious studies of the structure of ocean liner rates. Furthermore, despite a continuing concern within Latin America over freight rates on routes to the United States and to Europe, demonstrated by repeated resolutions at inter-American conferences calling for lower rates and for studies of rates, little work has been done in this field. One of the few studies carried out was prepared by a special committee for the Economic Conference of the Organization of American States, held in Buenos Aires in 1957.[7] Despite the fact that the Spanish text of the committee's report is 412 pages long, the only question examined is whether freight rates between the United States and Latin America tend to be stable. The committee made no attempt to determine whether the rates are too high or too low or whether the structure of rates is conducive to economic development in Latin America.

The statistical work carried out for the committee is impressive: 6,869 annual liner freight rates between the United States and Latin America for the period 1947 through 1953 were analyzed by the staff of the Organization of American States. The results are shown in the table on page 136.[8]

It is difficult to know what to conclude from these results of the months of work required to prepare the table. The study seems to show that the rates set by the shipping conferences tend to be stable or to increase slowly on routes between the United States and Latin America. To the extent that these same ships carry cargo within the LAFTA region, it is reasonable to believe that the same conclusion is applicable to this commerce.

[7] Economic Conference of the Organization of American States, *Report of the Ad Hoc Committee to Study the System of Establishing Freight and Insurance Rates in Inter-American Trade,* Doc. 9 (July 1957).

[8] *Ibid.,* pp. 28-31.

	Number of Rates	
Rates Unchanged for:		
2 years	882	
3 years	2,043	
4 years	386	
5 years	132	
6 years	220	
7 years	204	
	———	
		3,867
Rates Increased by:		
Less than $6	2,051	
Between $6 and $9	368	
$9 and Over	149	
	———	
		2,568
Decreased Rates		289
Open Rates		145
		———
		6,869

Within Latin America it is commonly accepted, on the basis of a Chilean study,[9] that on the average the maritime freight rate represents 12.5 percent of the c.i.f. value of goods traded within the area and 15 percent of the f.o.b. value. For Chile alone, the freight rate represented a somewhat smaller percentage on exports to other LAFTA nations, 9.92 percent of the c.i.f. value and 11.9 percent of the f.o.b. value. These percentages do not vary widely from those that have been calculated for Brazil's imports from all countries, where freight charges between 1958 and 1961 as a percent of the c.i.f. value of imports fluctuated between 9.0 and 9.5 percent.[10] These general averages, however, can be grossly misleading because of important variations on different routes and among different products.[11]

Considering the relation of rates within the LAFTA area to

[9] Tomás Sepúlveda Whittle, "Transporte Marítimo en la Asociación Latino-Americana de Libre Comercio," (Valparaiso, Chile: ICARE, Seminario sobre Mercado Común Latino-Americano, November 1961), pp. 3-4.

[10] U.N. Conference on Trade and Development, *Ocean Shipping and Freight Rates and Developing Countries, op. cit.*, p. 35. The International Monetary Fund is cited as the source of these estimates.

[11] For the purpose of this study an attempt has been made to collect a group of representative freight rates both within the LAFTA area and between this area and the United States, Europe, and Japan. The results are presented in Appendix Tables C-1—C-5, with an explanation of the methods used in preparing them.

rates from foreign ports to this area, the following observations can be made on the basis of the data presented in Appendix C:

1. Rates to Callao, Peru. Although New York is 3,368 nautical miles from Callao while Rio de Janiero is 4,909 nautical miles from the same port, the rates from Rio de Janiero to Callao are consistently less than rates from New York.

2. Rates to Valparaiso, Chile. Rates from the selected LAFTA ports to Valparaiso are consistently less than the rates from the United States, Japan, and Europe. The only exception refers to unboxed automobiles, where it is obvious that the foreign rate on this product is out of line with the rate on other products from these same countries.

3. Rates to Buenos Aires and Montevideo. Rates from Callao and Valparaiso to Buenos Aires and Montevideo are consistently and considerably less than rates from U. S. ports. The rates from Buenaventura, Colombia and Guayaquil, Ecuador for merchandise "not otherwise specified" are extremely high. Although this catchall product category is frequently assigned a higher rate than for other products, it appears clear that rates are high between the northern ports of South America's Pacific coast and the southern Atlantic ports. Rates from both U. S. Atlantic and Pacific ports tend to be higher to Chile and Peru than those from these same ports to Buenos Aires and Montevideo, especially for products which pay freight on a weight basis, despite the fact that the distance is greater to Buenos Aires.

4. Rates to Rio de Janeiro. The rates to Rio de Janiero tend to be lower from the LAFTA countries than from foreign countries, although there are important exceptions, as in the case of automobiles and tractors.

In summary, if the rates within the LAFTA area are close to those shown in Appendix Tables C-1–C-5, the rates within the area are not higher than rates from foreign countries to the area. This conclusion, however, refers solely to the southern part of LAFTA, that is, Peru, Chile, Argentina, Uruguay, and Brazil. There is partial evidence that the rates between the southern part of LAFTA and the northern part, at least to Ecuador and the Pacific ports of Colombia, are very high. The inclusion of the surcharges shown in Appendix Table C-6 to the basic rates would not change the conclusions, because these surcharges are greater in the case of cargo destined to LAFTA ports from foreign ports than in the case of cargo traded within the LAFTA area.

Effect of Imbalances of Trade Flows on Freight Rates

It would be anticipated on the basis of the analysis of Table 7-3 that rates would differ substantially in clockwise and counterclockwise directions. This, however, is not the case, as the rates quoted for transport between the following pairs of countries are the same in both directions: Peru-Chile, Peru-Argentina, Peru-Uruguay, Peru-Brazil, Chile-Argentina, Chile-Uruguay, Chile-Brazil. Several explanations come to mind as to why the trade disequilibrium is not reflected in rates. First, if particular commodities are always traded in only one direction, higher rates can be set on the commodities which move in the direction of the greater flow. Although the rate is supposedly applicable to the same goods transported in the direction of the lesser flow, this rate is in fact a paper rate. This hypothesis could only be tested by weighting freight rates by the tonnage traded between each pair of countries for each commodity, but casual inspection of the tariffs would not seem to support the hypothesis. Second, the frequency of sailings may be determined by service considerations, and the vessels may always operate with substantial excess capacity, in both directions. In this case, the marginal cost of transporting an additional ton in the direction of the greater flow would not be higher than that in the opposite direction. Third, and closely related to the second hypothesis, the rates quoted by the LAFTA-shipping line may take into account those charged by foreign liners operating within the same area which may operate with substantial excess capacity.

Price Discrimination in Freight Rates

Although cost factors can partially explain differences in the rate per ton established for different commodities, the major explanation is usually found in the existence of competition within the transport industry or between alternative sources of supply of the commodity, and in the existence of differing demand elasticities for transport from product to product, which often appear to be related to variations in the unit value of these products. Because of the small size of the sample of rates presented in Appendix Tables C-1—C-5 and the way the sample was selected, it is impossible to apply variance analysis techniques to study rate discrimination among different products. Instead, a far more simple method has been used. On the routes where rates had been obtained for nearly all the products selected, a ratio was calculated which relates the average of the two highest rates on that route to the average of the two lowest rates. Within the LAFTA area, the rates for merchandise not otherwise specified were excluded because comparable rates had not been obtained for routes from the United States to the LAFTA area. Separate calculations were made for rates applied on a volume basis and on a weight basis, because the two are not comparable.

The results of the calculations are shown in Table 7-4. It is immediately clear from this table that the range of rates is far great-

TABLE 7-4. *Range of Freight Rates on Selected Shipping Routes*[a]

Routes	Ratio of Two Highest Rates to Two Lowest Rates	
	Rates Based on Volume	Rates Based on Weight
Foreign Rates		
U. S. Atlantic and Gulf to Callao, Peru	1.70	2.65
U. S. Pacific to Callao	2.25	2.31
U. S. Atlantic and Gulf to Rio de Janeiro and Buenos Aires	1.90	2.45
U. S. Pacific to Rio de Janeiro and Buenos Aires	1.54	2.80
LAFTA Rates		
Callao to Buenos Aires	1.13	1.64
Callao to Rio de Janeiro	1.12	1.68
Callao to Valparaiso	1.11	1.40
Buenos Aires to Rio de Janeiro	—	1.60
Valparaiso to Buenos Aires	1.16	1.49
Valparaiso to Rio de Janeiro	1.14	1.66

[a] See text for explanation.

er for the commodities selected on routes to LAFTA from the United States than on routes within the LAFTA area. It seems probable, therefore, that rates presently applied within LAFTA differ less from the cost of transport of particular commodities than is the case of rates applied from the United States, where discrimination among commodities is far more significant. It should be emphasized, however, that one important reason that might explain this difference is that some of the rates cited within LAFTA are paper rates, in the sense that little significant cargo moves under them. Furthermore, there may also be greater excess capacity within the LAFTA region than between this region and other continents.

Effect of Variations in Distance on Freight Rates

It has already been shown that the rates within the southern part of LAFTA are not higher than those from other continents to these countries. Are the rates within LAFTA, however, as low as might be hoped, given the physical proximity of these countries? It would be expected, of course, that because of the importance of port costs, which do not vary with the distance specific cargo is transported, the freight rate per nautical mile should vary inversely with the distance that the rate covers.

Tables 7-5 to 7-9 have been prepared on the basis of Appendix Tables C-1–C-5 by dividing each freight rate by the shortest navigation distance between each of the selected ports. The distances used are shown on the first line of Tables 7-5–7-9. Tables 7-5–7-9 thus indicate the ocean freight rate per nautical mile, per metric ton or per cubic meter, depending on the base to which the rate for each commodity is applied.

It is clear from Tables 7-5–7-9 that the hypothesis is only partially substantiated. The rates per nautical mile are high on very short routes, specifically Callao-Valparaiso and Buenos Aires-Rio de Janeiro. The rates per nautical mile to Valparaiso are low from the distant ports in Japan, England, and Europe. Nevertheless, in the instances where the distances within LAFTA are comparable to the distances from other continents, the intra-LAFTA rates per

TABLE 7-5. *Ocean Freight Rates per Nautical Mile to Callao, Peru, from Selected Ports*[a]

(Cents per metric ton or per cubic meter)

From:		U. S. Atlantic-New York	U. S. Pacific-San Francisco	Valparaiso	Buenos Aires	Montevideo	Rio de Janeiro
Distance (nautical miles)		3368 p	4595	1306	4065	3971	4909
Automobiles, unboxed	C.M.	0.87	0.69	1.38	0.54	0.73	0.61
Automobiles, spare parts	C.M.	0.87	0.62	1.38	0.53	0.62	0.52
Tractors, unboxed	C.M.	1.26	0.88	1.38	0.62	0.72	0.61
Radio & TV sets	C.M.	1.68	1.77	1.53	0.59	0.68	0.57
Refrigerators	C.M.	1.15	1.17	1.53	0.59	0.68	0.57
Steel plates	Ton	1.01	0.77	—	0.31	0.35	0.34
Steel bars	Ton	1.05	0.77	—	0.47	0.53	0.43
Copper cable	Ton	2.16	1.73	1.23	0.63	0.69	0.56
Newsprint	Ton	1.05	0.77	1.32	0.65	0.66	0.54
Wood pulp	Ton	0.82	0.65	1.07	0.54	0.55	0.45
Plate glass	Ton	1.47	1.42	1.76	0.57	0.73	0.65
Wheat in bags	Ton	0.85	—	1.23	0.47	0.57	0.53
Canned fruits	Ton	2.26	1.54	1.45	0.62	0.71	0.63
Merchandise n.o.s.	C.M./Ton	—	—	2.45	0.74	0.86	0.81

Source: Appendix Table C-1

[a] Rates do not include port surcharges. "p" indicates distance via Panama Canal.

TABLE 7-6. *Ocean Freight Rates per Nautical Mile to Valparaiso, Chile, from Selected Ports*[a]

(Cents per metric ton or per cubic meter)

From:		Tokyo-Yoko-hama	Callao	U.S. Pacific-San Francisco	U.S. Atlantic-New York	Buenos Aires	Monte-video	Rio de Janeiro	London	Rotter-dam
Distance (nautical miles)		9280	1306	5861	4633 p	2826	2732	3670	7399 p	7445 p
Automobiles, unboxed	C.M.	0.29	1.38	0.54	0.63	0.81	0.95	0.74	0.31	0.31
Automobiles, spare parts	C.M.	—	1.38	0.48	0.63	0.65	0.79	0.61	—	—
Tractors, unboxed	C.M.	0.49	1.38	0.69	0.92	0.81	0.95	0.74	0.45	0.53
Radio & TV sets	C.M.	0.48	1.53	1.34	1.22	0.74	0.88	0.68	0.68	0.64
Refrigerators	C.M.	—	1.53	0.92	0.84	0.74	0.88	0.68	0.47	0.53
Steel plates	Ton	0.31	—	0.60	0.76	0.58	0.70	0.50	0.53	0.47
Steel bars	Ton	0.31	—	0.60	0.76	0.51	0.64	0.49	0.50	0.51
Copper cable	Ton	—	1.23	1.30	1.57	0.80	0.90	0.67	—	—
Newsprint	Ton	0.38	1.32	0.60	0.76	0.75	0.86	0.52	0.40	0.47
Woodpulp	Ton	—	1.07	0.51	0.59	0.60	0.69	0.45	—	—
Plate glass	Ton	—	1.76	1.05	1.07	0.81	0.95	0.79	—	—
Wheat in bags	Ton	—	1.23	—	0.62	0.57	0.71	0.63	—	—
Canned fruits	Ton	—	1.45	1.20	1.64	0.78	0.92	0.76	—	—
Merchandise n.o.s.	C.M./Ton	—	2.45	—	—	0.81	0.95	0.79	—	—

Source: Appendix Table C-2.

[a] Rates do not include port surcharges. "p" indicates distances via Panama Canal.

141

TABLE 7-7. *Ocean Freight Rates per Nautical Mile to Buenos Aires, Argentina, from Selected Ports*[a]
(Cents per metric ton or per cubic meter)

From:		Buena-ventura	Guayaquil	Callao	Valparaiso	U.S. Atlantic-New York	U.S. Pacific-San Francisco
Distance (nautical miles)		5279	4701	4065	2826	5871	8748 p
Automobiles, unboxed	C.M.	—	—	0.62	0.81	0.42	0.49
Automobiles, spare parts	C.M.	—	—	0.53	0.65	0.56	0.43
Tractors, unboxed	C.M.	—	—	0.62	0.81	0.54	0.36
Radio & TV sets	C.M.	—	—	0.59	0.74	1.08	0.73
Refrigerators	C.M.	—	—	0.59	0.74	0.74	0.49
Steel plates	Ton	—	—	0.31	0.58	0.42	0.30
Steel bars	Ton	—	—	0.47	0.51	0.50	0.28
Copper cable	Ton	—	—	0.63	0.80	1.01	0.76
Newsprint	Ton	—	—	0.65	0.67	0.45	0.37
Wood pulp	Ton	—	—	0.54	0.60	0.44	0.40
Plate glass	Ton	—	—	0.57	0.81	0.60	
Wheat in bags	Ton	—	—	0.47	0.57	0.57	0.50
Canned fruits	Ton	—	—	0.62	0.78	1.11	0.88
Merchandise n.o.s.	C.M.	1.31	1.50	0.74	0.81	—	—
	Ton	1.63	1.88	0.74	1.06	—	—

Source: Appendix Table C-3.

[a] Rates do not include port surcharges. "p" indicates distance via Panama Canal.

TABLE 7-8. *Ocean Freight Rates per Nautical Mile to Montevideo, Uruguay, from Selected Ports*[a]
(Cents per metric ton or per cubic meter)

From:		Buenaven-tura	Guayaquil	Callao	Valparaiso	U.S. Atlantic-New York	U.S. Pacific-San Francisco
Distance (nautical miles)		5185	4607	3971	2732	5749	8624 p
Automobiles, unboxed	C.M.	—	—	0.73	0.95	0.42	0.50
Automobiles, spare parts	C.M.	—	—	0.62	0.79	0.57	0.44
Tractors, unboxed	C.M.	—	—	0.72	0.95	0.55	0.37
Radio & TV sets	C.M.	—	—	0.68	0.88	1.11	0.74
Refrigerators	C.M.	—	—	0.68	0.88	0.75	0.50
Steel plates	Ton	—	—	0.35	0.70	0.43	0.31
Steel bars	Ton	—	—	0.53	0.64	0.51	0.29
Copper cable	Ton	—	—	0.69	0.90	1.03	0.77
Newsprint	Ton	—	—	0.66	0.86	0.46	0.38
Wood pulp	Ton	—	—	0.55	0.69	0.45	0.41
Plate glass	Ton	—	—	0.73	0.95	0.62	—
Wheat in bags	Ton	—	—	0.57	0.71	0.58	0.51
Canned fruits	Ton	—	—	0.71	0.92	1.13	0.89
Merchandise n.o.s.	C.M.	1.33	1.53	0.86	0.95	—	—
	Ton	1.66	1.91	0.86	0.95	—	—

Source: Appendix Table C-4.

[a] Rates do not include port surcharges. "p" indicates distance via Panama Canal.

TABLE 7-9. *Ocean Freight Rates per Nautical Mile to Rio de Janeiro, Brazil, from Selected Ports*[a]
(Cents per metric ton or per cubic meter)

From:		Tokyo-Yokohama	U.S. Pacific-San Francisco	Buena-ventura	Guaya-quil	Callao	Valpa-raiso	Buenos Aires	U.S. Atlantic-New York	London	Rotter-dam
Distance (nautical miles)		11517	7641 p	6123	5545	4909	3670	1151	4770	5212	5259
Automobiles, unboxed	C.M.	0.32	0.56	—	—	0.61	0.74	—	0.51	0.26	0.35
Automobiles, spare parts	C.M.	—	0.49	—	—	0.52	0.61	—	0.69	—	—
Tractors, unboxed	C.M.	0.42	0.42	—	—	0.61	0.74	—	0.67	0.33	0.35
Radio & TV sets	C.M.	0.43	0.83	—	—	0.57	0.68	1.91	1.33	0.64	0.47
Refrigerators	C.M.	0.43	0.57	—	—	0.57	0.68	1.91	0.91	0.66	0.72
Steel plates	Ton	0.23	0.35	—	—	0.34	0.50	1.39	0.52	0.37	0.43
Steel bars	Ton	0.23	0.32	—	—	0.43	0.49	—	0.62	0.36	0.43
Copper cable	Ton	—	0.87	—	—	0.56	0.67	1.30	1.24	—	—
Newsprint	Ton	0.56	0.43	—	—	0.54	0.52	1.65	0.56	0.57	0.46
Wood pulp	Ton	—	0.46	—	—	0.45	0.45	—	0.55	—	—
Plate glass	Ton	—				0.65	0.79	2.39	0.74	—	—
Wheat in bags	Ton	—	0.58	—	—	0.53	0.63	1.43	0.70	—	—
Canned fruits	Ton	—	1.01	—	—	0.63	0.76	1.91	1.36	—	—
Merchandise n.o.s.	C.M.	—		1.16	1.33	0.81	0.79	2.17		—	—
	Ton	—		1.44	1.64	0.81	0.79	2.17		—	—

Source: Appendix Table C-5.
[a] Rates do not include port surcharges. "p" indicates distance via Panama Canal.

nautical mile compare favorably with those on routes from England and Europe and are consistently lower than those from the United States, perhaps reflecting high stevedoring costs in the United States. In several cases, the rates per nautical mile are lower within LAFTA than from the United States despite the fact that the distances are much shorter than from the United States. It would seem, in sum, that the rates per nautical mile are not high within LAFTA for reasonably long routes, when the standard of comparison used is the rates per nautical mile from the continents.

A further calculation was made to analyze the rates within the LAFTA area in relation to the distances between different pairs of ports. Taking as a base the rates between Callao and Valparaiso, the shortest route for which nearly complete rates had been obtained, it was arbitrarily assumed that 65 percent of these rates

TABLE 7-10. *Influence of Distance on Freight Rates Between Selected Ports*[a]
(Cents per nautical mile, per metric ton, or per cubic meter)

From:	Buenos Aires to Rio de Janeiro	Callao to Valparaiso	Valparaiso to Buenos Aires	Valparaiso to Rio de Janeiro	Callao to Buenos Aires	Guayaquil to Buenos Aires	Callao to Rio de Janeiro	Buenaventura to Buenos Aires	Guayaquil to Rio de Janeiro	Buenaventura to Rio de Janeiro
Distance (naut. miles)	1151	1306	2826	3670	4065	4701	4909	5279	5545	6123
Automobiles, unboxed, C.M.	—	0.48	0.40	0.42	0.25	—	0.37	—	—	—
Automobiles, spare parts, C.M.	—	0.48	0.24	0.29	0.24	—	0.28	—	—	—
Tractors, unboxed, C.M.	—	0.48	0.40	0.42	0.33	—	0.37	—	—	—
Radio and TV sets, C.M.	0.78	0.54	0.28	0.33	0.27	—	0.31	—	—	—
Refrigerators, C.M.	0.78	0.54	0.28	0.33	0.27	—	0.31	—	—	—
Steel plates, Ton	—	—	—	—	—	—	—	—	—	—
Steel bars, Ton	—	—	—	—	—	—	—	—	—	—
Copper cable, Ton	0.40	0.43	0.43	0.38	0.37	—	0.35	—	—	—
Newsprint, Ton	0.67	0.46	0.36	0.21	0.37	—	0.31	—	—	—
Wood pulp, Ton	—	0.38	0.27	0.20	0.32	—	0.26	—	—	—
Plate glass, Ton	1.09	0.62	0.28	0.38	0.20	—	0.35	—	—	—
Wheat in bags, Ton	0.53	0.43	0.20	0.34	0.21	—	0.32	—	—	—
Canned fruits, Ton	0.84	0.51	0.34	0.43	0.31	—	0.38	—	—	—
Merchandise, n.o.s.:										
C.M.	0.36	0.86	0.08	0.22	0.23	1.06	0.39	0.91	0.95	0.82
Ton	0.36	0.86	0.33	0.22	0.23	1.43	0.39	1.23	1.27	1.10

[a] See text for explanation.

correspond to costs within the ports of origin and destination and hence are unrelated to distance. Then the remaining 35 percent of the rate corresponding to each commodity was divided by the distance between Callao and Valparaiso. Next the same absolute amount of money assumed to represent port costs on this route for each commodity was subtracted from the rate on the same commodity on each other route, assuming that port costs do not vary greatly among the different routes. The amount subtracted varied between nine and fifteen dollars for the different commodities. Finally, the difference between the quoted rate for each commodity on each route and the assumed port cost for that commodity was divided by the navigation distance for that route. The results of this calculation are shown in Table 7-10. This table seems to show that the rates for the very short routes, specifically Buenos Aires-Rio de Janeiro and Callao-Valparaiso are still rather high, in the sense that the rates on different commodities per nautical mile still tend to diminish as the distance increases. It would not seem justified to apply a still higher handling charge, however, because the rates do not diminish consistently as the distances increase over these very short routes. It is also clear from Table 7-10 that the rates quoted appear to include a substantial surcharge on shipments to Brazilian ports both from Chile and from Peru. It is also evident that the rates per nautical mile are still high from the ports of Colombia and Ecuador.

Other Views of the Rate Problem

Before summarizing the material that has been presented on present shipping rates within the LAFTA region, which is based exclusively on an analysis of Appendix Tables C-1–C-5, brief reference will be made to other sources which have commented on this problem.

Resolution XXI, adopted at the Economic Conference of the Organization of American States in 1957, after noting the importance of increasing commerce within Latin America, states:

> The freight rates adopted on inter-Latin American maritime routes, the principal means of transportation in the region, often tend to discourage this diversified trade, because such rates are higher than those for similar products originating outside the area, thus weakening the competitive position of Latin American products. . . .

> The Economic Conference of the Organization of American States Resolves:

> To recommend to the interested parties that, in view of the requirements of the economic development of Latin America and the diversification of its trade, they sponsor the adoption of freight rates for the maritime routes of the region on a level with those prevailing in the maritime routes between Latin America and the other regions of the world for the same commodities, taking into consideration factors that have a bearing on the costs of the respective transportation.[12]

[12] Economic Conference of the Organization of American States, Buenos Aires, 1957, *Final Act,* pp. 47-48.

The resolution, of course, refers to the situation that existed in 1957, which may have been different from that in 1964. Nevertheless, there is no indication that any study has been made to substantiate the assertion that rates within LAFTA were higher than those from outside the area. Although the resolution specifically cites the report of the Ad Hoc Committee of Experts of the American Republics for the Study of the System of Freight and Insurance Rates, which has been discussed above, this report does not touch on the relative level of freight rates within Latin America and from outside the region. The analysis of the tables in Appendix C indicates that rates within the southern part of the LAFTA region are not higher than rates from abroad, but rates between the northern and southern parts might well be.

The conclusions based on an analysis of Appendix Tables C-1– C-5 are consistent with an assertion made by Tomás Sepúlveda Whittle in 1961:

> Thus it should be made clear, for the peace of mind of all of you, that the freight rates between Chile and the other members of LAFTA . . . compare favorably with the rates from European and North American ports to these countries, except in the case of lumber, where we use a revenue ton defined as 500 feet and they use 1,000 feet. I can honestly state that there is no problem of Chilean exports to LAFTA being at a disadvantage because of freight rates, which does not mean that we shall not try to reduce transport costs and to increase productivity.[13]

Nevertheless, it is also clear from the analysis in the present study that freight rate problems do exist on routes between the northern and southern parts of LAFTA and also that the rates over very short routes appear unduly high. Referring to the first aspect, only scattered observations are available, but they indicate that the problem of low traffic volumes is compounded by the structure of the ocean freight conferences. Fernando Cúen, discussing the maritime transport problems of Mexico, states that a Mexican company exporting gas stoves found that the freight rate from Acapulco to Panama was practically double that to Venezuela, because the shipping line belonged to the San Fran-

[13] Sepúlveda, op. cit., p. 5. Free translation. At that time Sepúlveda was General Manager of the Chilean Shipowners Association.

cisco Conference while it was in the Pacific but was out of it while in the Caribbean and hence was able to offer promotional rates to Venezuela. A Mexican importer wished to import tannin directly from Buenos Aires to Tampico. He found, however, that the direct freight rate was $54, whereas via New Orleans the rate was $8 less and via Southampton, England, $14 less. Another Mexican company wished to export pressed fiber board, but found that although it could quote the same f.o.b. price as a Finnish company, the rate from Mexico to Venezuela was $24, while the freight rate from Finland to Venezuela was only $17.[14]

Referring to the second aspect, there has been considerable criticism of the freight rates between Argentina and Brazil set by the shipping conference composed of the shipping companies of those two nations. In 1959, the Chamber of Sawmills and Lumber Yards[15] protested to the Argentine Minister of Economy that the conference was setting exorbitant rates and was imposing excessively restrictive conditions on the transport of lumber from Brazil to Argentina. The Chamber stated that the rate was $33.50 per 1,000 feet while the rate from Brazil to the United States was only $25. "A voyage of five weeks thus pays a lower rate than a voyage of five days. We have learned of cases where 'outsiders' have been willing to provide service between Brazilian and Argentine ports for $25, but exporters and importers have not been able to use this service because of the threats of the conference."[16]

In its answer to this protest, the conference stated that although the rate had been $33.50 until November 1959, it had dropped in that month to $28.50, and, in the case of shippers who use the conference exclusively, an additional discount is allowed which lowers the rate to $26.37 and from Pôrto Alegre to $23.97. The conference also points out that comparisons with the rate on lumber to countries outside the area are misleading, because the foreign rates do not include loading and unloading, and surcharges for delays are charged apart. The conference stated that

[14] Fernando Cúen, "El Problema del Transporte Marítimo de México Frente al Area Latinoamericana de Libre Comercio," in Selecciones de Estudios Latinoamericanos, *El Transporte Marítimo en la ALALC* (1962), pp. 11-12.

[15] Cámara de Aserraderos y Depósitos de Madera.

[16] Instituto de Estudios de la Marina Mercante Argentina, *La Marina Mercante Argentina, 1960,* pp. 27-28.

the rate between Brazil and Argentina could be lowered further if the shippers were to absorb the cost of loading and unloading.[17]

In 1961, the freight rates between Brazil and Argentina were criticized by the Mixed Argentine-Brazilian Commission that requested government action to assure that "the price differential between the rates charged by Argentine and Brazilian ships in relation to international rates be limited to an amount which is compatible with commercial considerations, avoiding in this way that the prices of the goods traded be increased excessively to the detriment of the producers and consumers of the two countries."[18] The private shipowners, however, claim that their economic condition is precarious because of imbalance and fluctuations in the cargo available, excessive costs and delays in the ports, and unfair competition from the state lines.[19]

Perhaps the best summary of the prevailing attitude toward maritime shipping within LAFTA is that of Enrique Angulo:

> Some of the problems which must be overcome if maritime transport is to be adequate have their origin within LAFTA while others come from outside the area: the irregularity of shipping services, so that often only with good fortune is it possible to obtain shipping space at a reasonable rate; transport costs which are higher within Latin America than between this region and the rest of the world, due to high freight rates which represent approximately 12.5 percent of c.i.f. value and 15 percent of f.o.b. value; disequilibrium in trade flows; taxes on freight rates which, according to Chilean figures for 1961, represent an additional 5.5 percent within the LAFTA area; the disastrous situation in the ports, which has led shipping conferences to impose surcharges which reach 35 percent of the freight rate; and excessive documentation and other bureaucratic requirements which affect the operation of the vessels.[20]

The analysis that has been carried out in this study of shipping services and freight rates within the LAFTA area would not

[17] *Ibid.*, pp. 28-29.

[18] Instituto de Estudios de la Marina Mercante Argentina, *La Marina Mercante Argentina, 1961*, p. 46.

[19] Instituto de Estudios de la Marina Mercante Argentina, *La Marina Mercante Argentina, 1962*, p. 347.

[20] Enrique H. Angulo, "El Transporte y el Comercio Interlatinoamericano," in Miguel S. Wionczek (ed), *Integración de la América Latina* (Mexico and Buenos Aires: Fondo de Cultura, 1964), pp. 183-84. Free translation.

seem to lead to quite so pessimistic a view of maritime transport. It does seem clear that rates within the southern part of LAFTA are not higher than rates between this area and the rest of the world. Nevertheless, it is also probable that service is unsatisfactory and rates unduly high between the northern and southern parts of LAFTA. This problem arises both because of limited volumes of cargo traded and because of policies of international shipping conferences. It is also probable that rates are unduly high on short routes, most importantly between Brazil and Argentina. Although this problem is due in part to the restrictive bilateral agreement between the two countries, it is due primarily to high port costs and excessive delays in loading and unloading. There can be no doubt that at the present time, maritime transport does represent an obstacle to attaining the objectives of LAFTA. Some regions of LAFTA are isolated from other regions and present transport costs do not reflect sufficiently the geographical proximity of the member countries.

The Incidence of Port Costs on Freight Rates

Before continuing to examine the probable effect of the proposed draft maritime transport agreement on shipping rates and service within LAFTA, it is important to understand the significance of present port costs and conditions in the LAFTA region. At different times in this study, port costs of 51, 65, and 75 percent of total carrier costs have been assumed. The incidence in total maritime costs would be even higher, as the shipper must pay the cost of handling the cargo within the port itself, which is not included in the freight rate. The percentage incidence of port costs is not, of course, a constant on all routes; the percentage would be expected to fall as the distance increases of a particular commodity movement. Bulk commodities are likely to have lower handling costs in ports than general cargo, but the freight rate is also likely to be lower, so that a priori, little can be said about the effect on the incidence of port costs within total costs. Port costs also vary considerably among nations and among ports within a nation. It has been asserted that loading charges in New York average $12.88 per payable ton of 2,240 pounds or forty cubic feet, while charges in New Orleans average only $8.57. These stevedoring charges can be compared with rates which average $5.67 in Rotterdam, $4.47 in Liverpool, and $2.50 in Tokyo-Yokohama.[21]

Little quantitative information has been published on port costs within Latin America. It is commonly accepted, however, that these costs are high when compared with costs in other ports of the world, if ship turnaround time is included. One study is available which analyzes port costs in relation to the total freight rate paid for general cargo unloaded in the port of Montevideo, Uruguay by 713 ships during 1962. The results of this study, which was prepared by the Center of Transatlantic Navigation in Montevideo, are summarized below.[22]

More than 40 percent of total freight paid to foreign ships for Uruguayan general cargo imports never leaves Uruguay. If the port costs in the originating country were only half those in Uruguay, the total incidence of port costs in the freight rate would be more than 60 percent, which is considerably higher than the 51 percent shown in Table 6-4. On different routes to Uruguay the percentage varies from a low of 31 percent for the route from Continental Europe to a high of 55 percent on the less important routes to the west coast of North and South America, the Far East, Australia, India, and Africa. The wide variations both in the freight rate per ton, and in port costs per ton, are explained in part by the composition of imports transported over each route and the variation in the average tonnage handled per ship call. Another part of the variation in the freight rates is due to competition and the practices of the shipping conferences. Finally, a further part in the variation in port costs per ton handled is due to differing policies

---

[21] *Discriminatory Ocean Freight Rates and the Balance of Payments,* Hearings before the Joint Economic Committee, 88 Cong. 1 sess. (1963), Pt. 3, p. 338.

[22] The purpose of this study was to analyze potential foreign exchange savings to Uruguay if it were to use national ships for its international commerce. The study concludes that the potential savings represent only 18.3 percent of total freight paid to foreign liners on the route from ports on the east coast of the United States and Canada. Centro de Navegación Transatlántica, "Estudio del movimiento marítimo que ocasionaron en Montevideo las importaciones realizadas durante el año 1962, y lo que este movimiento marítimo significó para el país" (Montevideo, August 1963).

among shipping lines with respect to working overtime while in Montevideo.

In Table 7-11, the $862,000 in port costs incurred by foreign liners transporting general cargo imports to Montevideo from the east coast of the United States and Canada in 1962 are broken

TABLE 7-11. *Port Costs Incurred by Foreign Liners Carrying Cargo to Montevideo from the East Coast of the United States and Canada, 1962*[a]

	Cost Incurred (U. S. dollars)	Percentage Distribution
Group I:		
Stevedoring, including social security for stevedores	$414,566	48.1
Coopers	31,707	3.7
Subtotal	446,273	51.8
Group II:		
Charges for use of berths	20,371	2.4
Watchmen, police protection, fire protection	9,555	1.1
Special services rendered by customs and port authority	102,059	11.8
Rental of stevedoring equipment and miscellaneous costs	30,628	3.5
Subtotal	162,613	18.8
Group III:		
Pilotage	33,299	3.9
Social security payments for pilotage	8,641	1.0
Tug services	57,389	6.7
Navigational aids tax	7,929	0.9
Public health, stamped paper, immigration, lookouts, Center of Transatlantic Navigation, launches, automobiles, telegrams, postage, long distance telephone calls	22,817	2.6
Subtotal	130,075	15.1
Group IV:		
Advances to crew, doctors, medicine, hospitals, hotels, fresh water, laundry, newspaper advertisements, repairs, supplies, etc.	123,039	14.3
Total	$862,000	100.0

Source: Centro de Navegación Transatlántica, Montevideo, Uruguay, August 1963.

[a] Expenditures in Uruguayan pesos converted to dollars at the rate of 11 pesos per U. S. dollar. Table covers 170 ship calls during 1962.

down into the important components. The costs have been separated into four categories (which are not used in the original study). The costs included in the first group, stevedores and coopers, vary about proportionally with the tonnage handled, provided that a consistent policy of working overtime is assumed. As can be seen, the costs in this group represent 51.8 percent of total port costs. The costs included in the second group are affected by the amount of tonnage handled but probably do not vary proportionally with tonnage. In addition, part of the costs in this group should be charged against the goods loaded in Montevideo and destined for other ports.

The costs included in the third group are likely to vary little with tonnage handled and are practically a fixed cost per ship call. They thus represent a common cost for imported goods and exported goods carried by a single ship. The final group of costs are not a part of handling charges of the cargo in the port, although they do represent costs which are paid in Uruguay and hence represent a foreign exchange saving.

If it is assumed arbitrarily that all of the costs in group one, two-thirds of the costs in group two, one-half of the costs in group three, and none of the costs in group four should be considered port costs attributable to imported goods, then the weighted average of total port costs would fall from 45.0 percent on the route from the east coast of the United States and Canada to 32.4 percent. From this simple calculation, based on arbitrary assumptions about the distribution of common costs between inbound and outbound cargo, it is clear that the total incidence of port costs within freight rates applied within the LAFTA area is easily more than 50 percent for general cargo, and on short routes could reach the 65 percent assumed in Table 7-10. These costs, furthermore, do not include that part of ship depreciation, crew wages, fuel, etc., attributable to the stay in port.

Studies that relate total port costs—those borne by the carrier and the shipper—to maritime transport costs are even scarcer than those that analyze the relation between the cost borne by the carrier and the freight rate. One such study has been carried out for the port of Valparaiso by the Institute of Economic Research of the University of Chile,[23] concluding that in 1963 the expenditure incurred by foreign liners per ton of general cargo was 7.2 escudos in prices of 1959 (roughly seven dollars). The cost per ton for the same type of cargo borne by the port authority (and passed along to shippers to a greater or lesser degree) for handling within the port was 1.98 escudos, also in prices of 1959. Although the costs may be high in Valparaiso, it is clear that handling charges borne by the shipper-consignee have reached more than 25 percent of the cost borne by the carrier for stevedoring and related charges.

Shipping Rates and Service and the Draft LAFTA Treaty

Bearing in mind the deficiencies of maritime transport within the LAFTA area, it is now time to turn to the critical question whether the adoption of the General Agreement on Ocean and Inland Water Transport, described above in Chapter VI, would contribute to overcoming these deficiencies and to attaining the objectives of LAFTA.

At the outset, it must be recognized that the draft treaty prepared at the April 1964 meeting of the Transport Advisory Commission contains a number of ambiguities and unanswered questions which are inevitable in any international agreement that represents a compromise among sharply differing positions. For this reason, it is impossible to predict the *probable* effects that the treaty would have until it is known how the treaty would in fact be applied, that is, until all the questions have been answered and the ambiguities have been clarified. If the treaty were adopted and applied so as to benefit solely the LAFTA shipping companies, without consideration of the needs of the region for better transport, it is clear that the agreement would be a first step toward the eventual abandonment of the idea of economic integration. If the treaty were to mean nothing more than an extension

[23] Carlos Hurtado and Arturo Israel, *Tres Ensayos sobre el Transporte en Chile* (Santiago, Chile: Instituto de Economía de la Universidad de Chile, 1964), pp. 144, 147.

to the entire region, of the chaos that exists under the bilateral
agreement between Brazil and Argentina, there is clearly nothing
to be said in its favor.

Attention here, therefore, will be focused on only three aspects of the draft treaty: LAFTA cargo is almost entirely reserved
for vessels operated by established LAFTA shipping companies;
the reserves are nearly exclusively on a bilateral basis; and rates
would be established by shipping conferences. The basic question
raised is whether an intelligent application of these principles
could lead to improved maritime service within LAFTA at a reasonable cost.

Reservation of Cargo for LAFTA Ships

If the principle of multilateral reserves were accepted, it is
possible to see how the application of the first principle, that
LAFTA cargo be reserved for LAFTA ships, could improve maritime transport within the region. The application of multilateral
reserves would aid in correcting the damage already being done
by existing bilateral agreements, such as that between Brazil and
Argentina. This would permit, for example, Chilean ships to
combine the carriage of goods between Brazil and Argentina
with transport between Brazil and Chile. This effect alone
would contribute substantially to rationalizing transport services.

The importance of frequent, regular, and stable liner services
among all the LAFTA nations has been stressed repeatedly in this
study. These services do not now exist because they would not pay.
Neither will they pay until they have been established for a long
enough period to encourage potential exporters to search for new
markets, and potential importers to search for new sources of supply. As an alternative to state subsidies, or in combination with
subsidies where necessary, shipping lines that are willing to provide liner service should be granted assistance which channels to
them what cargo is presently available. LAFTA cargo should not
be reserved for *any* ship belonging to an established LAFTA
shipping company. It should be reserved for liner ships that follow fixed schedules and that charge rates published in publicly
available tariffs. It is irrelevant whether this service is provided

by companies dedicated exclusively to LAFTA or by companies which combine LAFTA service with service to other continents. It is also irrelevant whether the service comes from established companies or from companies which are newly formed. The only important factor is whether frequent, regular, and stable service is provided.

Because of the nature of the cargo which now makes up the greater part of intra-LAFTA commerce, shipping service by present LAFTA shipping companies is essentially tramp service. The transition from tramp service to liner service may well require that a significant portion of the transport of some bulk products be reserved for liner vessels. As state agencies are responsible in many instances for the export and import of products such as wheat, it should be possible to assure that these cargoes are channeled to the liners. So far as possible, the transport should be spread out over as long a period of each year as is economically feasible so as to maintain constant cargo flows. The importance of bulk cargo as the basis for regular liner service has been pointed out by Plácido García Reynoso,[24] whose observation is amply supported by studies which have been made of ocean shipping in other areas:

> Tramp and other casual competition flourishes on large movements of more or less homogeneous cargoes. If such cargoes are important in any trade, there is a marked tendency for casual competition to nibble into general cargo as well. The carriage of "non-tramp" cargoes may be potentially profitable enough to justify special arrangements for those cargoes congenial to bulk carriage. By negotiating with blocs of shippers who somehow can control the large volume cargoes, it may be possible for liner companies to give them service and rates that are attractive enough to keep their custom intact, yet still come out ahead on the carriage of the general cargo, control of which is thereby made possible. In sum, if such strategic core cargoes can be so controlled a shelter will have been constructed for general cargo.[25]

[24] Instituto de Estudios de la Marina Mercante Argentina, *La Marina Mercante Argentina, 1962*, p. 181.

[25] Allen R. Ferguson and others, *The Economic Value of the United States Merchant Marine* (The Transportation Center at Northwestern University, 1961), p. 403.

It is probable that on several routes sufficient cargo is already available to permit economical and profitable liner service if present cargo were channeled to a few companies. Nothing is done to solve the problem of inadequate transport on small-volume routes, however, if selected companies are merely granted a remunerative monopoly on high-volume routes. Monopoly privilege should be accompanied by a corresponding obligation to provide service over unprofitable routes, a principle that can also be applied to foreign liners.

Bilateral Reserves

With respect to the second aspect, bilateral reserves are clearly incompatible with the purpose and philosophy of the Montevideo Treaty and would inevitably prove a serious obstacle to improving service and lowering maritime costs within the LAFTA area. It is unfortunate that for so many years the question of bilateral versus multilateral reserves should have absorbed the bulk of the attention given to maritime problems within LAFTA. Fortunately, the sterile and political resolution in favor of bilateral reserves in the 1964 draft treaty was modified by the meeting of government maritime experts in May 1965 when reserves were advocated on a multilateral basis. From an administrative point of view, it is difficult to imagine a control system that could be devised which could apply bilateral reserves along the lines of the first article of the draft treaty. Commerce within the LAFTA area is already plagued sufficiently by bureaucratic obstacles without the addition of still another layer of permits and regulations which would increase not only the cost of trade but also the uncertainty.

From an economic point of view, bilateral reserves would be a disaster. The rates established over particular routes would have no relation to real transport costs within the area, and instead would reflect the operating costs of the particular shipping companies permitted to share in the trade and the trade flows and seasonal fluctuations affecting commerce between only two countries. The analysis which has already been carried out of present cargo flows, where both limited volumes and tonnage imbalances are common characteristics, amply supports the straightforward conclusions of the Economic Commission for Latin America:

> It is evident that a system of cargo distribution on a bilateral basis can lead to a bad or insufficient utilization of the cargo capacity of vessels and services, especially when it is considered that this system would signify fractioning a volume of cargo which is already barely sufficient or in many instances insufficient for an economical operation of regular, frequent and stable services. This problem is even more serious in the case of traffic with directional imbalances between particular countries and evidently contributes to increase the costs and the corresponding freight rates.[26]

Rate-Making and Shipping Conferences

If a system of multilateral reserves were applied intelligently to intra-LAFTA cargo, it seems clear that the formation of strong shipping conferences would be desirable to establish rates within the LAFTA area. Studies of maritime shipping throughout the world have consistently concluded that conferences tend to stabilize rates, regularize service, and prevent discrimination among shippers. These are evidently elements that are needed within the LAFTA region if economic integration is to be successful, provided that rates are not stabilized at a level higher than that required for adequate service. If freight rates are not set by a conference or conferences, the only other alternatives are that each company fix its own rates, that governments unilaterally establish rates, or that governments fix rates on a bilateral or multilateral basis.

If freight rates are set by shipping companies collectively through freight conferences, a review of rates by governments is far easier than if each company were to set its own rates. Furthermore, even though rates might theoretically be the responsibility of each company acting independently, experience in the past has shown that carriers will tend to associate informally to fix freight rates. For this reason, there are advantages to having these agreements explicit and the rates set by a formally established organi-

[26] U.N. Economic Commission for Latin America, *Los Problemas del Transporte en América Latina; posibles estudios en función del mercado común*, E/CN. 12/C. 1/14 (March 28, 1959), p. 13. Free translation.

zation to which interested shippers can recur to request rate reductions. Even though rates are established by conference, it would be possible to take into account significant differences in the quality of service offered by different companies. Moreover, the establishment of conference rates need not imply absolute price rigidity in the face of strong seasonal fluctuations in the cargo offered.

Independent governments cannot independently and simultaneously fix freight rates, because one country's exports are another country's imports. Neither is rate setting on a multilateral or bilateral basis advisable, both because of the danger of political considerations governing the decisions and because of the complexity of ocean shipping. Government agencies, as is clear from the experience of countries where governments have set rates for coastwise shipping, are not prepared to deal with the multitude of factors described earlier in this chapter which affect freight rates. Only operating shipping lines are in a position to recommend a structure and level of freight rates appropriate for the different LAFTA routes.

To recommend that freight rates be set by shipping conferences is to accept implicitly the desirability of discriminatory pricing among the different commodities transported so as to take into account the differing price elasticity of demand for transport among these goods. This pricing policy recognizes that a major part of the voyage costs of a vessel are common costs, for the different commodities carried between the various ports, and that there is no way to assign these common costs to particular shipments, although handling charges in ports are assignable to specific goods. Discriminatory pricing is based on the principle that these common costs should be distributed according to the ability to pay of specific cargo. The alternative to this pricing policy would be either to charge all the goods the same rate, based on average transport costs, or to charge all goods according to the marginal cost with a subsidy to cover the difference between marginal and average costs.

Although value of service pricing has been criticized in recent years, and a pricing policy more nearly related to costs has frequently been advocated, it is clear that value of service pricing is the policy which should be followed within the LAFTA area.[27] Specifically, this policy would mean that the freight rate on any product should be sufficient to cover all handling charges and other assignable costs, and in addition, should reflect the price elasticity of demand of that product for transport. The price elasticity for transport, in turn, will depend on the incidence of the freight rate on the f.o.b. value of the good and on the price elasticity of demand for the good itself.[28] This pricing policy will contribute more effectively to the establishment of regular liner service within the LAFTA area than either of the alternatives.

Good maritime service within LAFTA is by no means guaranteed, or even probable, if nothing more is done than to grant liners a partial monopoly on transport and to permit conferences to establish freight rates. Studies of the effect of conferences show that two conflicting dangers must be avoided. On the one hand, the conference is likely to abuse its monopolistic position and to establish rates which are unduly high, and on the other, excessive competition among member carriers is likely to lead to wasteful excess capacity.[29]

It is essential that the tariffs established and published by the conferences be subject to review by an international commission of the LAFTA members. This commission would be empowered as the representative of the LAFTA nations to analyze and approve the level and structure of rates established by the conferences. This review is essential to assure that the rates set are not unduly high. With respect to the structure of rates, the commission should take care to see that the application of value of service freight rates does not wipe out differences in f.o.b. prices among potential exporters. It should also be the task of the commission to assure that the transport policy adopted is consistent

[27] Daniel Marx, Jr., *International Shipping Cartels: A Study of Industrial Self-Regulation by Shipping Conferences* (Princeton University Press, 1953), App. A. George W. Wilson, *Essays on Some Unsettled Questions in the Economics of Transportation* (Indiana University, Foundation for Economic and Business Studies, 1962), Chap. 5. It is unfortunate that Wilson's stimulating book has not received the attention that it deserves. John R. Meyer and others, *The Economics of Competition in the Transportation Industries*, Harvard Economics Studies, Vol. CVII (Harvard University Press, 1959), Chap. 7.

[28] Wilson, *op. cit.*, p. 157.

[29] Marx, *op. cit.*, p. 291.

with the general policy of LAFTA in developing new industries and expanding commerce in the region. Specifically, the commission should be concerned that shipping companies do not consider traffic as static but rather that traffic can be increased by a judicious structure of rates. Furthermore, the commission must be aware of the effect on the location of economic activity of differing rates for raw materials and finished goods.

To avoid the danger of excessive competition and high average costs due to poor use of ships, both the conferences and the multinational commission should again be given ample responsibility. The conferences should present to the commission a range of maximum and minimum sailings which its members are prepared to make over each route. These sailings, based primarily on the nature and volume of cargo available on different routes, cannot be determined independently of the reserve policy adopted and the level of freight rates. It would be the responsibility of the commission to assure that maximum service is provided, taking into account both the use of ship capacity and freight rates.

The desirability of governmental supervision of conference activities has been indicated frequently throughout the world. The problem has always been to advise a suitable mechanism by which this might be done. Attempts of the Federal Maritime Commission of the United States to unilaterally regulate freight rates in U. S. commerce have been sharply resisted by traditional maritime nations. The success of the United States, however, in requiring all conferences to file rates and to be approved by the commission is a clear indication that the task is not impossible.

In summary, the draft treaty prepared in 1964 is clearly unacceptable, from the point of view of its effect on rates and service, in proposing bilateral cargo reserves, as was recognized by the May 1965 meeting of LAFTA maritime experts. In addition, the earlier document contains a number of ambiguities and unanswered questions that make it impossible to predict whether its application even on the basis of multilateral reserves would be beneficial. Nevertheless, it also seems clear that the principle of multilateral reserves and the formation of shipping conferences to establish rates and to assure regular, frequent, and stable liner services could be beneficial. For this to be possible, it would be necessary for the LAFTA nations to delegate regulatory powers over maritime transport within the LAFTA area to an international regulatory commission. If the LAFTA members are not yet prepared for this type of political innovation, neither are they in a position to benefit from the proposed cargo reserves. If the draft agreement or a similar agreement is adopted without adequate provision for the control of rates and service, great harm will be done to economic integration.

While a judicious application of a maritime policy along the lines of that incorporated in the draft LAFTA maritime convention could result in an improvement of present transport within South America, it is not clear that this is the best policy to achieve the objectives sought. The proposed treaty, after all, is still essentially concerned with the development of the Latin American merchant marine and only secondarily with improving maritime service and lowering freight rates. If attention is focused solely on transport as a function and the desire of the LAFTA nations to increase their shipping capacity is ignored, alternative policies easily come to mind. Transport along the west coast and between the east and west coasts of South America is reasonably adequate. The most important problem at the present time is the poor service and high rates between the northern and southern parts of the continent. Here, perhaps, a policy of direct subsidies to companies willing to provide regular liner service would make a greater contribution to the problem than an indirect policy of cargo reserves. On the east coast, the major difficulty lies in the ports, where cargo handling costs are high and ship turnaround time is slow. No policy of cargo reserves can be expected to improve this situation, and both here and throughout the rest of South America port inefficiency must be attacked directly. Were the Latin American countries willing to abandon their desire for a larger merchant fleet, or were they at least willing not to use the LAFTA agreement for this purpose, a transport policy based on direct subsidies to liners plus a massive and coordinated assault on the port problem might well be the best way to provide the regular, frequent, and economical ocean transport which the economic integration of Latin America requires.

CHAPTER VIII

Other Transport Modes and
Economic Integration

THE PRESENT DEPENDENCE ON ocean transport for intra-South American trade and the gravity of the problems that must be overcome for maritime shipping to fulfill its function as common carrier for products and over distances for which railroad transport is used on other continents indicate that LAFTA has done well to dedicate initial attention to this transport mode. At the same time, the opportunities presented by other transport media—river, highway, railroad, and air—must not be ignored. In some areas, these modes already are of importance in LAFTA commerce, and improvements in their organization together with new investments could indicate significant impetus to increased trade and closer integration. Furthermore, these transport modes, especially highways and railways, present a series of advantages which make their development desirable wherever and whenever they can compete economically with ocean transport.

In order to have a better understanding of the potential of international land transport within South America, it is useful to describe the present facilities. New investments to improve the structure of the continental transport systems must take into account the highways and railways that already exist. Similarly, it is useful to trace briefly the highlights of the development of land transport in South America because the willingness of the South American countries to invest in one or another mode of transport will depend in part on their experience in the past with these media and the problems they have encountered.

The Development of Railroads in South America

Railway construction in South America began around 1850 and was essentially completed by 1930. Appendix A Table A-2 traces railway extension in the South American countries and in the United States while Figure 8-1 presents graphically the total mileage at different times in the past. The similarity of the temporal patterns of development in North and South America is quite remarkable: when the South American graph is lagged two decades so as to make the year 1900 in South America coincide with the year 1880 in the United States, the development in both areas after those years is nearly identical.

Except in Colombia and Bolivia railroad construction since 1930 has not represented important percentage additions to the previous railway systems, although construction in both Argentina and Brazil since that time has been significant in absolute terms. In the United States, railroad mileage has decreased since 1920, and in Peru and Venezuela in South America peak mileage was reached relatively early with declines afterwards. The case of Brazil is interesting because railroad abandonment has taken place simultaneously with important new construction. Probably only in Venezuela, however, does there exist a real possibility of beginning in the future the development of a wholly new railroad system.

Types of Railroads

The construction of railroads in South America, financed primarily by British and French capital or by South American governments, was directed at four primary objectives which explain the present spatial pattern of the railway systems.[1] The first type of railroad connects mining centers and agricultural areas with ocean and river ports and is designed to facilitate exports. Although the examples of this type most commonly cited are the system

[1] U.N. Economic Commission for Latin America, *El Transporte en América Latina*, E/CN.12/703 (February 1965), Vol. I, p. 9.

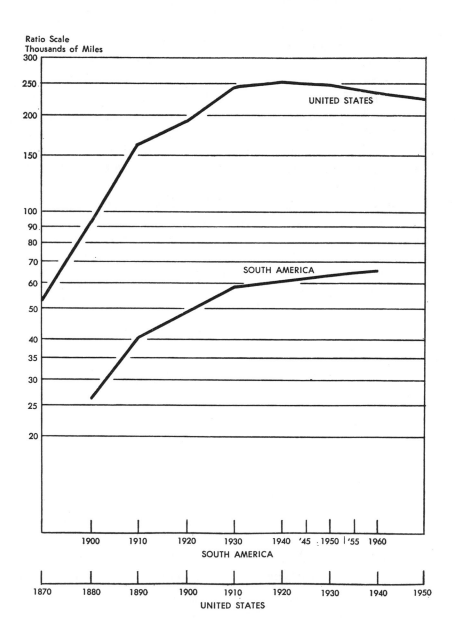

FIGURE 8-1. *Development of Railroads in South America and the United States*

that connects the port of Santos, Brazil, with the coffee-producing areas of its hinterland and the systems of Argentina and Uruguay that center on the ports of Buenos Aires, Bahia Blanca, and Montevideo, there are many others, such as the mineral railways on the west coast in Chile and Peru. In the case of Bolivia, the export-oriented railways are international, leading from Bolivia to the Chilean ports of Arica and Antofagasta and to the Peruvian port of Mollendo. Export railways will continue to be built in the future, especially in Brazil and Venezuela.

The second type of railroad in South America is designed to connect the inland capital of the country with an import port. This type was built many years ago in Chile, between Valparaiso and Santiago, and in Ecuador, between Guayaquil and Quito. In recent years, the construction of the Atlantic Railroad in Colombia to provide Bogotá with a direct connection to the ocean was for a similar purpose, as is partially true in the case of the railway lines constructed to Brasília, the new capital of Brazil. In the case of Bolivia, the railroads to the Peruvian and Chilean ports serve both the purpose of facilitating exports and that of connecting the capital to the sea for imports.

The third type of railroad was designed to link areas of low population density in far-off and isolated regions with the important administrative and commercial centers, prompted at times to assure national hegemony. This objective seems to have been important in the construction of the northern longitudinal railroad in Chile, which links the central provinces with the desolate northern regions taken from Bolivia and Peru in the Pacific War in the last decades of the nineteenth century. Similarly a number of the Argentinian and Brazilian railroads seem designed for this purpose, as in the case of the Rio Grande do Sul Railroad in Brazil, at least in part, and perhaps the General Urquiza Railroad in Argentina.

The fourth type of railroad includes short stretches designed for specific purposes, such as to circumvent unnavigable portions of rivers, as was the case of the Madeira-Mamoré Railroad in Brazil and the La Dorada Railroad in Colombia, or to link up relatively unimportant centers, as in the case of the Santa Catarina Railroad in Brazil.

FIGURE 8-2. *Major Railways in South America*

Perhaps a fifth type of railroad in South America should be added to the four types described by the Economic Commission for Latin America, especially because of its relevance for the present study. This type is designed to facilitate trade within South America by linking adjoining countries. The clearest examples are the Transandean Railroad (Transandino por Juncal) between Los Andes in Chile and Mendoza in Argentina, which began operating in 1910, and the line between Antofagasta, Chile, and Salta, Argentina, which was completed in the 1940's. The lines from Santa Cruz in Bolivia to Yacuiba, Argentina, and to Corumbá, Brazil, which are even more recent, also appear to fit into this category, as do the numerous branches constructed in Brazil to link with lines in Uruguay and Paraguay. To some extent, however, the objective of building railroads to facilitate intra-South American trade overlaps the first objective, facilitating access to export ports from mining and agricultural producing regions. The line from Salta, Argentina, to Antofagasta, Chile, for example, was intended in part to facilitate Argentine exports via Chilean ports.

From this description of the different motives for which railroads were constructed in South America, the results of which can be seen in Figure 8-2, it is clear that probably nowhere on the continent was there a conception of the desirability of developing an integrated national system of transport, with the exception of southern Chile, where the geographical shape of the country inevitably made the railroad an integrating factor. Furthermore, even when railroads were constructed for the purpose of developing a more integrated system, as perhaps was the motive for building the Rosario-Puerto Belgrano Railway in Argentina, now a part of the General Bartolomé Mitre Railroad, it was difficult to obtain sufficient traffic because this type of railroad did not respond to the transport needs of the time. Halsey wrote of this railroad in 1916:

> . . . The Rosario-Puerto Belgrano Ry . . . crosses most of the important railways running out of Buenos Aires. It is a broad gauge line and extends from Rosario to near Bahia Blanca (about 500 miles).

Although capitalized at about $30,000,000 it handles but little business and is now in receivers' hands.[2]

However well the railroad structure of South America may have served that continent's transport requirements during the last decades of the nineteenth century and the first decade of the twentieth, it is clear that it is not adequate at the present time. President Arturo Frondizi's description of the problem in Argentina several years ago could well be generalized as applicable in a number of the South American countries:

> The Argentine railway system no longer serves the needs of our economy. It was laid out for another Argentina, for the Argentina whose foreign trade was limited to the export of meat, hides, wool and grain and to the import of machinery, fuel and manufactured products. That country no longer exists. Now there are manufacturing centers throughout all the interior, oil wells in the north and south, iron ore and coal and other mines distributed throughout the entire country. The railroad must connect these centers adequately and rapidly, without the necessity of transshipment in Buenos Aires. It must be able to transport iron and coal from the south to the north and livestock and fruit from one province to another.[3]

Problems in Construction

The construction of railroads in South America for specific and limited purposes had other effects in addition to the spatial pattern of the resulting networks. As each railroad represented an independent business venture, they were built to the tastes and standards of their largely foreign owners. Within this framework, considerable diversity of gauges was inevitable, not only from country to country but even within single countries. The haphazard way in which gauges were selected is well illustrated by Halsey in his description of the first Argentinian railway, a six-mile line from Buenos Aires to the suburb of Flores, which opened in 1857:

[2] Frederic M. Halsey, *Railway Expansion in Latin America* (Jas. H. Oliphant & Co., 1916), p. 30.

[3] Instituto de Estudios de la Marina Mercante Argentina, *La Marina Mercante Argentina, 1962* (Buenos Aires, 1962), p. 70 (translation).

Its owners, not being oversupplied with funds, availed themselves of an opportunity to purchase a quantity of second-hand locomotives and cars which had been captured by the British during the siege of Sebastopol in the Crimea. This equipment had been built for an extremely broad gauge, viz: five feet, six inches. The Argentine Company laid its tracks to accommodate these cars and to this day the five feet six inches gauge is in general use throughout central and eastern Argentina.[4]

Although by 1927, the one-meter gauge accounted for slightly more than one-half of total South American railroad mileage, the other half was made up of eight different gauges, of which the most important was the five feet six inch gauge used in Argentina and Chile.[5] In Chile alone, there were seven gauges in use in 1927. The only countries that escaped this disparity of gauges were Paraguay and Bolivia, each of which had a single national gauge, and Uruguay, where a single gauge accounted for nearly the entire national system. Gauge diversity was, of course, important in the United States at one time, but there its devastating effect on transport efficiency was recognized and corrected while a similar policy has never been adopted in South America.

Even where different railroads were connected and had the same gauge, as in the southern part of Brazil and the northern part of Chile, different companies adopted different braking systems and couplings. When these railways were absorbed by national state-owned companies, it was impossible to use much of the existing equipment on through-trains, and heavy investments have been required to standardize equipment, a process which is still not completed.

Low-cost construction standards were common where railroads were built for narrow and specific purposes instead of forming part of an integrated railway system. This problem was compounded by difficult topography nearly everywhere except in the Argentine pampas, Uruguay, and parts of southern Brazil. Even in Brazil, however, access from the Atlantic Ocean to the plateau region can be provided only at great cost. The greatest obstacle is, of course, the Andes, which makes railway construc-

[4] Halsey, op. cit., p. 10.
[5] Santiago Marín Vicuña, Política Ferroviaria de la América (Santiago, Chile: Imprenta Universitaria, 1927), p. 115.

tion in Colombia, Ecuador, Peru, and Bolivia an engineering nightmare. Within the United States, the Rockies are also an impediment, and are considerably wider than the Andes. In height, however, there is no comparison: the Great Northern Railroad crosses the continental divide at about 5,000 feet and the Union Pacific Railway at about 8,000 feet. These altitudes can be compared with those of some of the South American railways:[6]

Guayaquil and Quito Railroad in Ecuador	11,841 feet
Central Railroad of Peru	15,665
Southern Railroad of Peru	14,688
Arica-La Paz Railroad between Chile and Bolivia	13,986
Antofagasta and Bolivia Railroad	13,000
Chile-Argentine Transandean Railroad	10,452

The combination of rugged terrain and low construction standards have led to high maintenance and operating costs and low commercial train speeds. In these countries, service is inevitably poor and expensive, but improving the situation is also expensive. Ecuador proposed purchasing diesel locomotives to avoid the necessity of breaking trains, since existing locomotives limited trains to 150 gross tons on the steep grades. The use of longer trains, even with new locomotives, would require extending the switchbacks which had been designed to accommodate trains composed of only a few cars.[7]

Another factor of significance in understanding the past development of railroads in several areas of South America is the influence of the military. As late as the 1930's, Bolivia and Paraguay were at war over the Chaco, and Ecuador is now by no means satisfied with the location of its frontier with Peru. Throughout South America the military in each country has been traditionally concerned with a possible invasion from the neighboring countries. As a result of these defense considerations, the military in Argentina consistently opposed an effective direct railway link between that country and Brazil, a policy greatly assisted by the natural barrier of the Paraná and La Plata rivers.

[6] R. H. Whitbeck, *Economic Geography of South America*, 2nd ed. (McGraw-Hill, 1931), p. 12.

[7] Junta Nacional de Planificación y Coordinación Económica, *Resumen del Plan General de Desarrollo Económico y Social del Ecuador* (Quito, 1963), pp. 175, 178.

When the northern railway was proposed in Chile, the natural coastal route was ignored, and the line was laid far from the coast in the mountains in order that it be out of shelling range from ships offshore.

Other aspects of the development of South American railways and the problems with which they are faced today are similar to those occurring throughout the world. The tremendous advantage of railroad transport in South America over alternative media was obvious until World War II and led to the extension of branch lines to areas where the density of traffic was low and to a proliferation of stations every few miles along the lines. The traffic generated on many branches and by many stations was inadequate to cover the costs they occasioned. In effect, they were subsidized by lines and stations where traffic was greater. So long as the railroad monopoly was not threatened by competition, the dead weight that this overextension represented was not evident.

The Highway Revolution

The end of World War II marked the end of the railroads' monopoly of transport within South America. Although coastwise shipping had traditionally been competitive with the railroads, its zone of influence was restricted, especially because of the dearth of navigable rivers to provide access to more interior regions, except for the area served by the La Plata River and its tributaries. Highway transport had existed before and during World War II, and was already of national importance in a number of countries such as Brazil, Venezuela, and Colombia, but the impossibility of obtaining motor vehicles during the war had held back the natural evolution of this mode. The war had also made it impossible to replace or expand railroad equipment at the same time that exceptional demands were being made of the railroads' transport capacity. The railroad situation, in turn, added to the postwar pressure to increase highway transport.

With the end of the war, massive investments were begun in highway construction and improvement, and have continued to

TABLE 8-1. *Development of Highways in South America*
(Miles)

Country	Paved[a]	Stabilized[b]	Not Stabilized But All-Weather[c]	Total All-Weather
Argentina				
1945	1,232	6,447	18,178	25,857
1950	2,473	13,381	28,583[d]	44,437[d]
1960	3,853	19,200[d]	24,233[d]	47,286[d]
1962	3,868	20,412[d]	26,098[d]	50,378[d]
Brazil				
1938	214	19,014[de]	—	19,228[d]
1952	—	—	—	26,098[d]
1960	8,388	37,282[de]	—	45,670[d]
1962	10,216	37,282[de]	—	47,498[d]
Uruguay				
1960	168	1,342[d]	3,977[d]	5,487
1963	172	1,491[d]	3,884[d]	5,547
Paraguay				
1962	162	503	625	1,290
Chile				
1945	9,163[f]	—	6,835[d]	15,998[d]
1950	984	9,601	7,146[d]	17,731[d]
1960	1,963	13,648	9,507[d]	25,118[d]
1963	3,018	14,546	10,563[d]	28,127[d]
Bolivia				
1960	333	1,355	1,886	3,574
1962	355	2,268	—	—
Peru				
1945	1,694	10,812[de]	—	12,506[d]
1950	1,818	11,682[de]	—	13,500[d]
1960	2,668	5,861	7,275	15,804
1963	2,554	5,809	7,502	15,865
Colombia				
1945	465[g]	7,891[de]	—	8,356[d]
1952	—	—	—	9,693[d]
1959	1,864	2,843	10,341	15,048
1962	2,896	—	—	—
Venezuela				
1944	757	2,080	1,071	3,908
1950	1,250	4,097	—	—
1960	5,165	6,042	5,224	16,431
1962	7,281	6,690	3,223	17,194
Ecuador				
1960	399	2,902	1,649	4,950
1963	669	3,058	1,649	5,376

Source: U. N. Economic Commission for Latin America, *Estudio Económico de América Latina, 1963*, E/CN. 12/696/Rev. 1 (1964), p. 105, Table 81. U.N. Economic Commission for Latin America, *Los Transportes en América Latina*, E/CN.12/673 (1963), p. 13, Table 4.

[a] Includes concrete and asphalt pavement.
[b] Includes stabilized, gravel, and roads with bituminous seal.
[c] Includes roads not stabilized but with adequate drainage.
[d] Estimate.
[e] Includes stabilized and non-stabilized but all-weather.
[f] Includes paved and stabilized.
[g] 1948.

TABLE 8-2. *Foreign Loans to South America for Highways*[a]
(Millions of U. S. dollars)

Country	Loans Given	Amount Used
Argentina		
Before 1960	2.8	2.5
1960–63	98.9	27.8
Brazil		
Before 1960	5.9	5.9
1960–63	12.5	—
Uruguay		
1960–63	22.6	—
Paraguay		
1960–63	6.0	0.1
Chile		
1960–63	25.0	4.8
Bolivia		
Before 1960	33.4	33.4
1960–63	7.2	—
Peru		
Before 1960	5.0	5.0
1960–63	53.3	8.9
Colombia		
Before 1960	47.4	47.4
1960–63	39.0	9.4
Venezuela		
1960–63	76.3	6.8
Ecuador		
Before 1960	40.2	40.1
1960–63	2.7	—
Total		
Before 1960	134.7	134.3
1960–63	343.5	57.8
Total	478.2	192.1

Source: U.N. Economic Commission for Latin America, *El Transporte en América Latina*, E/CN.12/703 (February 1965), Vol. II, pp. 386, 388–89, Table 119.

[a] Table includes loans authorized and in force to June 30, 1963 for the World Bank and the International Development Association; to December 31, 1963 for the Inter-American Development Bank; and to January 31, 1964 for the Export-Import Bank. The table also includes some $81.3 million of loans granted in 1962–63 by AID alone or in combination with another lending institution.

the present. The growth in all-weather road mileage is shown in Table 8-1, although it must be recognized that the data shown are at best crude estimates. For some countries highway development has been dramatic: between 1944 and 1962 Venezuela increased the mileage of its paved highways more than nine and one-half times and the mileage of its all-weather roads nearly four and one-half times. According to the figures shown in Table 8-1, Brazil had only 214 miles of paved roads in 1938; by 1962 this had grown to 10,216 miles, the largest paved highway system in South America. Impressive gains were also made in Argentina, Chile, and Colombia. A few countries have lagged behind, notably Paraguay, but in general the two postwar decades have been characterized by dynamic programs of highway development throughout the continent.

The efforts of the South American countries to improve their highways have found strong support from the international lend ing agencies. As can be seen in Table 8-2, the ten South American republics have received nearly $500 million in loans for this purpose, more than 70 percent of which were granted during the period 1960-63. The amount received by Brazil ($18.4 million) is small in comparison with the loans to the other nations and had Brazil been on better terms with the lending agencies during the period 1960-63, the total would undoubtedly have been much larger.

Investments in highways were paralleled during the two postwar decades by equally dramatic increases in the stock of motor vehicles in South America. Table 8-3 shows the growth in the number of cars, buses, and trucks in the South American countries from 1945 to 1963. Increases in the total stock of vehicles between these years ranged from a low increase of two and one-half times in Argentina to a high of 13.7 times in Venezuela. The percentage increase in the number of trucks in the ten republics (from 310,000 in 1945 to 1,500,000 in 1963) was considerably greater than the increase in automobiles (from one-half million in 1945 to two million in 1963).

The initiation of vehicle assembly plants, followed rapidly by the establishment of local industries producing component parts

TABLE 8-3. *Stock of Motor Vehicles in Selected Years*

(Thousands of units)

	Argentina	Brazil	Uruguay	Paraguay	Chile	Bolivia	Peru	Colombia	Venezuela	Ecuador	Total
Automobiles											
1945	303.7	114.4[a]	27.7[b]	1.1[c]	28.5	3.7[b]	16.6	15.3	16.2	1.0[c]	528.2
1950	318.1	200.1	40.1	1.7	39.8	3.3	32.0	32.2	69.6	1.4	738.3
1960	473.5	537.8	87.0[d]	4.3	57.6	14.3[d]	79.8	86.9	268.7	19.7	1,629.6
1963	623.8[e]	674.9	98.0	4.3[f]	62.4	14.3[d]	105.4	108.0[e]	325.2	23.1	2,039.4
Buses											
1945	7.2	8.0[a]	1.3[b]	0.2[c]	2.5	0.4[b]	1.5	3.7	1.6	0.8[c]	27.2
1950	11.4	25.8	1.6	0.2	4.2	0.5	3.4	6.8	5.0	1.0	59.9
1960	14.3	55.9	2.6[d]	0.4	5.5	1.2[d]	7.0	20.4	6.8	3.4	117.5
1963	15.6[e]	62.1	2.6	0.4[f]	7.5	1.2[d]	9.0	22.5[e]	7.9	3.9	132.7
Trucks											
1945	141.5	88.7[a]	12.4[b]	0.9[c]	20.0	7.2[b]	11.5	10.1	16.0	1.2[c]	309.5
1950	243.2	172.0	21.4	1.4	27.8	8.1	24.0	22.3	60.9	1.6	582.7
1960	413.7	540.0	65.0[d]	3.0	63.2	23.1[d]	56.9	74.7	94.5	5.2	1,339.3
1963	513.0[e]	571.7	74.0	3.0[f]	69.3	23.1[d]	70.5	78.2[e]	128.5	6.1	1,537.4
Total Stock											
1945	452.4	211.1[a]	41.4[b]	2.2[c]	51.0	11.3[b]	29.6	29.1	33.8	3.0[c]	864.9
1950	572.7	397.9	63.1	3.3	71.8	11.9	59.4	61.3	135.5	4.0	1,380.9
1960	901.5	1,133.7	154.6[d]	7.7	126.3	38.6[d]	143.7	182.0	370.0	28.3	3,086.4
1963	1,152.4[e]	1,308.7	174.6	7.7[f]	139.2	38.6[d]	184.9	208.7[e]	461.6	33.1	3,709.5

Source: U. N. Economic Commission for Latin America, *El Transporte en América Latina*, E/CN. 12/703 (February 1965), Vol. I, p. 232, Table 69.

[a] 1946; [b] 1947; [c] 1948; [d] 1959; [e] 1962; [f] 1960.

for vehicles, provided added impetus to the "vehicularization" of South America. Argentina's production of 117,000 cars in 1961 represented one-fourth of its entire stock of automobiles in 1960. Table 8-4 shows the assembly and production of vehicles in five South American countries in recent years. This factor is important in explaining the increase in the total number of vehicles, and in addition has permitted these countries to replace worn-out trucks, cars, and buses with a consequent improvement in operating efficiency. Furthermore, now that assembly plants are being replaced by production plants, which are able to produce some 60 percent of the value of production in Argentina and 80 percent of the total weight of production in Brazil, "vehicularization" has taken on an independent life of its own in these countries, with strong pressure groups that will favor ever greater expenditures on new and improved highways.

TABLE 8-4. *Production and Assembly of Motor Vehicles*[a]
(Units)

Year	Argentina	Brazil	Chile	Peru	Venezuela
1960					
Automobiles	72,343	57,357	1,926[b]	—	6,452
Trucks	16,485	75,721	391[c]	474	3,882
Total	88,828	133,078	2,317	474	10,334
1961					
Automobiles	117,055	72,683[b]	2,715[b]	—	8,842
Trucks	22,721	72,911[c]	1,224[c]	646	2,945
Total	139,766	145,674	3,939	646	11,787
1962					
Automobiles	116,915	97,134[b]	5,359	—	8,768
Trucks	12,099	94,060[c]	1,256[c]	775	2,898
Total	129,014	191,194	6,615	775	11,666
1963					
Automobiles	97,437	99,945[b]	6,309[b]	—	19,491[d]
Trucks	7,987	74,181[c]	1,630[c]	—	6,919[d]
Total	105,424	174,126	7,939	—	26,410[d]

Source: U.N. Economic Commission for Latin America, *Estudio Económico de América Latina, 1963*, E/CN.-12/696/Rev. 1 (1964), pp. 112, 114, Table 93.

[a] In Argentina, about 60 percent of the total value of production is produced nationally. In Brazil, about 80 percent of total weight of production is produced nationally.

[b] Includes jeeps and station wagons.

[c] Includes pickup and panel trucks.

[d] Production in month of December estimated.

Despite the advances which have been made in the last two decades, the continent as a whole is still clearly in a different world from that of Western Europe and the United States. As can be seen in Table 8-5, only in Argentina, Uruguay, and Venezuela in 1962 was the number of vehicles per one thousand inhabitants comparable to that in Italy around the same year or to France in 1950, and Argentina and Uruguay have well-developed railroad systems. The gap, furthermore, between these three most motorized countries of South America and the rest of the continent is enormous, as no other country had even a third as many vehicles per thousand inhabitants as the first three.

TABLE 8-5. *Vehicles per Thousand Inhabitants in Selected Countries*

Country	Automobiles			Total Stock of Vehicles		
	1950	1960	1962	1950	1960	1962
Argentina	18.5	22.6	28.7	33.3	43.0	53.0
Brazil	3.8	7.6	8.8[a]	7.6	16.1	17.0[a]
Uruguay	18.3	35.3[b]	38.0	28.7	62.9[b]	66.9
Paraguay	1.2	2.4	—	2.4	4.4	—
Chile	6.6	7.6	7.6[a]	11.8	16.6	17.0[a]
Bolivia	1.1	4.0	—	3.9	10.4[b]	—
Peru	4.0	7.9	9.6[a]	7.4	14.2	16.9[a]
Colombia	2.8	5.6	6.6	5.2	11.8	12.8
Venezuela	14.0	36.4	40.0[a]	27.2	50.5	56.8[a]
United States	263.1	329.0	338.7	322.6	391.5	399.2
France	35.7	133.5	147.6	50.0	169.2	182.1
Greece	1.0	5.2	6.7	3.7	9.5	12.6
Italy	7.2	40.2	59.9	12.2	51.2	72.9

Source: U.N. Economic Commission for Latin America, *El Transporte en América Latina*, E/CN.12/703 (February 1965), p. 235, Table 71.

[a] 1963.
[b] 1959.

Highway Development and Railroad Problems

However incipient the highway revolution might appear to be in South America, it has raised havoc with the South American railroads. Two UN studies[8] show what has happened to railroad freight tons and ton-kilometers from 1945 to recent years in eight South American countries (Paraguay and Venezuela are not included). The railroads in Argentina and in Uruguay carried in 1963 less than half as many tons of freight as they did in 1945. In Bolivia as well, there has been an absolute decline in both tons and ton-kilometers of freight traffic. In Chile, the tonnage has increased because of the development of iron ore exports in the north, but because of the short average distances, total ton-kilometers fell between 1945 and 1962. In Colombia, the reverse oc-

[8] U.N. Economic Commission for Latin America, *Los Transportes en América Latina*, E/CN.12/673 (1963), p. 33, Table 10. U.N. Economic Commission for Latin America, *Estudio Económico de América Latina, 1963*, E/CN.12/696/Rev. 1 (1964), p. 98, Table 73.

curred—total tonnage fell between 1945 and 1963 while ton-kilometers increased significantly (the average length of haul increased from 114 kilometers to 241 kilometers, reflecting in part the importance of the newly opened Atlantic Railroad). In Peru and Ecuador, the situation is not basically different from that in Colombia. Of the eight countries shown, only Brazil experienced really significant increases in both tonnage carried and ton-kilometers during this period, and even here both tons and ton-kilometers fell between 1960 and 1962. For the railroads, the highway revolution was real indeed.

If the highway systems in South America were being improved and the stock of vehicles was increasing at the same time

TABLE 8-6. *Development of Freight Traffic by Different Means of Transport*[a]
(Index numbers and percentages on the basis of ton-kilometers)

Country	Index Numbers				Percentage Composition		
	Rail-roads	Highway Trucking	Coastal and River	Total	Rail-roads	Highway Trucking	Coastal and River
Argentina							
1945	95	24	106	78	62.2	8.5	29.3
1950	100	100	100	100	51.1	27.3	21.6
1955	96	124	129	111	44.1	30.7	25.2
1960	94	160	162	127	38.0	34.5	27.5
Brazil							
1950	100	100	100	100	28.6	41.6	29.8
1955	116	203	123	154	21.5	54.7	23.8
1960	153	365	172	248	17.7	61.5	20.8
Chile							
1950	79	—	74	—	—	—	—
1954	100	100	100	100	—	—	—
1959	95	148	187	145	27.6	14.8	57.6
Colombia							
1951	100	100	100	100	21.2	43.6	35.2
1955	106	165	107	135	16.6	53.1	30.3
1960	140	201	130	163	18.2	53.9	27.9

Source: U. N. Economic Commission for Latin America, *El Transporte en América Latina*, E/CN. 12/703 (February 1965), Vol. I, p. 99, Table 24.
[a] Highway trucking in Chile and Colombia includes only interurban traffic.

that railway traffic was stagnant or declining, there were presumably important shifts in traffic to the highways. Highway freight traffic statistics are difficult to obtain and must always be used with great caution, but the scanty data available are consistent with the hypothesis. Table 8-6 indicates that the increase in highway transport was also at the expense of coastal and river transport in addition to the railroads. The highways' participation in estimated total freight ton-kilometers in Argentina increased from 8.5 percent in 1945 to 34.5 percent in 1960. Similar, if less dramatic, increases are also evident in Brazil and Colombia. The decline in river and coastal traffic is in general far more significant than Table 8-6 would indicate, because this water transport is now largely concentrated on a few bulk products transport of which has increased greatly in recent years, as is the case for petroleum in Argentina.

Had the highway revolution signified nothing more than the appearance of a new mode of transport, whose technological characteristics permitted it to carry out some transport functions more efficiently than the railways, so that the railways could relinquish these functions to the trucks and buses in an orderly fashion, the revolution would unquestionably be desirable. Trucks and buses can produce a different service because of their flexibility and the size of the transport unit, and it is to the advantage of any economy to make use of all technological advances which are suitable considering their needs and relative factor costs. There is no question that highway transport can permit a reduction in the total resources which must be dedicated to the transport sector when trucks and buses are used in those activities for which they represent a real cost saving to the economy. For short hauls, for transport in areas where traffic densities are low, and in the transport of high-value or perishable goods where speed is important, trucks are superior to the railroads, and traffic of this nature should be transferred to them.

Railway Rate Structure and Government Interference

Unfortunately, the deficiencies of the South American railroads were such that an orderly shift of some traffic to the highways at the same time that the railways cut back their own service was impossible. Some of the problems of the railroads have already been mentioned—the overextension of branch lines and proliferation of stations, the diversity of gauges and equipment, and the run-down condition of the way and rolling stock at the end of World War II. But there were many others. Some of these problems were by no means unique to South America, but rather plagued railroads throughout the world when their traditional monopoly was destroyed by the highway revolution. Of these general problems, two merit mention.

First, around the world a railway rate structure had been developed which related the freight rate for each product to the value of the product, that is, freight rates were in general *ad valorem*. Freight rates were based primarily on the ability to pay of particular products rather than on the cost to the railways of transporting them. As a result, the railways' large fixed costs were not distributed proportionally among all products carried but rather were covered by high rates charged the higher valued products. In general, this policy might well have been advantageous to the national economies because it permitted the railways to transport low-valued products that could not have been moved had these products been forced to pay a full fair share of the railways' fixed costs.

Second, the governments of most Western nations imposed strict controls on the rates charged by railways and the services they provided. Furthermore, in those countries where the railways were owned by the government, it was common for railway executives to be named for political reasons and for railway employment to be expanded as politicians paid off their political debts. Facing no effective competition and smothered by governmental interference, railways tended to wait for traffic to come to them and never developed commercial aggressiveness.

Under these conditions, it is easy to anticipate what happened when trucks appeared and offered a faster and more flexible service. Even though shippers would have been willing to pay rates to truckers higher than they had been paying to the railroads, in order to obtain this superior service, truckers were able to quote rates lower than the railroads. The high rates that railways had set for valuable products presented an attractive target for the trucks, and they rapidly skimmed off the cream of the traditional railway monopoly. Because the railways had depended on these high-valued goods to cover the major part of their fixed costs, the loss of this traffic had an immediate impact on railroad finances. The traffic that was lost was not restricted to short distance transport or to areas with a low traffic density, which appropriately should have shifted to the trucks, but frequently included long-haul main-line traffic. This problem was aggravated by the fact that often the first highways to be built, paved or improved, paralleled the main railway lines with the densest traffic.

Precisely because of their long monopoly, the railroads had difficulty throughout the world in adjusting to the new competition. It was obvious that the entire railway rate structure needed to be revamped, but government controls made this a slow and difficult process. In many countries throughout the world (although not generally in South America) controls were imposed on trucks, as they had earlier been imposed on railways, and part of the potential benefits of the highway revolution were lost.

Although the trucks had an obvious advantage for transport to regions which generated little railroad traffic, the railways in many countries were unable to abandon uneconomic branch lines. Political pressure was brought to bear to prevent the railways from "abandoning these communities." In many instances, however, the communities had long since abandoned the railways, which were then forced to run empty trains at high cost. In many parts of South America, however, an outcry against abandoning communities, typically unfound in the advanced western nations, held considerable truth, as they were served solely by railroad and had no highway access. Thus with the common policy of constructing highways either alongside important railway trunk lines, or in areas not served by railways, the railways in South America saw the lucrative mainline traffic lost at the same time that they were forced to maintain service to low density localities.

As a result of these factors, the average traffic density, already low in many countries, tended to decline even further. It is frequently stated that for railway transport to be justified, there must be a minimum of 400,000 to 500,000 ton-kilometers of traffic annually per kilometer of way. Whatever the difficulties involved in trying to obtain a single criterion which is adequate to isolate where one or another transport mode should be used, it does appear that there is a lower limit on traffic density before a railroad should be considered. Whether this lower limit is 500,000 ton-kilometers per kilometer of way or some other cannot be pursued here, but it is clear from the low average densities of traffic for some South American countries shown in the table below that sub-

Country	Average Density*	Probable Maximum			Probable Minimum		
		Section	Length*	Density*	Section	Length*	Density*
Argentina	345				Ex-Patagónico	773	19
Brazil	334	Vitoria-Minas	569	4,566	Belem-Bragança	332	5
Chile	233						
Peru	180	Cerro de Pasco	175	537	Ilo-Moquegua	98	0.3
Colombia	216	Bogotá-Pto. Salgar	200	366	Nariño	72	17

* Density in thousands of ton-kilometers per kilometer of way; length in kilometers.

stantial parts of the railroad systems should be abandoned.[9] The highest density of the five national averages shown (for the year 1960) is that of Argentina: 345,000 ton-kilometers per kilometer of way. The average density in Peru, which has the lowest of the five, is only 180,000. Just how much abandonment is required goes beyond the scope of the present study. Other studies have suggested that as much as 3,100 miles should be abandoned in Brazil and 8,700 miles in Argentina.[10]

Inflation

Some problems of the South American railroads are less similar to those in other parts of the world. One of the most important of these is inflation, which has beset all the South American countries except Venezuela and Ecuador. The effects of inflation on the railroads are various. In the first place, their costs,

[9] U.N. Economic Commission for Latin America, *El Transporte en América Latina, op. cit.*, Vol. I, p. 155.

[10] U.N. Economic Commission for Latin America, *Los Transportes en América Latina, op. cit.*, p. 8.

of course, rise. Governments, however, are reluctant to permit comparable increases in rates and fares, in part because they hope to be able to retard the rate of inflation by holding down the cost of basic foodstuffs and other raw materials, and in part because of fear of political repercussions if passenger fares are raised. Although this policy might occasionally be justified for a short period of time for strategic reasons, it makes no sense over a decade. The primary result of the governments' policy has been to accelerate railroad deficits and to make it more difficult for the railways to replace obsolete plant and equipment so as to improve service. In the second place, inflation is almost inevitably accompanied by balance of payments difficulties and government policies to restrict the use of foreign exchange. Again the effect has been to make more onerous the efforts of the railways to carry out necessary maintenance and renovation.

Nationalization

A second more localized South American problem arose from the nationalization of previously privately owned—generally foreign owned—railroads. Although some railroad systems have been government owned since they were built, as is the case of most of the Chilean railroads, and some systems still remain in private hands, as in Peru, other major systems were nationalized shortly after World War II. In Brazil and Argentina, nationalization took place primarily between 1948 and 1952. These countries thus followed the worst of all possible policies: by permitting the original construction to be carried out by independent private companies, they lost the opportunity to have an integrated and coordinated national system. By nationalizing in the decade after World War II, just as the highway revolution was sweeping the continent, the governments were left with the task of bringing run-down railroads into line with the nations' new needs.

Governments are ill-suited for this type of task, and the problems in both Brazil and Argentina rapidly worsened. Government ownership is a serious obstacle to the closing of branch lines and unnecessary stations made redundant by the highway revolution. The task is at best difficult when a privately owned railroad is pressuring a government to permit it to reduce or abandon service. When the initiative itself must come from the government, it is even less likely to succeed.

Furthermore, the governments are under constant pressure to increase both employment and salaries in the state railways. Employment in the Brazilian federal railway system increased from 135,000 in 1948 to 162,000 in 1957, falling somewhat after that year although traffic continued to increase.[11] Between 1953 and 1962, the average salary in the Brazilian federal railways increased 96 percent in real terms.[12] In Argentina, the number of railroad workers increased from 147,000 in 1945 to 210,000 in 1955, and in this case traffic during the period was nearly constant.[13] The times called for retrenchment, for cost reduction, for branch line abandonment, for payroll cutting, but these measures seemed impossible to the governments concerned.

The result of these many problems can be seen in Table 8-7, where the revenues, expenditures, and operating ratios of railroads in seven South American countries are shown. In each case, the railways were showing profits in 1945 (a possible exception is Uruguay, for which information is not shown), and in each case the railroads were in serious financial difficulties in 1962. In some countries, the impact of the highway revolution was felt immediately, the railways of Argentina, Brazil, Uruguay, and Chile showed substantial losses by 1950, but the reckoning came inevitably. In 1962, the four countries just named covered less than half of railroad expenditures with railroad earnings, and the situation continues to deteriorate. In several countries, the railroad losses, which must be absorbed by subsidies from the national budgets, put severe pressure on government finances. In 1961, railroad losses accounted for 30 percent of the budgetary deficit in Brazil and for 42 percent in Chile.[14] In Argentina, the railroad losses have reached more than $300 million annually and repre-

[11] Pedro Cipollari, "El Problema de los Déficits en los Ferrocarriles del Brasil," *Desarrollo Económico*, Vol. 2, No. 1 (Primer Trimestre, 1965), p. 35.

[12] *Ibid.*

[13] U.N. Economic Commission for Latin America, *El Transporte en América Latina, op. cit.*, Vol. II, p. 305, Table 104.

[14] U.N. Economic Commission for Latin America, *Estudio Económico de América Latina, 1963, op. cit.*, p. 121, Table 100.

TABLE 8-7. *Financial Results of Railroad Operations*[a]

(Millions of local currency in current prices)

Year	Argen- tina	Brazil	Uru- guay	Chile[b]	Bolivia[c]	Peru	Colom- bia
1945							
Revenue	795	3,164	—	1,764	—	—	49
Expenditures	649	3,058	—	1,750	—	—	34
Coefficient	82	97	—	99	—	—	69
1950							
Revenue	1,791	4,199	26	3,092	668	120	62
Expenditures	2,217	5,711	35	4,234	545	125	64
Coefficient	124	136	135	137	82	104	103
1955							
Revenue	4,175	9,218	29	17,183	8,298	224	59
Expenditures	5,341	14,743	56	25,998	7,568	230	65
Coefficient	128	160	193	151	91	103	110
1960							
Revenue	17,051	23,348	41[e]	78,858	65,700[d]	347	102
Expenditures	26,749	44,833	82[e]	121,147	94,074[d]	385	115
Coefficient	157	192	200[e]	154	143[d]	111	113
1962							
Coefficient	207	260	253	203	—	124	126
1963							
Coefficient[f]	—	287	347	—	—	129	—

Source: U. N. Economic Commission for Latin America, *Los Transportes en América Latina*, E/CN.12/673 (1963), p. 49, Table 17. U. N. Economic Commission for Latin America, *Estudio Económico de América Latina, 1963*, E/CN.12/696/Rev. 1 (1964), p. 121, Table 100.

[a] Because of the differences in the accounting practices of different railroads, the coefficients are not strictly comparable.

[b] In millions of pesos.

[c] Only the railroads of the Andean system.

[d] 1959.

[e] 1957.

[f] Estimates.

sent around 10 percent of total government expenditures.[15] Where once the railroads were affected by the inflation in these countries, now they contribute to it by forcing national governments to expand the money supply to cover their operating losses.

[15] Bank of London and South America, *Fortnightly Review*, Vol. 29, No. 715, March 7, 1964, p. 162.

Obviously enough, both the national governments and railroad managements in these countries are well aware of the gravity of the problem and are striving to overcome it. They are faced, however, with a cumulative situation to which there are no easy answers. The disastrous financial situation makes it difficult to obtain funds to replace and modernize plant and equipment. As a result, service is very poor and can be provided only at high cost. Shippers, dismayed by car shortages and long delays before their goods reach their destination, prefer highway transport, so that railroad traffic and revenues decline still further, reducing the possibility of obtaining capital funds. Despite the fall in traffic, both the nature of railroad operations and political pressures make it difficult to reduce employment or to lower costs in other ways. A point is finally reached where no rate increase could hope to bring revenue into line with costs, and successive governments can do little more than hope to be able to keep the situation from worsening. Even this hope, however, is doomed, and the railroads continue their downward spiral.

Possible Solutions

Few people would deny that the railroads should continue to be a heavily used mode in many of the South American countries, especially in Argentina, Brazil, and Chile. The problem is one of coordination between highway and rail transport so that the railroads carry the cargo for which they are the appropriate mode without bankrupting the national treasury. Policy lines to resolve this problem are various. National planning is being given increased importance so that transport requirements can be predicted with greater precision, and investment decisions regarding one transport mode are made simultaneously with those of the others. Sizable investments are programmed for railroads in a number of the development plans that have been completed. Table 8-8 indicates the planned distribution of transport investment funds in seven countries. Argentina dedicated more than half its transport investment funds to the railroads, Chile more than a third, and Brazil more than a fifth. These investments are essential if the railways are to be able to improve the quality of

TABLE 8-8. *Average Annual Investments Programmed for the Transport Sector*

(Millions of U. S. dollars)

Country	Rail-Roads	High-ways	Ports and Navigation	Aviation	Motor Vehicles	Total	Total Without Vehicles
Argentina, 1962–64	242.5	169.6	32.7	—	—	—	444.9
Brazil, 1963–64	88.9	216.1	80.0	24.7	230.0	639.7	409.7
Chile, 1961–65	41.4	48.3	18.8	9.1	34.9	152.5	117.6
Bolivia, 1963–64	1.7	15.7	0.4	4.7	—	—	22.5
Peru, 1962–66[a]	2.0	34.7	11.9	1.1	—	—	49.7
Colombia, 1962–66	14.2	40.3	5.2	3.9	100.0[b]	163.6	63.6
Venezuela, 1963–66	—	141.5	11.4	8.0	26.5	187.4	160.9

Source: U. N. Economic Commission for Latin America, *Estudio Económico de América Latina, 1963*, E/CN. 12/696/Rev. 1, (1964), p. 118, Table 97.

[a] Railroads, 1962–65; ships, 1963–66.

[b] 1962–71.

their service to attract and keep traffic and to reduce operating costs.

Branch line abandonment and the elimination of unnecessary workers are required, however politically unpopular this might be, and in general governments tacitly acknowledge this obligation and make what progress they can. At times, these governments must feel like Sisyphus, as on occasion they have found it politically necessary to reopen branch lines already closed. Early in 1964, the Argentine state railways announced that more than a thousand miles of lines in the Province of Buenos Aires, closed in 1961 during the Frondizi administration, would be reopened.[16]

For the railroad dilemma to be resolved, it is essential that the South American countries adopt highway policies that tend toward a rational use of the nations' railways without aborting the significant contribution which the trucks and buses can make to economic development. Greater priority for highways paralleling low density railway lines is required if these railroad branches are to be abandoned. Wide fluctuations in the imports of motor vehicles must be avoided if freight rates are not to fluctuate widely from year to year in response to changes in the vehicle stock.

[16] *Ibid.*, No. 716 (March 21, 1964), pp. 209-10.

Weight limits to protect the investment in highways, realistic gas-oline prices, and reasonable highway user taxes are also neces-sary. While there is little to be said in favor of setting truck rates or restricting the area over which trucks can operate, the licensing of common carriers might well be desirable in a number of coun-tries.

Finally, it must be recognized that the railways' problems are multiplied and solutions are more difficult when the national econ-omies are stagnant. Workers can more easily be removed if job opportunities exist in other sectors of the economy. A rational dis-tribution of traffic between the highways and railways is more likely if total traffic is increasing than if it is constant or declining. In this sense, successful economic integration in South America, by promoting general economic growth, can do much to assist in-directly in overcoming presently overwhelming transport prob-lems.

International Railroad Transport Within South America

Considering the preoccupation of each country to resolve its own internal transport problems, it is not surprising that the South American governments have paid relatively little attention to improving land transport links with their neighbors. This lack of concern with access to other South American countries was un-derstandable when intra-South American trade itself was consid-ered to be of slight importance. Now, when closer economic inte-gration is being looked upon as a potential dynamic source of economic development throughout the continent, international transport facilities and service can no longer be ignored. Al-though it is true that transport investments alone will not suffice to guarantee increased commerce among the South American re-publics, and that transport policies must form a part of a larger group of policies all of which are designed to facilitate trade, it is also true that transport improvements are essential if closer eco-nomic integration is to become a reality.

More than seventy-five years ago visionaries looked at South

America as a continent, a single geographical area, rather than as merely the collection of ten independent and isolated republics, and speculated on the development that might be possible if adequate transport were provided. These men, among whom was Andrew Carnegie, were intimately aware of the revolutionary economic opportunities that had been created in the United States by the construction of the transcontinental railroads, and they believed that South America could obtain the same rewards. North Americans were also concerned by the fact that at the end of the last century South America's trade was primarily oriented toward Europe, from where it purchased manufactured goods in exchange for exports of raw materials. In no small measure, this pattern of trade reflected the near monopoly which England had of ocean shipping to South America. From the dual origins of wishing to increase trade between North and South America and to exploit more fully South America's resources, in addition to the more nebulous impetus which came from a desire for greater political and social integration among the Americas, came the proposal for the Pan American Railway, which would stretch from New York to Buenos Aires.

Despite the encouraging support which the proposal for a Pan American Railway received more than half a century ago, including funds appropriated by the U. S. Congress to survey the route, the project was never realized. Basically, geography and population settlements foredoomed the proposal to failure. At the First International Conference of American States, held in Washington in 1889-1890, the project was given official approval by the American countries represented at the conference. But the route that was recommended and which was later ratified by the Intercontinental Railway Commission followed the Andes so as both to connect up the principal cities of Colombia, Ecuador, Peru, and Bolivia, and to make use of the bits and pieces of railroad which had already been built in these countries. This route ran directly parallel to the ocean shipping routes and in addition would have entailed incredibly high construction and later operating costs. In no way could it be compared with the transcontinental railway lines in the United States which for much of their length cross flat, rich farmland. The alternatives of locating the line to the east of the Andes, either along the slopes and foothills, or further to the east so as to cut through the Amazon basin, were equally impossible, as here the land was unpopulated, and was either mountainous and forested or unhealthful jungle. A north-south railroad was clearly a century ahead of its time, and it is not surprising that capital could not be found to embark on such a venture.

In the southern part of the continent, however, where geography, population settlements, and agricultural opportunities were more similar to conditions in the United States, railroad construction pushed ahead rapidly and international railways became a reality. When the Transandean line was completed in 1910, South America had its first transcontinental line, as it was then possible to travel by rail from Buenos Aires to Valparaiso, Chile. This train trip took two days, in 1916, to cross the 886 miles from ocean to ocean as compared with the 11 days previously required to travel by sea.[17] The railroad, however, was never given much use, despite the great expectations when it was built. In 1962, only 79,500 metric tons moved between the two countries by rail over this route, of which 75,400 tons were livestock transported from Argentina to Chile.[18] The fact that cargo must be transshipped both in Mendoza, Argentina and Los Andes, Chile is undoubtedly a significant factor in explaining the low traffic volumes. Traffic on the international segment of the other transcontinental route which connects Buenos Aires and Antofagasta, Chile through Salta, Argentina is even lighter: 42,255 metric tons in 1962, of which 38,277 tons were live animals imported into Chile.[19] In this case, there is no change of gauge to impede through transport.

On the eastern side of the continent, real efforts were made for about ten years before the outbreak of World War I to establish a truly integrated international railroad system that would link Brazil, Uruguay, Paraguay, Bolivia, Argentina, and Chile. The driving force behind this attempt to "Harrimanize" the railroads of southern South America was a North American, Percival

[17] Halsey, op. cit., pp. 13-14.
[18] Annual Report of the Transandean Railway to the Chilean Government, 1962.
[19] Annual report of Chilean State Railways.

Farquhar.[20] In 1906, Farquhar incorporated the Brazil Railway in the state of Maine in the United States, and, using European capital, began buying, leasing, and constructing railroads in Brazil. By 1911, Rio de Janeiro was linked by rail to Montevideo, a distance of 2,000 miles,[21] and Farquhar began even more ambitious undertakings. In 1912, he incorporated the Argentine Railway Company, also in the permissive state of Maine, to acquire railroads in Argentina and to construct extensions to fill out his system. He also obtained concessions in Bolivia and Uruguay and even briefly controlled the Antofagasta and Bolivia Railway, which he wanted to make a part of a transcontinental system to connect Chile and Brazil. With the outbreak of war, however, he was no longer able to obtain new European capital and his empire collapsed. Never again was a serious and concerted effort made to use the transport potential that existed in the many disconnected railways in that part of the world.

Table 8-9 shows the international railroad connections which presently exist in South America. Venezuela, Colombia, and Ecuador do not appear in the table because their railroad systems are national systems and do not reach the frontier, although at one time a short line crossed the border between Venezuela and Colombia. Figure 8-3 shows the international links more clearly than does Figure 8-2. Of the 14 international connections, 5 are of lines with different gauges, making transshipment obligatory. In other cases, as on the Transandean Railway, although the crossing itself at the frontier is of the same gauge, the railways change gauge internally within the country, making through shipments impossible.

Interest in railroad transport to contribute to closer integration still exists, as is evidenced by the recently completed link between Santa Cruz, Bolivia and Yacuiba, Argentina. For Bolivia, of course, railroad transport represents its lifeline to the outside

[20] The material which follows on Percival Farquhar is taken primarily from Frederic M. Halsey, *The Railways of South and Central America* (Francis Emory Fitch, Inc., 1914). For a biography of Farquhar, see Charles Anderson Gauld, *The Last Titan: Percival Farquhar, American Entrepreneur in Latin America* (Institute of Hispanic American and Luso-Brazilian Studies, Stanford University, 1964).

[21] Whitbeck, *op. cit.*, p. 290.

TABLE 8-9. *International Railway Connections in South America*

Connections	Gauges (meters)
Paso de los Libres, Argentina	1.435
Uruguaiana, Brazil	1.000
Posadas, Argentina (ferry crossing)	1.435
Encarnación, Paraguay	1.435
Mendoza, Argentina	1.000
Los Andes, Chile	1.000
Salta, Argentina	1.000
Antofagasta, Chile	1.000
La Quiaca, Argentina	1.000
Villazón, Bolivia	1.000
Yacuiba, Argentina	1.000
Santa Cruz, Bolivia	1.000
Jaguarão, Brazil	1.000
Rio Branco, Uruguay	1.435
Livramento, Brazil	1.000
Rivera, Uruguay	1.435
Quaraí, Brazil	1.000
Artigas, Uruguay	1.435
Corumbá, Brazil	1.000
Santa Cruz, Bolivia	1.000
Antofagasta, Chile	1.000
La Paz, Bolivia	1.000
Arica, Chile	1.000
La Paz, Bolivia	1.000
Arica, Chile	1.435
Tacna, Peru	1.435
Guaqui, Bolivia (lake crossing by ferry)	1.000
Puno, Peru	1.435

Source: U. N. Economic Commission for Latin America, *El Transporte en América Latina*, E/CN. 12/703 (February 1965), p. 29, Table 7.

FIGURE 8-3. *International Railways in South America*

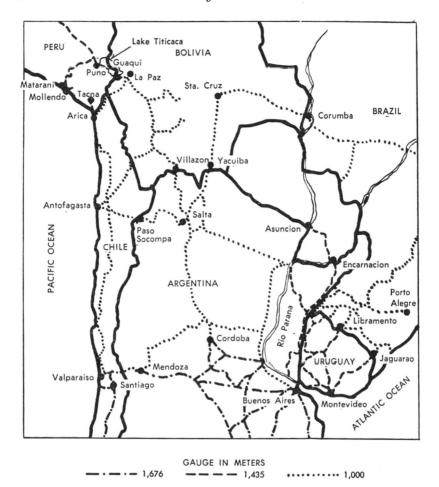

world, but it may well be that the South American countries are becoming aware of the opportunity which has been ignored and will make better use of facilities that already exist. In many instances, new investments would be necessary before good service would be possible, as between Antofagasta and Salta, but at the present time probably the principal problem is administrative rather than physical, at least in those instances where a common gauge exists, and perhaps even in the other cases. Lack of agreements on the interchange of rolling stock, unrealistic freight rates, excessive paperwork on exports which makes carload shipments uneconomical as compared with ocean shipments, delays and losses in customs and at transshipment points all contribute to the presently low traffic volumes.

The stimulus provided by the formation of the Latin American Free Trade Association has led to new interest in international railway transport. In March 1964, representatives of the railroads of Argentina, Bolivia, Brazil, Chile, Ecuador, Paraguay, and Uruguay met at Chapadmalal, Argentina, to establish the Latin American Association of Railroads (ALAF). Perhaps, if this association is successful in carrying out its program, Farquhar's vision will at last become a reality and South America's railways will be "Harrimanized."

International Highway Transport

As enthusiasm for the Pan American Railway diminished after World War I, its logical successor was the Pan American Highway. In Latin America, the Pan American Railway had always been supported primarily because of its potential contribution to communications, and especially to facilitate international passenger movements, rather than as an economical way to transport freight. When the automobile was no longer just a rich man's toy, it rapidly became evident that international highway transport could more easily be used than railways for passenger transport from country to country. In the early 1920's, auto clubs were established throughout South America, and these gave strong support to the Pan American Highway idea. This support was echoed in the United States, where the automobile manufacturers were quick to see the potential market for vehicles if highways in Latin America were improved.

In 1923, at the Fifth International Conference of American States, held in Santiago, Chile, the Pan American Highway received official international approval. The resolution on "Cooperation in the Improvement of Communications" reads in part:

5. To recommend the States belonging to the Pan American Union, especially when the necessary railroad communications are lacking, to improve as rapidly as possible the transportation facilities be-

tween their most important cities by means of automobiles, and between such cities and the principal ports permanently open to international traffic, and between the principal cities and the capitals of neighboring States;

6. To recommend the same States to forward to the Pan American Union at Washington, within a period of six months after the adjournment of this Conference, a report regarding automobile roads at present in service, as well as those under construction, and those projected;

7. To recommend the negotiation of conventions relative to automobile transportation, in order to define the international juridical status of automobiles and to regulate the circulation of same between the various countries;

8. That an Automobile Road Conference be held at the time and place which the Governing Board of the Pan American Union may determine, which shall study the most adequate means for carrying out an efficient program for the construction of this class of roads in the various countries of America, and between such countries.[22]

The first Pan American Highway Congress met at Buenos Aires in 1925, in accord with the resolution just cited, after an informal meeting of U. S. and Latin American engineers in Washington in 1924. In Buenos Aires, the Pan American Highway Congress was established on a permanent basis and the Pan American Confederation for Highway Education (later this name was changed to Pan American Highway Confederation) was founded with headquarters in the Pan American Union in Washington. At the Second Pan American Highway Congress, held in Rio de Janeiro in 1929, a convention on automotive traffic was drafted. The convention was ratified by nearly all the American republics at the Pan American Conference on the Regulation of Automotive Traffic, held in Washington in 1930.[23] The Ninth Pan American Highway Congress met in Washington in 1963, continuing the work begun nearly four decades earlier in Buenos Aires.

[22] James Brown Scott (ed), *The International Conferences of American States, 1889-1928* (Oxford University Press, 1931), pp. 276-77.
[23] *The International Conferences of American States, First Supplement, 1933-1940* (Carnegie Endowment for International Peace, 1940), pp. 404-06; 468-69.

It is probable that in the United States during the 1920's the Pan American Highway was imagined as a single route uniting the different American republics patterned after a proposal for the Pan American Railway. Such a proposed route was exhibited in 1927 in Washington for the benefit of the congressional representatives to the Sixth International Conference of American States to be held the following year in Havana, Cuba, Senator Ralph H. Cameron also suggested a route earlier in 1927, which had the appearance of a highway system, but clearly only the single route down the Pacific Coast, across the Andes from Santiago to Buenos Aires, and up the Atlantic Coast was at all feasible in 1927. Even today it would be difficult to find proponents of the direct highway from Bogotá across the Amazon Basin to Buenos Aires.

From the start, however, persons more knowledgeable about South America had conceived of the Pan American Highway as a system of highways rather than as a single route. The concept of a system is already clear in the regulations of the Pan American Confederation for Highway Education, adopted in 1925, and at the Second Pan American Highway Congress. Resolutions were adopted recommending that each country prepare a study of its highway system to isolate the points where the systems of neighboring countries should join. These studies were to be sent to the Pan American Union, which would endeavor to promote agreements between countries on international highway crossings of the frontiers.[24] Nevertheless, Carlos Anesi, in his book on the Pan American Highway written in 1938, could still say that even though the American republics accepted the basic principle that the Pan American Highway System should be composed of the highways which connect the capitals of neighboring countries, the exact routes had as yet not been determined.[25]

When the routes proposed by Anesi in 1938 are compared with the Pan American System now accepted as official, and which is shown in Figure 8-4, it is clear that few changes have

[24] Segundo Congresso Panamericano de Estradas de Rodagem, 1929, *Boletim Official No. 17* (Aug. 28, 1929), pp. 67, 79.

[25] Carlos P. Anesi, *La Carretera Panamericana* (Buenos Aires: Compañiá General Fabril Financiera, 1938), p. 45.

FIGURE 8-4. *Pan American Highway System, South America*

LEGEND

═══════ Paved

─────── All Weather

─ ─ ─ ─ Dry Weather

• • • • • Impassable

TABLE 8-10. Summary of Pan American Highway System, 1938 and 1963[a]

Section of Highway	1938[b] Total Length Miles	1938[b] All Weather Miles	All Weather Per-cent	Dry Weather Miles	Dry Weather Per-cent	In Construction Miles	In Construction Per-cent	1963[b] Total Length Miles	Paved Miles	Paved Per-cent	All Weather Miles	All Weather Per-cent	Dry Weather Miles	Dry Weather Per-cent	Impassable Miles	Impassable Per-cent
Venezuela	764	764	100.0	—	—	—	—	583	583	100.0	—	—	—	—	—	—
Colombia	1,771	1,522	85.9	—	—	249	14.1	1,646	772	46.9	447	27.2	—	—	427	25.9
Ecuador	719	435	60.5	—	—	284	39.5	721	56	7.8	665	92.2	—	—	—	—
Peru	2,268	1,082	41.2	1,426	54.3	120	4.5	1,909	1,542	80.8	367	19.2	—	—	—	—
Chile	1,711	694	40.6	991	57.9	26	1.5	2,094	1,017	48.6	957	45.7	120	5.7	—	—
Bolivia	3,086	2,306	74.7	599	19.4	181	5.9	655	6	0.9	576	87.9	73	11.2	—	—
Argentina	3,431	1,660	48.4	1,764	51.4	7	0.2	3,005	2,023	67.3	456	15.2	526	17.5	—	—
Paraguay	640	224	35.0	101	15.8	315	49.2	208	45	21.6	42	20.2	121	58.2	—	—
Uruguay	394	316	80.2	78	19.8	—	—	365	214	58.6	141	38.7	10	2.7	—	—
Brazil	3,741	2,191	58.6	1,550	41.4	—	—	2,826	1,863	65.9	963	34.1	—	—	—	—
Total	18,885	11,194	59.3	6,509	34.5	1,182	6.2	14,012	8,121	58.0	4,614	32.9	850	6.1	427	3.0

Source: Appendix Table A-8.
[a] Overlapping sections have been omitted.
[b] Figures for 1938 All Weather include paved. For 1963, they do not include paved.

occurred in the last quarter of a century. The state of the system in 1938, as described by Anesi, is compared with that in 1963 in Appendix Table A-3. In Table 8-10 this material is summarized by country. The progress made in paved and all weather roads is evident. Within a few years the entire system within South America should either be paved or at least all-weather. The seriousness which the South American governments have attached to the system is all the more remarkable because the costly investments carried out have been financed nearly entirely by these countries with little foreign assistance. While the United States has spent more than $135 million on that section of the highway which passes through the Central American countries, it has contributed little to financing the highway system in Mexico and South America.[26]

When the Pan American Highway System was proposed in the 1920's, little importance was given to its use in the transport of freight within South America. Important segments of the route are heavily used today within the separate countries by trucks and buses, but there is remarkably little traffic across national boundaries, apparently bearing out the original belief of the South Americans that the principal users of the system would be private automobiles. What international traffic does exist is concentrated primarily in those areas where frontier regions of adjoining countries have developed considerable commerce. This highway transport is over relatively short distances, and long distance movements are uncommon (but not unknown). This situation will change, however, if South America is successful in bringing about closer economic integration, especially in the production of industrial products. The contribution of highway transport would not be adequately measured by the number of ton-miles of transport, as these will remain far inferior to those generated by ocean transport, but it will be significant for products of relatively high value through regions where the population is reasonably dense.

For this to be possible, sizable investments in highway construction and paving will be necessary to permit large trailer

[26] U.S. Senate Committee on Public Works, *Report on Progress on Inter-American Highway, 1962*, 87 Cong., 2 Sess. (1962), p. 3.

trucks to operate economically. Just as important, however, is the elimination of administrative obstacles that plague international highway transport at present. Frequently, trucks from one country are not even permitted to enter a neighboring nation and costly transshipment is required at the frontier. Surely nothing can be so irrational as to invest millions of dollars in highways and then to build bureaucratic roadblocks that make it impossible to use them.

International River Transport

In several areas of South America, river transport is already of considerable importance and, if it were properly coordinated with ocean, highway, railroad, and air transport, could contribute greatly to economic integration. The River Plate and Amazon River systems are among the largest river systems of the world, but despite their potential, they have been ignored as an area where moderate investments could have a high rate of return. The study of river transport in general in South America has been left largely to lawyers, concerned with international treaties, and to engineers, concerned with the relative merits of different types of barges. While funds can be found to study the feasibility of a highway to stretch along the eastern slope of the Andes from Venezuela to Bolivia, a project whose payoff would be realized only in the far future, river transport, with a few significant exceptions (as in Venezuela[27]) remains untouched.

The River Plate system, composed of the River Plate itself, and the Paraná, Paraguay, Upper Paraná, and Uruguay Rivers, in addition to other navigable tributaries, could well become the cornerstone for efficient transport between the Argentine part of the industrial heartland and large parts of the supporting hinterland lying in Argentina, Paraguay, Uruguay, Bolivia, and Brazil.[28]

[27] U.N. Economic Commission for Latin America, *El Transporte en América Latina, op. cit.,* pp. 94-96.

[28] Economic Conference of the Organization of American States, 1957, *Transportation and Economic Growth: The La Plata River System,* Document 11 (Pan American Union, 1957). U.N. Economic Commission for Latin America, *El Transporte en América Latina, op. cit.,* pp. 80-88; 91-92.

Within Argentina there are more than 2,000 miles of navigable rivers which form part of this system and in Paraguay more than 1,300 miles. Over just one route of this system, mineral ores are transported nearly 2,000 miles from Corumbá, on the border between Bolivia and Brazil, down through Paraguay to the port of Nueva Palmira in Uruguay for transshipment abroad. In view of the enormous impact which efficient river transport between Regions I and II could have on economic integration and development, it can only be termed shameful that improvements in the waterways have been so long delayed, due in no small measure to narrow political considerations. The feasibility of economical and intensive river transport in this part of South America has long been known, but this knowledge has not been transformed into the preparation of investment projects and their subsequent realization.

Although much of the region drained by the Amazon River system can be developed only with great difficulty, tributaries of the Amazon can be used effectively to develop the eastern portions of Peru and Bolivia. Ships of 2,000 gross registered tons reach Iquitos in Peru after a voyage of 2,000 miles up the Amazon from the Atlantic Ocean. Within Bolivia, it has been estimated that there are more than 6,300 miles of navigable rivers, many of which form part of the Amazon system. The enormous cost of building highways in eastern Peru and Bolivia and in western Brazil, in addition to the low population densities, indicates that serious consideration should be given to the possibilities of a transport system based on a combination of river, air, and highway transport, where the natural advantages of each are used in the development of an adequate and efficient network.

In other parts of the continent, there are additional opportunities awaiting study to permit a more efficient use of natural waterways. In the northern part of the continent, for example, the Meta River could be used for transport between Venezuela and Colombia.[29] One of the most important conclusions of even a casual study of transport and economic integration in South America is that a high priority should be given to developing

[29] *Ibid.*, pp. 88-91.

FIGURE 8-5. *Air Passenger Traffic in South America, 1927–1963*

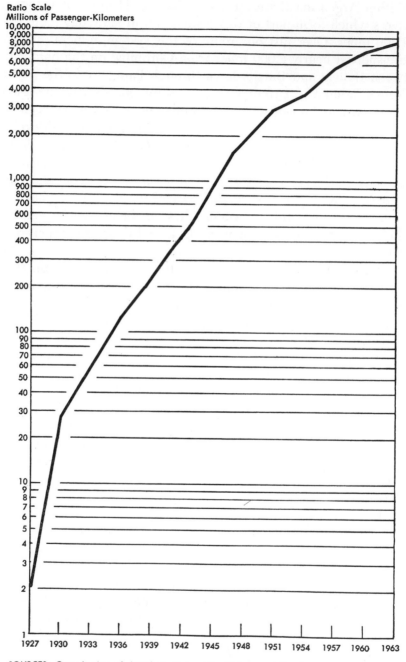

Ratio Scale
Millions of Passenger-Kilometers

SOURCES: Organization of American States, *The History and Development of Civil Air Transportation in Latin America 1919-1961*, UP/G.36/15 (Washington: Pan American Union, 1964), Tables 3, 5 and 7; International Civil Aviation Organization, "Traffic 1960-1963," *Digest of Statistics* No. 106, p. 66.

river transport and to integrating this mode with the other transport media.

International Air Transport

Despite the ease with which the Pan American Highway displaced the Pan American Railroad in the imagination of the Latin Americans forty years ago, the fact that the international highway system is still not completed is due in no small measure to the emergence of air transport. Had air transport been better developed in the 1920's when highway transport was looked on as the most promising means to improve communications within South America, the Pan American Highway System might even have been abandoned in favor of a vast international system of airports and air routes.

For most international passenger transport within South America, air transport is clearly the most appropriate mode. Even though bus and private automobile transport will become increasingly important between adjoining countries, only air transport can provide the rapid passenger service among the capitals and larger cities of South America that is indispensable for successful economic integration. The difficult topography, long distances between urban centers, and lack of developed surface transport media, furthermore, have also encouraged the development of air transport within many of the countries of South America. Figure 8-5 shows the growth of air passenger traffic in Latin America from 1927 to 1963, and although the concepts and coverage are not uniform over the period,[30] the rapid growth at least to 1960 is quite clear.

From 1951, data are available that show the development of air passenger traffic in each of the South American countries corresponding to scheduled services provided by South American

[30] The figures from 1927 through 1943 refer to passenger-kilometers performed in Latin America, that is, Central America and the Caribbean as well as South America, by all airlines—Latin American and non-Latin American. The figures for 1947 through 1963 refer to passenger-kilometers performed anywhere in the world by airlines registered in Latin America and reporting to the International Civil Aviation Organization.

FIGURE 8-6. *Passenger Kilometers Performed by Scheduled South American Airlines Reporting to ICAO, 1951–1963*

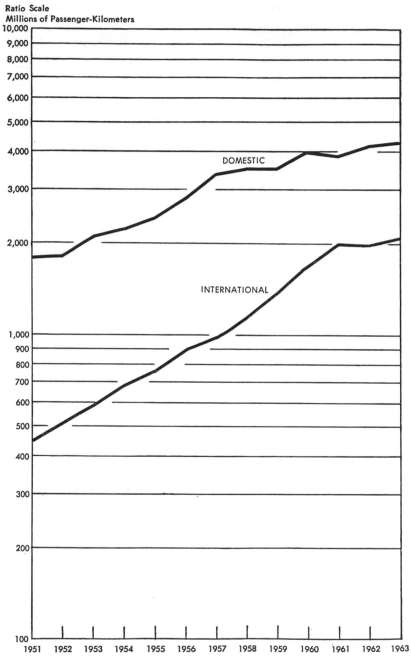

SOURCES: International Civil Aviation Organization, ''Traffic 1947-1961,'' *Digest of Statistics No. 90*, pp. 76-99; International Civil Aviation Organization, ''Traffic 1947-1959, 1960-1962,'' *Digest of Statistics No. 99*, pp. 67 and 70; International Civil Aviation Organization, ''Traffic 1960-1963,'' *Digest of Statistics No. 106*, pp. 70 and 74.

airlines reporting to the International Civil Aviation Organization (ICAO). Appendix Table A-4 traces this development, separating the domestic and international operations of the airlines registered in each of the countries. In this table, the passenger-kilometers for international flights refer to those performed on flights that originate and/or terminate at airports located in the territory of a country other than the one in which the airline is registered. Domestic flights are those that originate and terminate at airports located in the territory of the country in which the airline is registered. Figure 8-6 presents graphically the passenger-kilometers performed in domestic and international operations.

The predominance of Brazil, especially with respect to domestic operations, is immediately evident in Appendix Table A-4. In 1951, Brazil accounted for 59 percent of the passenger-kilometers performed in domestic operations by all the South American countries. Although Brazil's share fell somewhat over the period covered in the table, it still represented 53 percent in 1963. When the domestic and international traffic of the other two leading countries, Argentina and Colombia, is added to that of Brazil, the total for the three countries represents 81 percent of total traffic in 1963. The drop between the third leading country, Argentina, and the fourth, Venezuela, is substantial, as Venezuela in 1963 had only slightly more than one-half the total traffic of Argentina.

Considerable variation exists among the different countries in the passenger-kilometers performed in domestic and international operations. In Brazil and Colombia, for example, domestic service is by far the most important, while in Argentina international operations are now more important than domestic service. In Uruguay, whose total traffic is relatively small, international operations are far more important than domestic operations. For the continent as a whole, as can be seen in Figure 8-6, international operations increased from 1951 to 1963 considerably more rapidly than domestic operations. While in 1951 international operations represented only 20 percent of total passenger-kilometers performed, this had increased to 32 percent by 1963.

The same factors of difficult topography, widely scattered urban centers and undeveloped surface transport that were noted above as contributing to the growth of air passenger transport

FIGURE 8-7. *Freight Carried by South American Airlines, 1951-1963*

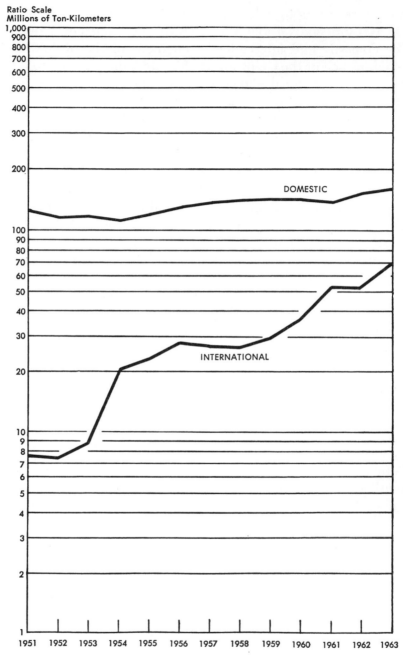

SOURCES: 1951-1961: International Civil Aviation Organization, "Traffic 1947-1961," *Digest of Statistics No. 90,* pp. 76-99; 1962-1963: International Civil Aviation Organization, "Draft Report on Study of Air Freight in the Latin American Region," AT-WP/811 (January 28, 1965, Appendix 5.

have also been key elements in the development of air freight transport in South America. Data before 1951 are unreliable, but after that year sufficient information is available to trace the ton-kilometers of freight carried by scheduled South American airlines in their domestic and international operations. These data are presented graphically in Figure 8-7 and are broken down by country in Appendix Table A-5.

Between 1951 and 1963, domestic air freight transport increased in South America at a considerably slower rate than domestic air passenger transport. Average annual rates of growth of air transport in South America from 1951 to 1963 are shown in the following figures.[31]

	Freight Traffic	All Traffic
Domestic Service	2.0	7.5
International Service	20.0	14.0
Both Services	4.6	9.0

As in the case of passenger traffic, air cargo transported in international operations increased far more rapidly than in domestic services, which in the case of cargo was practically constant over the period. As a result, for South America as a whole, ton-kilometers of air freight carried in international service increased from 5.7 percent of all air freight traffic in 1951 to 30.2 percent of air freight traffic in 1963.

Air freight traffic in South America is considerably more important than the average for the entire world. In 1963, freight traffic on the average throughout the world represented 19 percent of scheduled air traffic.[32] All the South American countries except Argentina and Uruguay exceeded this percentage. In the case of Venezuela, air freight represented 45 percent of total scheduled air traffic in 1963. Revenue from air freight reached 14.4 percent of total revenue in a sample of nineteen Latin American airlines in 1962, 58 percent above the world average.[33]

[31] Derived from Tables A-4 and A-5.

[32] International Civil Aviation Organization, "Draft Report on Study of Air Freight in the Latin American Region," AT-WP/811 (Jan. 28, 1965), p. 10, Table 1.

[33] Ibid., p. 13; Table 4, p. 45.

TABLE 8-11. *Air Freight Entering and Leaving Countries of South America, September 1–30, 1963*

(Metric tons)

From \ To	Argen- tina	Brazil	Uru- guay	Para- guay	Chile	Bolivia	Peru	Colom- bia	Vene- zuela	Ecua- dor	Total
Argentina	—	55.7	44.0	57.1	1,173.2	4.7	46.2	—	2.7	—	1,383.6
Brazil	31.8	—	66.0	3.2	—	—	19.0	—	3.4	—	123.4
Uruguay	85.3	38.1	—	—	—	—	—	—	—	—	123.4
Paraguay	14.5	1.9	—	—	0.1	1.6	22.8	—	12.3	—	53.2
Chile	439.4	—	—	0.3	—	5.2	68.5	—	—	—	513.4
Bolivia	0.1	—	—	1.8	0.4	—	9.6	—	—	—	11.9
Peru	12.1	19.8	—	3.7	68.5	33.1	—	17.2	—	24.5	178.9
Colombia	—	—	—	—	—	—	19.2	—	12.6	43.1	74.9
Venezuela	3.4	19.7	—	9.4	—	—	—	18.4	—	—	50.9
Ecuador	—	—	—	—	—	—	33.2	13.4	—	—	46.6
Total	586.6	135.2	110.0	75.5	1,242.2	44.6	218.5	49.0	31.0	67.6	2,560.2

Source: Organization of American States, Second Meeting of Governmental Experts in Civil Aviation, *Inter-American Transborder Air Traffic and Capacity, Scheduled Services September 1–30, 1963, inclusive,* UP/G. 36/13 (Washington, D. C.: Pan American Union, June 12, 1964).

As in the case of air passenger transport in South America, there is considerable concentration of cargo transport within a few countries. Brazil and Colombia alone accounted for 80 percent of the ton-kilometers of air freight carried in domestic service by the South American airlines in 1963, and Brazil and Venezuela accounted for 73 percent of the freight transport in international service. For the Latin American region as a whole, seven airlines transported half of the scheduled air freight in 1963: VARIG, PARENSE, and VASP (Brazil), AVIANCA (Colombia), RANSA (Venezuela), LAN (Chile), and AERONAVES (Mexico).[34]

Because three-fourths of scheduled air freight traffic is carried in the holds of passenger aircraft in Latin America, estimates of costs are necessarily somewhat ambiguous, as the service provided is determined by the demands for passenger service. Nevertheless, rough estimates indicate that the average direct operating cost for nineteen Latin American airlines in 1962 was 12.8 cents per ton-kilometer available, about 14 percent above the world average. Average indirect cost was 10.6 cents, making a total average cost of 23.4 cents per ton-kilometer available, about 16 percent above the world average. Freight rates in general do not appear to be unduly high, but both costs and rates could be

[34] *Ibid.*, p. 18.

reduced by the use of modern airplanes specifically designed for cargo transport.[35]

Despite the relatively well developed cargo services within many of the South American countries and between these and the United States and Europe, there is still little traffic from one South American country to another. Table 8-11 shows air freight entering and leaving the countries of South America from other nations of the continent during September 1963. Of the total of 2,560 metric tons transported in that month, the traffic from Argentina to Chile amounted to 1,173 tons. While Table 8-11 does not show the origin and final destination of air cargo transported, but rather the tonnages moved between pairs of countries along the established air routes, it is probable that the single most important traffic during that month was the transport of meat from Argentina to Chile. Throughout the rest of the continent, the absolute quantities of air freight transported from one South American country to another were small.

Conclusion

Although it is essential that an international highway system be developed in South America, and also that use be made of the railway connections which exist but are little used, it is also clear that in many areas air cargo transport offers a significant opportunity for economical and efficient transport. Between Region III (Chile) and Region I, the industrial heartland, for example, air transport provides a promising alternative to the slow maritime route around Cape Horn and to the costly land transport over the Andes and across the Argentine pampa. Industrial integration, especially if it takes the form of industrial complementation, with parts of a single product produced in separate countries for final assembly elsewhere, will put a high premium on the speed and security of transport. For products whose value in relation to their weight is high, as is the case with electronic equipment, adding machines, typewriters, etc., air cargo transport may be the best means of transport. In other areas as well, such as be-

[35] *Ibid.*, pp. 6-7, 26, 32, 44.

tween Peru and Venezuela, and for products not usually associated with air transport, such as fruits and vegetables, this mode may well play a role that it does not have in any other continent of the world.

In the United States, in Europe, and in other areas, air transport matured after long-distance highway and rail transport were well established. For transport among the nations of South America, this is not the case. Here it is possible to jump from ocean transport to air transport over many major routes with a development of land transport in the future when traffic densities are sufficiently high to make its use economical. The pattern of development that would result from this sequence of transport investments will be different in South America from that which would occur should this continent follow the traditional development path of presently industrialized large countries. As Burden has explained:

> Great transcontinental railroads, the dream of progressive Latin Americans of the nineteenth century, will now never be built. Dozens of villages along their projected routes are doomed to slumber, forever deprived of the chance of becoming large and flourishing towns whose names would have been bywords to every world traveler. At the same time other tiny settlements not on the route of the proposed railroads will grow to world importance because they are to be stopping points on the trunk airlines of the future.[36]

Air transport, however, should not be considered a panacea for the transport problems of Latin American economic integration. If organized on the basis of large and modern aircraft, air transport can be competitive with highway transport even when this is organized on the basis of large trailer trucks operating over paved highways if the distances are sufficiently great. If the highway trucks can carry only 5 tons of cargo and operate over unpaved mountainous roads, air transport can be competitive over quite short distances.[37] Air transport suffers from the same fundamental defect which affects maritime transport; it contributes solely to the development of the area within the radius of attrac-

---

[36] William A. M. Burden, *The Struggle for Airways in Latin America* (Council on Foreign Relations, 1943), p. 188.

[37] Organization of American States, *El Papel de la Aviación Civil en los Proyectos de Colonización*, UP/G.36/17 (Pan American Union, 1964).

tion of the airport. Because of the overwhelming incidence of terminal costs in ocean transport, there is always an important stimulus operating to reduce the number of port calls and to concentrate cargo in as few ports as possible. In air transport, the analogous factor is the cost of raising the airplane off the ground. Only if distances are long between airports and the full capacity of large aircraft can be used, is air transport economical. For this reason, dependence on air transport would tend to perpetuate the present pattern of population and industrial production concentrated into a few "hypercephalic" urban centers. As Burden has noted:

> A trunk railroad or highway is likely to produce a "ribbon" development of towns along its entire route and to encourage the development of contiguous feeder lines. A community situated anywhere on such routes has transportation immediately available merely by flagging a train or buying a motor car. The stops on trunk airlines, on the other hand, are usually 500 or more miles apart. The vast intermediate stretches remain as isolated as they were before the air route was installed unless, because of their natural importance, they justify some local service. . . . A railroad or highway automatically provides transportation for literally all points along its route, regardless of whether that territory justifies high-speed transportation or not, while airlines must be more consciously directed toward specific transportation needs of particular localities.[38]

One of the important objectives pointed out above of economic integration in South America is the geographical dispersion of the development attained. Air transport can contribute to this objective if it is used to penetrate undeveloped areas more economically than is possible through costly highway construction, especially over mountain barriers and in cases where the territory between presently populated centers and the new frontier area has little economic potential. International air transport is also desirable in many areas, as has already been noted. But because air transport is not a development sower, in the same sense as are highway and railroad transport, it is desirable to invest in land transport just as soon as traffic density is sufficiently high to permit an economic return on the investment.

[38] Burden, *op. cit.*, p. 188.

CHAPTER IX

A Transport Policy for the Economic Integration of South America

THROUGH THE USE OF REGIONAL ANALYSIS, this study has attempted to highlight the fact that economic meaning can be given to the integration of South America only when the spatial aspects of the different South American countries and of the South American continent as a whole are considered. Despite the impatience of the leaders of the Latin American republics with the slow course of the Latin American Free Trade Association, and their astute criticism of the formulas laid down in the Montevideo Treaty for the progressive lowering of the intrazonal trade barriers, the fact remains that there are severe geographical obstacles to economic integration that must be overcome if the South American countries are to follow the path of the European Common Market.

In the chapter on present intrazonal trade patterns, it was pointed out that present trade within South America is largely concentrated in trade between adjoining countries and in primary products. These countries, nevertheless, have looked on the economic integration of the South American continent (plus Mexico) as a way to escape the severe limitations which the lack of world markets for primary products has imposed on their capacity to import the essential capital goods they require. By creating a market for industrial goods that encompasses an entire continent, these nations hope to produce efficiently goods that are a prerequisite to continuing industrial expansion and that presently must be imported from outside the region.

The creation of a market, however, is not solely a legal matter. Whatever treaties and conventions are signed, they will remain mere pieces of paper unless the goods produced in one Latin American country can be placed in the marketplace of another at prices comparable to those of the same goods imported from Europe, the United States, and Japan. Among the many factors that will determine the succcess of the LAFTA effort is transport. Without regular, frequent, and economical transport, there is no hope of overcoming the natural geographical barriers which have contributed to present trade patterns within the region.

The regional approach used in this study pointed out the diversity of transport problems and opportunities among the regions which have been delineated in South America. The maritime problems which affect trade between Argentina and Brazil are quite different from those between Argentina and Colombia. Similarly, the opportunities for substituting maritime transport between Chile and Peru are less than those between Chile and Argentina. While the information presently available on transport and development potential in South America does not permit a definitive statement regarding investment priorities, it is possible on the basis of the material presented in this study to sketch broadly a structure of transport appropriate for economic integration.

Table 9-1, which is based on the nine regions delineated in Chapter II, is a preliminary attempt to indicate transport priorities both within and among the regions of South America.[1] The diagonal of this double-entry table corresponds to internal transport within each of the nine regions while the remaining squares correspond to interregional transport. Within each square, priorities are indicated by the ordering of the transport media. This ordering does not represent the ordering of the ton-miles which will be transported by each of the transport modes. It shows, instead,

[1] For an earlier attempt of the author to suggest investment priorities in transport in South America see "El Transporte y el Desarrollo Económico en Sudamérica," *Desarrollo Económico*, Vol. 1, No. 4 (November-December 1964), pp. 15-23.

TABLE 9-1. *Indicated Transport Investment Priorities in South America*

Regions: Both Origins and Destinations	I	II	III	IV	V	VI	VII	VIII	IX
I. Industrial Heartland in Brazil, Argentina and Uruguay	Highway/ Railway River Ocean	River Railway Highway	Highway Ocean Railway	Ocean	Highway & River/ Railway	Ocean	Ocean	River & Ocean	Highway Ocean Railway
II. Supporting Hinterland		Railway/ Highway/ River	Highway/ Railway	Ocean	Highway & River/ Railway	Ocean	Ocean	River & Ocean	Ocean/ Highway
III. Chile			Highway Railway	Ocean Railway	?	Ocean	Ocean	Ocean	Ocean
IV. Highlands of Bolivia and Peru				Highway Railway	Highway	Ocean	Ocean	Highway & River Ocean	Ocean
V. Eastern slope of the Andes					Highway/ River	?	?	River	?
VI. Colombia and Venezuela						Highway/ Railway Ocean	Highway/ Ocean	River & Ocean	Ocean
VII. Ecuador							Highway Railway	River & Ocean	Ocean
VIII. Amazon Basin								River	River & Ocean
IX. Northeast Brazil									Highway Railway

Explanation: Ordering indicates priority for investment and development. A slash between two media indicates equal priority. An "&" between two media indicates that they are used together. Ocean refers both to ports and to the organization of shipping services. "?" indicates that priorities cannot be determined at present. The main diagonal is internal transport within each region. Other squares correspond to interregional transport. Only half the table is shown because the same transport media are used for transport in both directions.

214

the ordering with which attention should now be given to new transport investments and policies so as to make a maximum contribution to economic integration, especially in regard to industrial products. Air transport is excluded from the table even though it holds considerable promise for the economical transport of industrial products over many routes.

Table 9-1 indicates that for internal trade within each of the nine regions, highway transport has a clear priority in four regions and is given equal priority with railroad and/or river transport in another four regions. In Region VIII, the Amazon Basin, river transport has a clear priority. Again it should be emphasized that the priorities listed do not indicate where the principal transport problems are. In Chile, Region III, for example, highway transport is given first priority despite the fact that the major problem confronting the government in the transport sector is how to reduce the financial deficit of the state railways. The priority given highway transport indicates that investments in this mode in Chile are likely to make a greater contribution to internal development at the present time.

Of the thirty-six pairs of interregional combinations shown in Table 9-1, ocean transport alone or in combination with river transport is the only feasible transport mode in twenty cases. In six other cases, ocean transport will continue to be important, including one instance where it is given first priority for development purposes. The permanent role which is thus assigned ocean transport, despite the many disadvantages which this implies, is a clear indication of the geographic difficulties confronting economic integration in South America.

In the northern part of the continent, among Regions VI, VII, and VIII, and between these regions and the rest of South America, transport will continue to develop basically along the lines of the past with primary dependence on ocean transport and, in the case of the Amazon Basin, river transport. While it is possible and desirable to improve highway transport between Ecuador and Colombia and between Colombia and Venezuela, especially to stimulate the development of frontier areas, it is difficult to discern instances where a major change in transport could radically alter the development that is already taking place.

Region IV, the highland and coastal areas of Peru and Bolivia, will continue to be linked with the rest of the continent almost exclusively by ocean transport. Although highway transport between this region and Region V, the eastern slope of the Andes, will become increasingly important, and although Bolivia may be able to increase its trade somewhat with Chile using present railroad connections, the natural isolation of this region can be reduced only slightly.

Region IX, the northeast of Brazil, should improve its land transport connections with the rest of Brazil, but its links with the other South American countries will have to be by water. Region V is at present accessible by highway from Region IV, by railroad and river from Regions I and II, and by river from Region VIII. A proposal is under study by the Inter-American Development Bank to construct a highway parallel to the Andes through the entire region, but it is probable that this project is premature. For this reason, Table 9-1 contains a number of question marks indicating that the type of transport investment required to connect Region V with other regions is still in doubt.

For the transport planner, the most interesting transport problems are found in the southern zone of South America, encompassing Regions I, II, and III. Here the transport alternatives are wider, and, if economic integration is to be successful in South America, it must be based primarily on these three regions and especially on industrial integration between Argentina and Brazil. The development of river, highway, and railroad transport among these three regions to reduce the present dependence on ocean transport can contribute enormously to this integration and can also aid in spreading economic development geographically over a much wider area.

Ocean Transport and Economic Integration

Because of the present nearly complete dependence on maritime transport for intra-Latin American trade, the LAFTA secretariat has focused practically all the attention it has given to transport on this mode. As was shown in the analysis presented in Chapter VII, maritime transport among a number of regions, especially between those in the northern part of the South American continent (plus Mexico) and those in the southern zone, is deficient. Considering that ocean transport must fulfill in South America the role played by the transcontinental railroads of the United States in the economic integration of that continent one hundred years ago, it is evident that the LAFTA effort will not be successful unless maritime transport can be improved. The direction that has been followed by the Latin American countries in confronting this problem, nevertheless, has not been particularly fortunate. To a large degree, the action taken by LAFTA in this area has been guided by the Latin American shipping companies, both state and private, and insufficient attention has been given to the basic problem of providing regular, frequent, and economical liner service. The paragraphs which follow indicate ways in which this problem might more usefully be attacked.[2]

Improving Maritime Service versus Protecting LAFTA Ships

Considered as one economic activity among the many carried on in the LAFTA region, maritime shipping should be encouraged, and, to the extent that it is economically desirable to do so, regional producers should be relied on instead of foreign producers. Import substitution is as legitimate in this activity as it is in any other.

Nevertheless, it must also be remembered, that maritime transport is not just one activity among many. It represents a unique activity that affects all others. Ocean transport will maintain for many years to come its predominant position in intrazonal commerce. The structure of freight rates influences the location

[2] For an excellent statement of the different aspects of the maritime problem which should be considered in a LAFTA treaty, see Tomás Sepúlveda Whittle, *Hacia una Política Naviera para la Asociación Latinoamericana de Libre Comercio*, Memoria de prueba para optar al grado de Licenciado en Comercio y Ciencias Económicas, Universidad Católica de Valparaíso (Privately printed, 1965), pp. 77-80.

of many economic activities, the extent of the market, and the degree to which economies of scale can be used to advantage. The maritime shipping industry has the right to protection from outside competition only so long as this protection is consistent with the other objectives of the Latin America Free Trade Association.

It is unfortunate that during the last few years the maritime transport problem has been looked upon as one of protecting LAFTA ships rather than as one of improving maritime service. The service at the present time is inadequate for achieving the goals of LAFTA. The transport policy adopted by LAFTA should be designed to protect and develop liner services which operate with a fixed schedule rather than to assist shipping companies in general.

Port Problems

Inefficient ports and undisciplined port workers represent, at present, the single most important obstacle in this transport sector to economic integration in South America. It will be possible for shipping companies to provide regular liner service, according to fixed schedules, only if they are assured of prompt reception in the various ports of call and of efficient handling of the cargo which they leave and take on. Freight rates within the LAFTA area can be maintained at a reasonable level only if port workers charge realistic rates for the work they do and if ships are not forced to remain in port for unduly long periods of time because of the low productivity of port workers.

It is probable that at the present time port costs differ sharply from country to country and even among different ports within the same country. Freight rates should reflect the costs in the specific ports served, that is, freight rates should not be set for a group of ports when port costs within this group vary widely. The producers and consumers within the zone of attraction of a high-cost port should be forced to pay higher rates than persons situated in areas served by lower-cost ports. Only in this way can community pressure be brought to bear so as to reverse the dangerous trend toward even higher port costs.

Important progress has already been made by the Inter-American Ports Conferences, sponsored by the Organization of American States, to simplify port procedures for reception of vessels and in the documentation required. The recommendations of these conferences and of the Permanent Technical Committee on Ports should be applied immediately throughout the LAFTA countries.

Operating Subsidies Versus Cargo Reserves

Direct intergovernmental action is necessary in South America to establish regular liner service among the LAFTA countries in those regions where it is presently deficient. The two basic alternatives which this state action can follow are: (1) direct subsidies to liners to assure regular service on low-volume routes, and (2) cargo reserves that would channel the existing traffic to favored carriers.

Subsidies have not been considered, as such, within the LAFTA organizations, despite the fact that they form the basis for the support given the private merchant marine in the United States, and in general, are less likely to introduce serious distortions in an efficient distribution of resources than quantitative restrictions such as cargo reserves. Some subsidized liner services already exist, as several of the subsidized state shipping companies provide service within the LAFTA area. Providing subsidies on a multinational basis, however, would create a number of problems and the shipping companies themselves have not recommended this alternative. Despite the theoretical advantages of subsidies, LAFTA members at present favor the alternative of cargo reserves.

Applied intelligently, cargo reserves could improve maritime service. Although the LAFTA members will not find that it is economically desirable to reserve all intra-LAFTA cargo for ships registered in the LAFTA countries, they should assert their right to control collectively the routing of this cargo and to use this policy alternative in those instances where it is clearly beneficial to do so. It is to be expected that the United States government and the European shipping conferences will consider retaliatory action should cargo reserves be implemented. At least in the case of the former, however, more detailed economic analysis and continued negotiation would, it is hoped, permit an acceptable agreement to be reached.

New LAFTA Maritime Transport Agencies

Whether LAFTA chooses to improve liner service through subsidies or through cargo reserves, it is essential that two new organizations be established: shipping conferences for intra-LAFTA ocean commerce and an international LAFTA regulatory body. Both agencies are essential for the development of liner services and for the adoption of freight rates in accord with the general objectives of the Free Trade Association.

The shipping conferences could propose freight rates for trade within the area and enforce the approved tariffs. They could also propose minimum and maximum service on each of the trade routes and distribute sailings among the conference members. It might be possible to have a single conference for the entire LAFTA region or, alternatively, separate conferences for each of the major trading areas. The conferences should be composed of the companies offering liner service in the region, including foreign liners.

The LAFTA Maritime Commission, on the other hand, should be a regulatory agency empowered to review the tariffs and services proposed by the conferences. It should also license carriers designated as liner companies in the region, both LAFTA and foreign companies. This commission could be composed of five members from the principal geographic regions: one representing Argentina and Uruguay, the second Brazil and Paraguay, the third Chile and Peru, the fourth Colombia and Ecuador, and the fifth Mexico and Venezuela. Several of the members should have had considerable experience in maritime transport. The LAFTA governments could delegate to this commission the power that is necessary to assure good maritime service at a reasonable cost within the area. The permanent technical staff of the commission could be part of the international LAFTA secretariat.

Adequate Maritime Transport Statistics

Both the conferences and the LAFTA Maritime Commission will function effectively only if they have current, accurate, and complete information on maritime shipping within the area. This information does not exist at the present time, and, in many countries, there is no mechanism adequate for this purpose. Basic to the solution of the problem would be the adoption of a common freight commodity classification, applied consistently throughout the area. The task of improving maritime statistics, although difficult, is by no means hopeless, as the success of Chile in applying data processing techniques to information obtained from ship manifests has shown. Work in this area should be closely coordinated with the other efforts of LAFTA to improve statistics on intrazonal commerce.

Determination of Basic Shipping Routes Within LAFTA

A critically important task, which should be undertaken jointly by the conferences and the LAFTA Maritime Commission, is the determination of basic shipping routes within LAFTA. These routes should provide the basis for the establishment of specific liner services. In determining these shipping routes, factors such as the following should be considered: volume of traffic, nature of cargo traded, seasonal fluctuations, cargo flow imbalances, new industries to be established, and minimum service consistent with promoting industrial integration among all member countries. In Appendix D to this study, a methodology based on linear programming techniques is presented to indicate one possible way to select an efficient pattern of shipping routes. Although the methodology shown is oversimplified and takes into account only a few of the factors that must be considered in determining these routes, it demonstrates that this complex problem can be resolved using modern computer oriented techniques.

Criteria for Establishing Freight Rates

Freight rates are discussed separately for expository convenience, yet it must be remembered that these rates cannot be established independently from decisions affecting the maritime service to be offered. For reasons explained in Chapter VII, individual freight rates should be determined on a value of service principle. The application of this policy would contribute to the maintenance of remunerative liner service, but the companies offering regular liner service should be protected from tramp and other irregular competitors.

The criteria to be followed in determining the level and structure of freight rates are: (1) that each complete service be remunerative to the carrier (although subsidies may be necessary on some routes); (2) that rates not be unduly high; and (3) that value of service rates not lead to an irrational distribution of industrial location.

Application of Cargo Reserves

The use of cargo reserves may not be the most efficient way to improve maritime service within LAFTA, but it could lead to better service than now exists. No defense can be made, however, for adopting bilateral reserves, and for reasons given in Chapter VII, only multilateral reserves should be considered by LAFTA members. It is true, however, that in the application of multilateral reserves, the legitimate desires of the different members to develop their own merchant fleets must be considered. This can be done without partitioning the LAFTA region into unrelated and chaotic markets for each route.

Should LAFTA decide to adopt a multilateral system of cargo reserves, one way the system might be applied is as follows. Once a tentative structure of shipping routes and freight rates has been determined by the conferences and the LAFTA Maritime Commission, each shipping company should be asked to indicate the minimum service it is willing to provide over the routes it selects if granted a license as a LAFTA common carrier. Potential LAFTA common carriers include LAFTA companies presently dedicated exclusively to LAFTA service, LAFTA companies that combine intra-LAFTA service with service to other continents, and foreign liner companies operating in the LAFTA area. These companies should make their offers on the basis of the shipping routes and the freight rates tentatively adopted, and would be assured, if they were selected, that all intra-LAFTA general cargo and a portion of bulk products such as wheat would be reserved for them. Bulk minerals and petroleum would be excluded from the reserve system.

When the offers of the potential liner companies have been received, they should be studied to determine whether the service offered by LAFTA ships alone would be sufficient for requirements of industrial integration on each route. In cases where LAFTA ships alone cannot promise adequate service, as might occur, for example, between the southern Pacific ports of South America and the Pacific ports of Mexico, foreign liners should be included among the selected companies. Where LAFTA and foreign companies combined are not willing to provide adequate service, consideration should be given to raising the rates on the routes affected or to offering subsidies. In cases where the offer of LAFTA companies may exceed the minimum service considered necessary, rates can be lowered on these routes, and bulk cargoes can be released to other ships than liners. It is clear that this process will be laborious and will require successive approximations before an adequate solution can be reached.

In the selection of the companies to be licensed as LAFTA common carriers, it will be necessary to take into consideration the necessity that as many as possible LAFTA countries are represented. This requirement is likely to lead to a final solution that does not represent an economic optimum, but is politically acceptable to all the countries concerned. Furthermore, the cost of taking into consideration political factors is far clearer when the procedure recommended here is followed, than when percentage quotas are assigned arbitrarily to each country from the outset.

Once a group of companies, from the LAFTA region and from abroad, have been selected to provide service, they should be licensed as LAFTA common carriers. To these companies would be channeled all intra-LAFTA general cargo and that part of bulk cargo which is needed to make specific routes remunerative. These companies would guarantee to follow a fixed schedule of sailings and to provide adequate capacity to transport cargo offered at published rates.

The application of multilateral cargo reserves along the lines suggested here makes unnecessary any processing of export and import permits to assign cargo routings. Exporters should be permitted to use any licensed LAFTA common carrier in trading with other LAFTA countries. The exporter would know in advance the precise sailing schedule of the companies that serve his port and that of the purchaser of his goods. If the LAFTA common carrier does not complete his schedule, then after a brief delay, the exporter would be free to use any carrier. Carriers would, of course, be permitted to change sailing schedules, but only with advance notice published in the countries served.

In order that all routes be remunerative, it might be necessary to reserve, for a particular carrier, cargo transported between two ports which are also served by other LAFTA common carriers. Similar adjustments could be made to make small volume routes remunerative by permitting carriers—mostly licensed foreign liners—to carry intrazonal cargo on some, but not on all, of their sailings. These adjustments would be under continual study both by the conferences and the LAFTA Maritime Commission so as to assure the necessary flexibility in intra-LAFTA transport.

The only major problem that might arise would be the division of bulk cargoes between the part reserved for LAFTA common carriers and that released to any carrier. This should be the only area in which it would be necessary to determine the routing of specific cargoes. Even here, however, the problem should not be overly difficult because of the importance of state agencies in the transport of these goods. It should also be possible to work closely with producer and consumer associations, as in the case of lumber transported between Brazil and Argentina.

River Transport and Economic Integration

Despite the paucity of data regarding international river transport within South America, it is clear that this mode offers exceptional opportunities and that its development could make a substantial contribution to economic integration. In the Amazon Basin (Region VIII) and in many parts of the eastern sections of Bolivia and Peru (Region V), population densities will be low for many years to come, thus the economic return on costly investments in trunk highways cannot be justified. These regions, however, are interlaced with navigable rivers, which, with relatively inexpensive investments in channel improvement, and appropriate vessels, together with complementary investments in feeder roads and landing strips, can serve the development requirements for many decades.

Similar opportunities for economical transport exist in the southern zone of the continent through the rational use of the River Plate system. Repeated stress has been placed in this study on the importance of economic integration within the industrial heartland (Region I) and between this region and its supporting hinterland (Region II). The River Plate and its tributaries are admirably suited for this purpose. Neither the cost nor the technical difficulties of improving river transport in this zone represent serious obstacles; the principal problems are political. If the Latin American countries take seriously the LAFTA effort, they must be willing to search for rapid and suitable solutions to these problems.

The development of river transport appears to be one of the areas in which technical and economic assistance from the United States could make a significant contribution. The Latin American countries have already expressed their doubts whether the United States favors economic integration in Latin America in the light of U. S. threats of retaliation should the LAFTA countries channel LAFTA cargo to LAFTA ships. River transport appears to be one area in which the United States can contribute effectively to economic integration without incurring opposition from U. S. private interests. The importance of river transport in the United States and the magnitude of the problems which U. S. engineers have overcome to make this possible are clear indications of capability in this area. This assistance could be directed toward improving channels, installing navigational aids, selecting appropriate river vessels, and giving advice on operations. It may also be that the United States could assist in the planning and execution of more ambitious international multipurpose projects, as those designed to produce electric power, control floods, and improve river transport.

Land Transport and Economic Integration

Despite the fact that ocean transport must continue to dominate in intra-LAFTA commerce for many decades to come, it must be recognized that in many ways this transport mode is less suitable than land transport. The LAFTA countries are faced not only with the task of connecting their economies with those of their neighbors but also with incorporating all of the geographic area within their boundaries into the national economy. All the LAFTA nations are concerned with extending present industrial development, now centered in a few isolated urban islands, to new regions. Ocean transport is not an appropriate means to attain this objective. On the contrary, reliance exclusively on ocean transport tends to increase industrial centralization. Because of the enormous incidence of port costs within total maritime transport costs, ships must keep to a minimum the number of port calls on each voyage. The establishment of new industrial centers is made more difficult when potential export products from these centers must be transported by sea. As was written of South America more than seventy-five years ago:

> It must be clear, then, to those who are at all familiar with the past history and present condition of the great majority of the countries under consideration, that, with only the present ocean-route avenues connecting them, to a limited extent, commercially along their coasts, and scarcely at all socially, long cycles of years must roll

around without essentially changing the characteristics of the different peoples, or materially assimilating them with each other . . . unless some new and very powerful factor, such as the proposed intercontinental railway, shall be introduced.[3]

The transcontinental railway, of course, was never built, and long cycles of years have rolled around with few essential changes in Latin America. A few semipowerful factors have been introduced, such as the establishment of international airlines, which have contributed to closer relationships within Latin America. To date, however, the most significant single event has been the establishment of the Latin American Free Trade Association. The potential impact of LAFTA has not been fully felt and has not even been envisioned except by a few outstanding Latin American leaders. The full impact, should the LAFTA effort be successful, will not be restricted to a somewhat increased trade in a few industrial products but rather will cut across the entire economic and social structure of the Latin American nations. Not just goods but capital and labor as well will move across national frontiers. New giant companies will come into being; plants and subsidiaries in a multitude of these countries will move their employees freely from nation to nation, and new impetus will be given to ancient dreams of political integration.

Ocean transport, even when complemented by air transport, is an inadequate base on which to build this new Latin America, and, for this reason, it is essential that international land transport, principally by highway, be developed within South America. Only land transport provides the ease and flexibility of goods and passenger transport at an economic cost which is required to spread development spatially within each country while at the same time bringing these countries together. Providing the basic facilities to permit highway transport is the single best way to provide economic access among South American countries, and, as was shown in Chapter III, present trade is largely concentrated between those pairs of countries where economic access is relatively good. While improved ocean transport is essential to permit goods to move within the LAFTA region, the completion of

[3] Hinton Rowan Helper and others, *The Three Americas Railway* (W. S. Bryon, 1881), p. 92.

the Pan American Highway System is a prerequisite for producers to discover new markets in adjoining countries and for consumers to learn of new sources of supply.

Important segments of the Pan American Highway System have already been completed, as was noted in Chapter VIII, and work continues on other segments. It can already be noted, however, that the use of some completed links (and also of many of the international railroads) is distressingly low. In large measure, this failure to make use of existing facilities is a result of burdensome bureaucratic obstacles at the frontiers and of controls and restrictions on international commerce and passenger movement in general. The elimination of these artificial barriers is crucial for the attainment of the LAFTA objectives.

Appendixes

Tables

TABLE A-1. *Categories Used in Classifying Commodities in Intra-South American Trade*

Origin	Raw Materials and Unprocessed	Semi-Processed	Processed and Manufactured
Animal	Live animals Wool and other fibers of animal origin Other	Hides, hair, plumes, pelts Meat: frozen, fresh, chilled Animal fat Other	Leather Meat: canned, salted, dried Dairy products Other
Agriculture	Wheat and other grains Raw and baled fibers Fresh fruits Legumes and vegetables Seeds Nuts Other	Flour Other milled grains Sugar: semi-refined and refined Dried fruits Coffee, cocoa, tea, yerba mate Other	Food, including canned fruits and vegetables, juices, etc. Tobacco Beverages: beer, wine, liquor, mineral water, etc. Vegetable oils Textiles: yarn, thread, cloth Confections Other
Forestry	Live plants	Logs, lumber, boards Rubber, cork, quebracho and other extracts Non-textile vegetal fibers Other	Furniture and other wood manufactures Plywood, fiberboard Cellulose pulp, paper, and paper products
Hunting and Fishing	Fresh seafood		Fish meal Canned, frozen, salted seafood Canned, frozen, salted game Fish oils
Minerals	Metal ores Crude oil Sand, stone, clay Non-metallic ores Natural gas	Refined and smelted metals Refined oil products	Rolled metal products Machinery and its parts Vehicles and their parts Cement, bricks, cinder blocks, and other construction materials Fertilizers Chemicals, drugs, plastics Glass, crystal
Miscellaneous			

TABLE A-2. *Development of Railroads in South America and the United States*
(Miles)

	1870	1880	1890	1900	1910	1920	1930	1940	1950	1960	1963
Argentina	457	1,572	5,895	10,352	17,496	21,177	23,825	25,802	26,635	27,292	25,006
Brazil	462	2,110	6,197	9,517	13,250	17,730	20,180	21,283	22,792	23,823	23,334
Uruguay	61	268	—	1,028	1,371	1,633	1,742	1,807	1,859	1,853	1,853
Paraguay	45	45	93	155	190	290	309	309	310	310	310
Chile	495	1,107	1,707	2,707	3,713	5,096	5,549	5,350	5,280	5,397	5,369
Bolivia	—	—	—	500	796	—	1,502	1,608	1,914	2,156	—
Peru	158	1,259	991	1,116	1,801	2,238	2,613	1,721	1,924	1,823	1,798
Colombia	—	—	—	340	614	—	994	—	1,901	2,213	2,184
Venezuela	—	—	—	529	542	—	646	—	620	295	—
Ecuador	—	42	51	311	466	621	703	687	698	716	717
Total	1,678	—	—	26,555	40,239	—	58,063	—	63,934	65,878	—
United States	52,922	93,267	163,605	193,346	240,293	252,845	249,052	233,670	223,779	217,552	—

231

Source: Bolivia, Colombia and Venezuela, 1900 and 1910: Frederic M. Halsey, *The Railways of South and Central America* (New York: Francis Emory Fitch, 1914), p. 169. The 1900 estimates for these countries are for the years 1900–1901 and the 1910 estimates are for 1912–1913. Colombia and Venezuela, 1930: Santiago Marín Vicuña, *Política Ferroviaria de la América* (Santiago, Chile: Imprenta Universitaria, 1927), p. 115. The mileage shown is for 1927 or an earlier year. U. S. and South American countries, 1870–1940: *Directory of Railway Officials & Year Book, 1962–1963* (Westminster, England: Tothill Press, Ltd., 1962), pp. 560–66. South American countries 1950–1960: U. N. Economic Commission for Latin America, *Los Transportes en América Latina,* E/CN. 12/673 (March 25, 1963), p. 7. U. N. Economic Commission for Latin America, *Estudio Económico de América Latina, 1963,* E/CN. 12/696/Rev. 1 (1964), p. 104, Table 80.

Section of Highway	1938				1963				
	Total Length	All Weather	Dry Weather	In Construction	Total Length	Paved	All Weather	Dry Weather	Impassable
Venezuela to Colombia									
La Guaira—Caracas	22	22	—	—	11	11	—	—	—
Caracas—Valencia	99	99	—	—	96	96	—	—	—
Valencia—Barquisimeto	136	136	—	—	116	116	—	—	—
Barquisimeto—border	507	507	—	—	360	360	—	—	—
Across Colombia to Ecuador									
Colombia/Venezuela border— Pamplona	56	56	—	—	48	48	—	—	—
Pamplona—Tunja	233	233	—	—	252	168	84	—	—
Tunja—Bogotá	97	97	—	—	85	70	15	—	—
Bogotá—Calarca	192	157	—	35	176	176	—	—	—
Calarca—Palmira	118	118	—	—	112	112	—	—	—
Palmira—Pasto	286	261	—	25	280	31	249	—	—
Pasto—Rumichaca (Colombia/Ecuador border)	79	79	—	—	60	—	60	—	—
Bogotá to Panama border									
Bogotá—Manizales	201	178	—	23	191	167	24	—	—
Manizales—border	416	250	—	166	442	—	15	—	427
Cauya to Murillo	93	93	—	—	—	—	—	—	—
Across Ecuador to Peru									
Rumichaca—Ibarra	82	82	—	—	82	—	82	—	—
Ibarra—Quito	82	82	—	—	85	—	85	—	—
Quito—Alausi	179	161	—	18	170	56	114	—	—
Alausi—Macara (Ecuador/ Peru border)	376	110	—	266	384	—	384	—	—
Across Peru to Chile									
La Tina (Ecuador/Peru border)—Chiclayo	316	54	262	—	268	268	—	—	—
Chiclayo—Lima	574	175	399	—	468	468	—	—	—
Lima—Nazca	323	227	96	—	292	292	—	—	—
Nazca—Concordia (Peru/ Chile border)	658	—	615	43	574	484	90	—	—
Nazca to Bolivia border									
Nazca—Desaguerdero (Peru/ Bolivia border)	757	626	54	77	634	357	277	—	—
Peru/Chile border to Puerto Montt, Chile									
Border—Arica	13	13	—	—	12	12	—	—	—
Arica—Zapiga	130	50	80	—	126	8	118	—	—
Zapiga—Antofagasta	347	189	158	—	328	103	225	—	—
Antofagasta—Santiago	1,008	345	663	—	859	338	426	95	—
Santiago—Puerto Montt	—	—	—	—	661	518	143	—	—
Zapiga to La Paz									
Zapiga—Chinchillani (Chile/ Bolivia border)	116	—	90	26	—	—	—	—	—
Chinchillani—La Paz	295	196	56	43	—	—	—	—	—
Peru/Bolivia border to La Paz									
Desaguadero—La Paz	68	68	—	—	71	6	65	—	—
La Paz to Rio de Janeiro									
La Paz—Puerto Suarez (Bolivia/Brazil border)	1,025	482	419	124	—	—	—	—	—
Corumba (Bolivia/Brazil border)—Rio de Janeiro	1,312	536	776	—	—	—	—	—	—

Section of Highway	1938				1963				
	Total Length	All Weather	Dry Weather	In Construction	Total Length	Paved	All Weather	Dry Weather	Impassable
La Paz to Asuncion									
La Paz—Esmeralda (Bolivia/ Paraguay border)	878	754	124	—	—	—	—	—	—
Esmeralda—Asuncion	410	224	—	186	—	—	—	—	—
La Paz to Buenos Aires									
La Paz—Villazon (Bolivia/ Argentina border)	—	—	—	—	584	—	511	73	—
La Quiaca (Argentina/Bolivia border)—Cordoba	—	—	—	—	796	448	273	75	—
Cordoba—Rosario	253	253	—	—	251	251	—	—	—
Rosario—Buenos Aires	222	222	—	—	192	192	—	—	—
La Paz—Yacuiba (Bolivia/ Argentina border)	820	806	—	14	—	—	—	—	—
Yacuiba—Cordoba	894	544	350	—	—	—	—	—	—
Santiago to Buenos Aires									
Santiago—Cristo Redentor (Chile/Argentina border)	97	97	—	—	108	38	45	25	—
Cristo Redentor—San Luis	296	296	—	—	295	228	67	—	—
San Luis—Buenos Aires	510	131	379	—	519	519	—	—	—
Buenos Aires to Asuncion									
Rosario—Santa Fe	99	99	—	—	103	103	—	—	—
Santa Fe—Puerto Pilcomayo (Argentina/Paraguay border)	655	78	570	7	547	201	—	346	—
La Enramada (Argentina/ Paraguay border)— Asuncion	7	—	7	—	5	—	5	—	—
Asuncion to Brasília									
Asuncion—Rio Parana (Paraguay/Brazil border)	223	—	94	129	203	45	37	121	—
Foz de Iguacu—Curitiba	524	—	524	—	437	41	396	—	—
Curitiba—São Paulo	308	308	—	—	250	250	—	—	—
São Paulo—Rio de Janeiro	312	312	—	—	268	268	—	—	—
Rio de Janeiro—Belo Horizonte	—	—	—	—	292	292	—	—	—
Belo Horizonte—Brasília	—	—	—	—	450	450	—	—	—
Rio de Janeiro to Buenos Aires									
Curitiba—Pôrto Alegre	574	324	250	—	448	448	—	—	—
Pôrto Alegre—Uruguaiana (Argentina/Brazil border)	437	437	—	—	443	—	443	—	—
Paso de los Libres (Brazil/ Argentina border)— Santa Fe	—	—	—	—	302	81	116	105	—
Paso de los Libres—Buenos Aires	502	37	465	—	—	—	—	—	—
Rio de Janeiro to Montevideo									
Pôrto Alegre—Jajuaro (Brazil/Uruguay border)	274	274	—	—	238	114	124	—	—
Rio Branco (Uruguay/Brazil border)—Montevideo	284	206	78	—	255	104	141	10	—
Montevideo to Colonia (across River Plate from Buenos Aires)	110	110	—	—	110	110	—	—	—

Sources: 1938, Carlos P. Anesi, *La Carretera Panamericana* (Buenos Aires: Compania General Fabril Financiera, 1938); 1963, Pan American Union, *The Pan American Highway System* (Pan American Union, 1963).

TABLE A-4. *Passenger Kilometers Performed by Scheduled South American Airlines Reporting to ICAO*

(Thousands)

Country	1951	1953	1955	1957	1959	1961	1963
Argentina							
Domestic	178,531	155,966	204,773	319,960	320,001	446,654	422,747
International	125,944	160,663	166,641	198,281	354,219	684,112	457,942
Total	304,475	316,628	371,414	518,241	674,220	1,130,766	880,689
Brazil							
Domestic	1,062,861	1,278,934	1,411,679	1,923,447	2,160,413	1,958,601	2,288,453
International	176,844	203,709	272,708	366,049	438,710	657,382	788,397
Total	1,239,705	1,482,643	1,684,387	2,289,496	2,599,123	2,615,983	3,076,850
Uruguay[a]							
Domestic	—	—	13,340	14,107	14,887	15,980	15,865
International	—	—	15,310	19,626	44,176	63,432	41,800
Total	—	—	28,650	33,733	59,063	79,412	57,665
Paraguay							
Domestic	—	—	—	8,250	9,850	9,550	9,250
International	—	—	—	—	—	2,700	7,325
Total	—	—	—	8,250	9,850	12,250	16,575
Chile							
Domestic	48,727	84,671	117,971	307,684	182,878	289,321	280,425
International	17,034	10,611	38,269[b]	130,500	138,506	137,786	101,592
Total	65,761	95,282	156,240	438,184	321,384	427,107	382,017
Bolivia							
Domestic	22,126	26,874	45,557	31,380	31,800	37,429	28,499
International	—	1,715	1,900	1,970	2,040	13,320	14,033
Total	22,126	28,589	47,457	33,350	33,840	50,749	42,532
Peru							
Domestic	62,152	78,519	91,325	103,977	99,750	96,660	96,420
International	9,874	—	1,255	9,000	27,500	89,720	104,640[c]
Total	72,026	78,519	92,580	112,977	127,250	186,380	201,060
Colombia							
Domestic	269,732	302,423	339,363	444,163	490,271	624,897	923,054
International	51,595	112,980	144,915	171,000	190,320	198,863	281,793
Total	321,327	415,403	484,278	615,163	680,591	823,760	1,204,847

Source: International Civil Aviation Organization, "Traffic 1947–1961," *Digest of Statistics No. 90*, pp. 76–99; and "Traffic 1960–1963," *Digest of Statistics No. 106*, pp. 70, 74.

[a] Became a member of ICAO in 1954.

[b] Línea Aérea Nacional only.

[c] Includes non-scheduled flights.

	1951	1953	1955	1957	1959	1961	1963
Venezuela							
Domestic	150,402	175,996	198,845	220,051	264,430	212,417	209,298
International	66,262	92,532	126,629	89,015	143,309	126,722	251,329
Total	216,664	268,528	325,474	309,066	407,739	339,139	460,627
Ecuador[a]							
Domestic	—	—	7,600	9,000	22,727	24,340	25,820
International	—	—	—	820	16,667[d]	19,245	17,670
Total	—	—	7,600	9,820	39,394	43,585	43,490
South America							
Domestic	1,794,531	2,103,383	2,430,453	3,382,019	3,597,007	3,715,849	4,299,831
International	447,553	582,210	767,627	986,261	1,355,447	1,993,282	2,066,521
Total	2,242,084	2,685,592	3,198,080	4,368,280	4,952,454	5,709,131	6,366,352

[d] Includes a small amount of domestic operations.

TABLE A-5. *Freight Carried by Scheduled South American Airlines Reporting to ICAO*

(Thousands of ton–kilometers)

Country	1951	1953	1955	1957	1959	1961	1963
Argentina							
Domestic	1,242	1,549	1,465	2,374	3,418	5,096	3,371
International	1,886	2,161	1,303	3,661	4,353	7,704	4,310
Total	3,128	3,710	2,768	6,035	7,771	12,800	7,681
Brazil							
Domestic	43,562[a]	47,509[a]	56,468[a]	69,939	78,310	74,023	90,568
International	2,750[a]	2,479[a]	3,306[a]	3,061	6,742	12,024	20,042
Total	46,312	49,979	59,774	73,000	85,052	86,047	110,610
Uruguay[b]							
Domestic	—	—	75	110	180	140	60
International	—	—	40	239	82	120	495
Total	—	—	115	349	262	260	555
Paraguay							
Domestic	d	d	d	600[c]	710[c]	690	625
International	d	d	d	d	d	50	70
Total	—	—	—	600	710	740	695
Chile							
Domestic	693[a]	1,386[a]	1,290[a,e]	8,245[a]	3,598	5,744	16,296
International	51[a]	58[a]	132[a,e]	2,100[a]	1,253	8,164	3,832
Total	744	1,444	1,422	10,345	4,851	13,908	20,128
Bolivia							
Domestic	2,440[c]	2,970[c]	4,760[c]	2,280[c]	2,560[c]	5,200[c]	1,321
International	—	300[c]	350[c]	260[c]	275[c]	600[c]	442
Total	2,440	3,270	5,110	2,540	2,835	5,800	1,763
Peru							
Domestic	4,536[a,c]	4,980[a,c]	5,250[a,c]	6,030[a,c]	6,600[a,c]	6,390[a,c]	4,895
International	220[a,c]	—	25[a,c]	200[a,c]	550[a,c]	800[a,c]	895[a]
Total	4,756	4,980	5,275	6,230	7,150	7,190	5,790
Colombia							
Domestic	66,607[a,c]	53,487[a,c]	44,501[a,c]	42,434[a,c]	40,996[a,c]	35,040	36,520
International	712[a]	2,276[a]	12,647[a]	10,000[a]	8,000[a]	5,941	8,633
Total	67,319	55,763	57,148	52,434	48,996	40,981	45,153

Sources: 1951–61, ICAO, "Traffic 1947–1961," *Digest of Statistics No. 90*, pp. 76–87; 1962–63, ICAO, "Draft Report on Study of Air Freight in the Latin American Region," AT-WP/811 (Jan. 28, 1965), App. 5.

[a] Includes non-scheduled flights.
[b] Became a member of ICAO in 1954.
[c] Includes excess baggage.
[d] Category not applicable.
[e] LAN only.

	1951	1953	1955	1957	1959	1961	1963
Venezuela							
Domestic	6,354[c]	5,755[c]	5,169[f]	5,132[c]	4,877	4,350	5,171
International	1,950[c]	1,546[c]	5,348[f]	7,434[c]	8,353	18,031	30,328
Total	8,304	7,301	10,517	12,566	13,230	22,381	35,499
Ecuador[b]							
Domestic	—	—	110[c]	130[c]	640	700[c]	695
International	—	—	d	10[c]	257[g]	300[c]	260
Total	—	—	110	140	897	1,000	955
Total							
Domestic	125,434	117,636	119,088	137,274	141,889	137,373	159,522
International	7,569	8,811	23,151	26,965	29,865	53,734	69,307
Total	133,003	126,447	142,239	164,239	171,754	191,107	228,829

[f] Includes mail.
[g] Includes a small amount of domestic operations.

Methodological Note on Population Projections

Population projections have a notorious tradition of going astray, even in countries like the United States where the underlying data are excellent. In South America, where the data are poor, and key variables shift abruptly and unexpectedly from one census to the next, projections are primarily educated guesses. The importance of the projections is so great, however, that they must be made, and all that users of the data can do is to consider explicitly the impact of possible wide divergences between the projections and reality. Tables B-1 and B-2 present estimates made by different agencies of the United Nations, at different times, of population in 1960 and of pro-

TABLE B-1. *Population of South America, 1960*

(Thousands)

Country	Estimates of Population in 1960 Made by				
	United Nations 1955[a]			ECLA 1962[b]	U. N. 1964[c]
	Low	Medium	High		
Argentina	19,602	20,036	20,470	20,956	20,956
Brazil	64,532	66,085	66,085	70,600	70,459
Uruguay	2,668	2,717	2,768	2,827	2,491
Paraguay	1,828	1,874	1,923	1,768	1,720
Chile	6,822	6,867	6,958	7,627	7,627
Bolivia	3,784	3,876	3,876	3,696	3,696
Peru	10,912	11,190	11,190	10,857	10,199
Colombia	14,941	15,324	15,324	15,468	15,468
Venezuela	6,509	6,669	6,669	7,331	7,394
Ecuador	4,057	4,160	4,160	4,317	4,355
Total	135,655	138,798	139,423	145,447	144,365

[a] U. N. Bureau of Social Affairs, Population Branch, *The Population of South America, 1950–1980*, ST/SOA/ Series A, Population Studies No. 21 (1955), pp. 51–63. Jungle population excluded in Peru and tribal Indians excluded in Venezuela.

[b] U. N. Economic Commission for Latin America, *Boletín Económico de América Latina*, Vol. VII, No. 1 (October 1962), p. 6, Table 3. Mid-year estimates. Jungle population included in Peru, Bolivia, Colombia, and Paraguay. Jungle population excluded in Brazil, Ecuador, Venezuela.

[c] U. N. Department of Economic and Social Affairs, *Provisional Report on World Population Prospects, as Assessed in 1963*, ST/SOA/Series R/7 (New York, 1964), p. 244, Table 14.2, and p. 261, Table 14.11. Jungle population included in Brazil (150,000), Peru (455,000), Venezuela (30,000), and Ecuador (80,000).

TABLE B-2. *Population of South America, 1980*

Country	Population Projection to 1980 Made by					
	United Nations, 1955[a]			ECLA, 1961[d]	ECLA, 1962[b]	U. N., 1964[c]
	Low	Medium	High			
Argentina	24,638	26,250	27,885	29,334	29,334	28,998
Brazil	98,311	105,527	113,402	107,902	126,800	123,716
Uruguay	3,040	3,212	3,386	3,355	3,355	3,126
Paraguay	2,797	3,212	3,727	3,065	3,065	2,981
Chile	9,092	9,879	10,235	12,300	12,300	12,378
Bolivia	6,158	6,627	7,147	6,000	6,000	6,000
Peru	18,896	20,370	21,992	20,371	20,371	17,500
Colombia	25,438	27,388	29,514	26,573	27,691	27,691
Venezuela	10,678	11,476	12,338	12,400	13,355	14,857
Ecuador	6,662	7,174	7,733	7,834	8,080	7,981
Total	205,710	221,115	237,359	229,134	250,351	245,228

[a] U. N. Bureau of Social Affairs, Population Branch, *The Population of South America, 1950–1980,* ST/SOA/ Series A, Population Studies No. 21 (1955), pp. 51–63. Jungle population excluded in Peru and tribal Indians excluded in Venezuela.

[b] U. N. Economic Commission for Latin America, *Boletín Económico de América Latina,* Vol. VII, No. 1 (October 1962), p. 6, Table 3. Mid-year estimates. Jungle population included in Peru, Bolivia, Colombia, and Paraguay. Jungle population excluded in Brazil, Ecuador, Venezuela, and Uruguay.

[c] U. N. Department of Economic and Social Affairs, *Provisional Report on World Population Prospects, as Assessed in 1963,* ST/SOA/Series R/7 (New York, 1964), p. 244, Table 14.2, and p. 261, Table 14.11. Jungle population included in Brazil (150,000), Peru (455,000), Venezuela (30,000), and Ecuador (80,000).

[d] U.N. Economic Commission for Latin America, *Boletín Económico de América Latina,* Vol. VI, Suplemento Estadístico (November 1961), p. 6, Table 2. Mid-year estimates. Jungle population included in Colombia, Paraguay, and Peru. Jungle population excluded in Brazil (45,000), Ecuador (39,000), and Venezuela (57,000).

jected population in 1980 in the South American countries. The upward adjustment in the estimate of Brazil's population in 1980 between the projection made in 1961 by the Economic Commission for Latin America (108 million) and the projection in 1962 by the same agency when Brazil's 1960 census became available (127 million) is especially dramatic.

For the purposes of the present study, projections are necessary not only by country in 1980 but also by region, using the regional classification of South America delineated in Chapter II. For the instances where country and regional boundaries coincide, no additional problem arises beyond that of selecting which estimate for 1980 to use. Here the latest estimate available, that of the United Nations published in 1964,[1] was used for both the estimate of the population in

[1] *U.N. Provisional Report on World Population Prospects, as Assessed in 1963,* ST/SOA/Series R/7 (New York, 1964).

TABLE B-3. *Population of Argentina, 1947, 1960, 1980*[a]

(Thousands)

Provinces	Population 1947	Population 1960	Rate of Increase 1947–60 (Percent)	Rate Used in Projection to 1980 (Percent)	Population 1980
Region I					
Federal District	2,981	2,967	negative	constant	2,967
Buenos Aires					
Metropolitan	2,709	4,157	3.35	3.2	7,805
Other	1,565	2,577	3.91	3.7	5,330
Santa Fe					
Metropolitan	656	803	1.56	1.5	1,081
Other	767	779	0.12	0.1	795
Subtotal	8,678	11,283			17,978
Region II					
Santa Fe other	280	284	0.12	0.1	290
Catamarca	147	172	1.22	1.2	219
Cordoba	1,498	1,760	1.25	1.2	2,234
Corrientes	526	543	0.26	0.2	565
Chaco	431	535	1.69	1.6	735
Chubut	92	142	3.37	3.2	267
Entre Rios	787	804	0.16	0.2	836
Formosa	114	179	3.52	3.3	342
Jujuy	167	240	2.84	2.7	409
La Pampa	169	158	negative	constant	158
La Rioja	111	128	1.14	1.1	160
Mendoza	588	826	2.64	2.5	1,353
Misiones	246	391	3.62	3.4	763
Neuquen	87	111	1.91	1.8	159
Rio Negro	134	193	2.81	2.7	328
Salta	291	413	2.73	2.6	689
San Juan	261	353	2.33	2.2	545
San Luis	166	174	0.40	0.4	189
Santa Cruz	43	53	1.62	1.5	71
Santiago del Estero	480	477	negative	constant	477
Tucuman	593	780	2.13	2.0	1,160
Territories	8	10	1.64	1.5	14
Subtotal	7,219	8,726			11,963
Total	15,897	20,009			29,941

Source: Dirección Nacional de Estadística y Censos, *Censo Nacional de 1960. Población. Resultados Provisionales* (Buenos Aires, 1961), pp. 12, 142–47, and Presidencia de la Nación, *IV Censo General de la Nación* (Buenos Aires, 1947), Tomo I, pp. 69–71.

[a] The rate of increase used in the projection to 1980 was calculated by taking 17/18 of the historical rate from 1947 to 1960. The data are based on the provisional census estimates which refer to population found present in each area on the day of the census, regardless of where their legal residence might be.

1960 as well as for the projection to 1980. The relationship of this 1964 estimate to earlier estimates can be seen in Tables B-1 and B-2.

Where country and regional boundaries do not coincide, as is the case in Argentina, Bolivia, Brazil, and Peru, it was necessary to estimate the population in each of the regions within each country. Again the 1964 United Nations estimates were used for both the population in 1960 and the total country projection to 1980. The methodology used in each country was not the same and so will be described country by country.

Argentina

The part of Argentina which was defined as falling in Region I is composed of the Federal District, the Province of Buenos Aires, and the following districts in the Province of Santa Fe: Belgrano, Caseros, Castellanos, Constitucion, General Lopez, Iriondo, La Capital, Las Colonias, Rosario, San Jeronimo, San Lorenzo, and San Martin. The remaining districts (*departamentos*) of Santa Fe and the other provinces were defined as composing that part of Argentina which falls in Region II.

Using the 1947 census and the preliminary results of the 1960 census, the annual compound rate of increase was calculated between the two census years for each province. The results can be seen in Table B-3. As it was believed that the Argentine population would not grow as rapidly between 1960 and 1980 as it had between 1947 and 1960, the historical rates of increase were reduced slightly by multiplying the historical annual rates by 17/18. This resulted in a projected total population of Argentina for 1980 below the 1964 United Nations estimate at the same time that the sum of the projected provincial totals was larger than the United Nations projection. Furthermore, the 1964 United Nations estimate of Argentina's population in 1960 was in excess of the provisional results of the 1960 census. In order to adjust for these differences, the Region I and II totals for 1960 were increased by 4.73 percent and the projections for 1980 shown in Table B-3 were reduced by 3.15 percent. In this way, the sum of the projected provincial estimates was made to correspond to the United Nations estimate used in Table 5-1.

Bolivia

Parts of Bolivia fall into three of the nine regions into which South America has been divided in this study. The district (departamento) of Santa Cruz lies in Region II, the districts of La Paz, Cochabamba, Oruro, Chuquisaca, Potosí, and Tarija in Region IV, and the districts of Pando and Beni in Region V.

The United Nations estimate of the population of Bolivia in 1960 and the projection to 1980 are subject to such a wide margin of error that little is gained by using an elaborate method to distribute the national totals by region. According to one recent source,[2] the population by region of Bolivia in 1961, and the estimated annual increase were as follows:

	Population 1961 (Thousands)	Rate of Increase (Percent)
Region II		
Santa Cruz	314.3	1.41
Region IV		
La Paz	1,140.0	2.13
Cochabamba	545.9	1.38
Oruro	260.7	1.85
Chuquisaca	315.4	1.48
Potosí	609.2	1.88
Tarija	141.5	1.00
Subtotal	3,012.7	1.80
Region V		
Pando	24.0	1.54
Beni	157.7	1.67
Subtotal	181.7	1.65
Total	3,508.7	

The estimate of the total population for 1961 is less than the United Nations estimate for 1960, which is 3,696 thousand. Assuming that the *regional* distribution in 1961 shown above is reasonably correct and that it was approximately the same in 1960, and assuming that the United Nations total estimate is approximately correct, the regional

[2] Harold Osborne, *Bolivia: A Land Divided* (London: Oxford University Press, 1964), p. 105.

population in 1960 would be:

Region II	333,000
Region IV	3,175,000
Region V	188,000
Total	3,696,000

If the 1960 regional population is projected to 1980 using the rate of increase in each region shown above, the total will not reach the 6 million predicted population estimated by the United Nations. It is therefore necessary to increase each of the regional growth rates in order to make the total 1980 population projection coincide with the United Nations estimate. It is assumed that the three regional growth rates should be increased proportionately, by slightly more than 40 percent. When this is done, the 1980 regional projection is as follows:

	Population in 1960 (Thousands)	Rate of Increase (Percent)	Crude Projection (Thousands)	Adjusted Projection (Thousands)
Region II	333	2.0000	495	490
Region IV	3,175	2.5625	5,266	5,212
Region V	188	2.3750	301	298
Total	3,696	2.5000	6,062	6,000

Brazil

The methodology followed to distribute the population of Brazil in 1960 and 1980 among the four regions into which it is divided in this study is similar to that used in the case of Argentina. The provisional results of the 1960 census published by the Brazilian government included the population of each state in 1950, 1960, and a projected rate of increase to 1970. The rate of projection used by the Brazilians was simply extended to 1980 in Table B-4. It was necessary, however, to adjust both the 1960 and 1980 figures in that table to make the totals coincide with the United Nations estimates. This was done by reducing the 1960 figures by 0.72 percent and the 1980 projection by 8.36 percent. The results by region are shown in Table 5-1.

TABLE B-4. *Population of Brazil, 1950, 1960, 1980*[a]

(Thousands)

States	Population 1950	Population 1960	Rate of Increase 1950–60 (Percent)	Rate Used in Projection to 1980 (Percent)	Population 1980
Region I					
Minas Gerais	7,718	9,799	2.4	2.2	15,249
Serra dos Aimores	160	384	9.2	8.9	2,103
Espirito Santo	862	1,189	3.3	3.1	2,186
Rio de Janeiro	2,297	3,403	4.0	3.8	7,192
Guanabara	2,377	3,307	3.4	3.1	6,118
São Paulo	9,134	12,975	3.6	3.4	25,256
Parana	2,116	4,278	7.3	7.1	16,818
Santa Catarina	1,561	2,147	3.2	3.1	3,958
Subtotal	26,225	37,482			78,880
Region II					
Rio Grande do Sul	4,165	5,449	2.7	2.6	9,029
Mato Grosso	522	910	5.7	5.5	2,646
Goias	1,215	1,955	4.9	4.6	4,837
Distrito Federal	—	142	—	—	—
Subtotal	5,902	8,456			16,512
Region VIII					
Rondonia	37	71	6.7	6.4	246
Acre	115	160	3.4	3.2	299
Amazonas	514	721	3.4	3.2	1,348
Rio Branco	18	29	5.0	4.8	75
Para	1,123	1,551	3.3	3.1	2,830
Amapa	37	69	6.3	6.0	220
Subtotal	1,844	2,601			5,018
Region IX					
Maranhão	1,583	2,492	4.6	4.4	5,945
Piaui	1,046	1,263	1.9	1.7	1,767
Ceara	2,695	3,338	2.2	2.0	4,943
Rio Grande do Norte	968	1,157	1.8	1.6	1,594
Paraiba	1,713	2,018	1.7	1.5	2,734
Pernambuco	3,395	4,137	2.0	1.9	5,978
Alagoas	1,093	1,271	1.5	1.4	1,672
Fernando de Noronha	1	1	9.1	8.0	6
Sergipe	644	760	1.7	1.6	1,035
Bahia	4,835	5,991	2.2	2.0	8,918
Subtotal	17,973	22,428			34,592
Total	51,944	70,967			135,002

Source: I. B. G. E., Servicio Nacional de Recenseamento, *Sinopse Preliminar do Censo Demografico* (Rio de Janeiro, 1962), pp. 8–9.

[a] Data do not include unregistered Indian population in inaccessible areas.

244

Peru

Two of Peru's 24 districts, Lareto and Madre de Dios, are classified as falling into Region V, the eastern slope of the Andes. The other 22 districts are in Region IV, the coastal and highland areas of Peru and Bolivia. On the basis of the 1940 and 1960 census data giving the population of each district, a weighted annual rate of increase was calculated for each region for the period 1940-60. The rates are 2.55 percent for Region IV and 3.63 percent for Region V, and when these are used to project the regional population according to the 1960 census to the year 1980, the projected population is:

Region IV	16,560,000
Region V	890,000
Total	17,450,000

Although the total projected population for 1980 is nearly identical to the United Nations projected estimate shown in Table 5-1, 17,500 thousand, the difference is larger between the 1960 census estimates of population in that year and the figure given by the United Nations. The census figure is 10,420 thousand, which includes jungle population of 101 thousand and estimated omitted population of 413 thousand. The United Nations figure is 10,199 thousand, which includes an estimated jungle population of 455,000. In order to make both the 1960 and 1980 figures coincide with the United Nations figures, the 1960 population was reduced by 2.12 percent and the 1980 projection was increased by 0.29 percent. The results are shown in Table 5-1.

Data on Ocean Freight Rates

An attempt has been made to collect a group of representative freight rates both within the LAFTA area and between this area and the United States, Europe, and Japan. The results are presented in Tables C-1 through C-5. Before these results can be analyzed, however, it is essential to understand how the tables were prepared.

TABLE C-1. *Ocean Freight Rates to Callao, Peru, from Selected Ports, circa 1964*[a]

(Dollars per metric ton or per cubic meter)

		U. S. Atlantic- New York,	U. S. Pacific-San Francisco	Valparaiso	Buenos Aires	Monte- video	Rio de Janeiro
Distance (naut. miles)		3368 p	4595	1306	4065	3971	4909
Automobiles unboxed	C.M.	29.15	31.80	18.00	22.00	29.00	30.00
Automobile spare parts	C.M.	29.15	28.27	18.00	21.50	24.50	25.50
Tractors unboxed	C.M.	42.40	40.64	18.00	25.00	28.50	30.00
Radio & TV sets	C.M.	56.54	81.27	20.00	24.00	27.00	28.00
Refrigerators	C.M.	38.87	53.89	20.00	24.00	27.00	28.00
Steel plates	Ton	34.17	35.27		12.50	14.00	16.50
Steel bars	Ton	35.27	35.27		19.00	21.00	21.00
Copper cable	Ton	72.75[b]	79.37[c]	16.00	25.50	27.50	27.50
Newsprint	Ton	35.27	35.27	17.30	26.30	26.30	26.30
Wood pulp	Ton	27.56[d]	29.76[e]	14.00	22.00	22.00	22.00
Plate glass	Ton	49.60	65.04[f]	23.00	23.00	29.00	32.00
Wheat in bags	Ton	28.66		16.00	19.00	22.50	26.00
Canned fruit	Ton	76.06	70.55	19.00	25.00	28.00	31.00
Merchandise n.o.s.	C.M./Ton			32.00	30.00	34.00	40.00

Source: See text.

[a] Rates do not include port surcharges. "p" indicates distance via Panama Canal.

[b] Bare cable. Insulated is $83.78.

[c] Bare cable. Insulated is $90.39.

[d] Not more than 40 cubic feet per 2,000 pounds.

[e] More than 40 but less than 45 cu. ft. per 2,000 pounds.

[f] Not more than 1 square yard.

1. Different sources were necessarily used to obtain rates over different routes. The rates from U. S. ports to the five South American ports selected were taken from conference tariffs on file with the Federal Maritime Commission in Washington. The rates from European and Japanese ports to Valparaiso, Chile, and Rio de Janeiro, Brazil, were taken from hearings before the Joint Economic Committee

of the United States Congress.[1] The rates from Buenaventura, Colombia, and Guayaquil, Ecuador, to Buenos Aires, Montevideo, and Rio de Janeiro are included in tariffs on file with the Federal Maritime Commission. The rates from Buenos Aires to Rio de Janeiro are from the tariff published by the Argentina–Brazil Maritime Shipping Con-

TABLE C-2. *Ocean Freight Rates to Valparaiso, Chile, from Selected Ports, circa 1964*[a]

(Dollars per metric ton or per cubic meter)

		Tokyo-Yokohama	Callao	U.S. Pacific-San Francisco	U.S. Atlantic-New York	Buenos Aires	Montevideo	Rio de Janeiro	London	Rotterdam
Distance (naut. miles)		9280	1306	5861	4633 p	2826	2732	3670	7399 p	7445 p
Automobiles unboxed	C.M.	26.50	18.00	31.80	29.15	23.00	26.00	27.00	22.76	22.71
Automobile spare parts	C.M.		18.00	28.27	29.15	18.50	21.50	22.50		
Tractors, unboxed	C.M.	45.72	18.00	40.64	42.40	23.00	26.00	27.00	33.39	39.58
Radio & TV sets	C.M.	44.17	20.00	78.62	56.54	21.00	24.00	25.00	50.09	47.65
Refrigerators	C.M.		20.00	53.89	38.87	21.00	24.00	25.00	35.07	39.58
Steel plates	Ton	28.54		35.27	35.27	16.50	19.00	18.50	39.27	35.14
Steel bars	Ton	28.54		35.27	35.27	14.50	17.50	18.00	37.20	37.95
Copper cable	Ton		16.00	76.06[b]	72.75[c]	22.50	24.50	24.50		
Newsprint	Ton	35.43	17.30	35.27	35.27	21.30	23.50	19.00	29.43	35.14
Woodpulp	Ton		14.00	29.76[d]	27.56[e]	16.85	18.85	16.35		
Plate glass	Ton		23.00	61.73[f]	49.60[f]	23.00	26.00	29.00		
Wheat in bags	Ton		16.00		28.66	16.00	19.50	23.00		
Canned fruits	Ton		19.00	70.55	76.06	22.00	25.00	28.00		
Merchandise n.o.s.	C.M./Ton		32.00			23.00	26.00	29.00		

Source: See text.

[a] Rates do not include port surcharges. "p" indicates distance via Panama Canal.

[b] Bare cable. Insulated is $87.08.

[c] Bare cable. Insulated is $83.78.

[d] More than 40 but less than 45 cubic feet per 2,000 pounds.

[e] Not more than 40 cubic feet per 2,000 pounds.

[f] Not more than 1 square yard.

ference. The rates between Valparaiso and Buenos Aires, and vice versa, are from the tariff published by the Argentina–Chile Maritime Shipping Conference. The remaining intra-South American rates are taken from the tariff published by a South American shipping company which provides liner service within the LAFTA area.

2. Nearly all the rates correspond to the first half of 1964. A few are for an earlier period.

3. There is no way of knowing whether shippers in fact pay the

[1] *Discriminatory Ocean Freight Rates and the Balance of Payments*, Hearings before the Joint Economic Committee, 88 Cong. 1 sess. (1964), Pt. 3, pp. 341-43.

published rates. Although the rates quoted between U. S. ports and South American ports are probably accurate, it is possible that rates paid between Buenos Aires and Rio de Janeiro are less than those shown here. The rates quoted by the South American shipping company providing regular service within the LAFTA area are probably less than the rates charged by foreign liners operating in the same region which provide a more rapid service.

TABLE C-3. *Ocean Freight Rates to Buenos Aires, Argentina, from Selected Ports, circa 1964*[a]

(Dollars per metric ton or per cubic meter)

		Buena-ventura	Guaya-quil	Callao	Valpa-raiso	U. S. Atlantic-New York	U. S. Pacific-San Francisco
Distance (naut. miles)		5279	4701	4065	2826	5871	8748 p
Automobiles, unboxed	C.M.			25.00	23.00	24.59[b]	42.84
Automobile spare parts	C.M.			21.50	18.50	32.69	37.54
Tractors, unboxed	C.M.			25.00	23.00	31.80	31.80
Radio & TV sets	C.M.			24.00	21.00	63.60	63.60
Refrigerators	C.M.			24.00	21.00	43.29	43.29
Steel plates	Ton			12.50	16.50	24.61	26.46
Steel bars	Ton			19.00	14.50	29.53	24.80
Copper cable	Ton			25.50	22.50	59.05	66.14
Newsprint	Ton			26.30	19.00	26.57	32.52
Wood pulp	Ton			22.00	16.85	26.08[c]	35.27[d]
Plate glass	Ton			23.00	23.00	35.43	
Wheat in bags	Ton			19.00	16.00	33.46	44.09
Canned fruits	Ton			25.00	22.00	64.96	77.16
Merchandise n.o.s.	C.M.	68.90	70.67	30.00	23.00		
	Ton	85.98	88.18	30.00	30.00		

Source: See text.

[a] Rates do not include port surcharges. "p" indicates distance via Panama Canal.

[b] KD or SU.

[c] Not more than 55 cubic feet per 2,240 pounds.

[d] Not more than 80 cubic feet per 2,000 pounds.

4. The products selected were chosen arbitrarily on the basis of the rates that were available and so as to include products with a wide variation in unit value. Even though a rate is shown for a particular route, it does not necessarily follow that goods are traded, that is, some of the rates may be merely "paper rates," subject to reduction should potential traffic emerge. Great care was taken to assure that identical products were selected for each route. Exceptions are shown in the footnotes to the table.

5. The rates shown in Tables C-1–C-5 do not include port surcharges, which are common in South America. The port surcharges

which were encountered in the sources used are shown separately in Table C-6 as these are subject to frequent change. To the extent that port surcharges have been incorporated into the published rates in some instances, and have been kept apart in others, the rates over different routes shown in Tables C-1–C-5 are not comparable.

6. Since some of the rates quoted in the original sources were based on short or long tons and on cubic feet, a conversion was made to

TABLE C-4. *Ocean Freight Rates to Montevideo, Uruguay, from Selected Ports, circa 1964*[a]

(Dollars per metric ton or per cubic meter)

		Buena-ventura	Guaya-quil	Callao	Valpa-raiso	U. S. Atlantic-New York	U. S. Pacific-San Francisco
Distance (naut. miles)		5185	4607	3971	2732	5749	8624 p
Automobiles, unboxed	C.M.			29.00	26.00	24.29[b]	42.84
Automobile spare parts	C.M.			24.50	21.50	32.69	37.54
Tractors, unboxed	C.M.			28.50	26.00	31.80	31.80
Radio & TV sets	C.M.			27.00	24.00	63.60	63.60
Refrigerators	C.M.			27.00	24.00	43.29	43.29
Steel plates	Ton			14.00	19.00	24.61	26.46
Steel bars	Ton			21.00	17.50	29.53	24.80
Copper cable	Ton			27.50	24.50	59.05	66.14
Newsprint	Ton			26.30	23.50	26.57	32.52
Wood pulp	Ton			22.00	18.85	26.08[c]	35.27[d]
Plate glass	Ton			29.00	26.00	35.43	
Wheat in bags	Ton			22.50	19.30	33.40	44.09
Canned fruit	Ton			28.00	25.00	64.96	77.16
Merchandise n.o.s.	C.M.	68.90	70.67	34.00	26.00		
	Ton	85.98	88.18	34.00	26.00		

Source: See text.
[a] Rates do not include port surcharges. "p" indicates distance via Panama Canal.
[b] KD or SU.
[c] Not more than 55 cubic feet per 2,240 pounds.
[d] Not more than 80 cubic feet per 2,000 pounds.

metric tons and cubic meters. This conversion introduced an additional problem, because the weight-measure ratio is not the same in the two instances. Within South America a revenue ton is defined as one metric ton or one cubic meter, whereas in most of the other trades a revenue ton is defined as 2,000 pounds or 40 cubic feet. Thus when a rate using pounds and cubic feet is given for a particular product and is to be applied on *either* weight or measure at the option of the carrier, two separate rates are generated when a conversion is made to the metric system, depending on whether the conversion is made according to weight or according to measure. To avoid this problem, a decision was

TABLE C-5. *Ocean Freight Rates to Rio de Janeiro from Selected Ports, circa 1964*[a]

(Dollars per metric ton or per cubic meter)

		Tokyo-Yokohama	U.S. Pacific-San Francisco	Buenaventura	Guayaquil	Callao	Valparaiso	Buenos Aires	U.S. Atlantic-New York	London	Rotterdam
Distance (naut. miles)		11517	7641 p	6123	5545	4909	3670	1151	4770	5212	5259
Automobiles, unboxed	C.M.	37.10	42.84			30.00	27.00		24.29[b]	13.30	18.55
Automobile spare parts	C.M.		37.54			25.50	22.50		32.69		
Tractors, unboxed	C.M.	48.59	31.80			30.00	27.00		31.80	17.01	18.55
Radio & TV sets	C.M.	49.91	63.60			28.00	25.00	22.00[c]	63.60	33.39	24.73
Refrigerators	C.M.	49.91	43.29			28.00	25.00	22.00[c]	43.29	34.63	37.99
Steel plates	Ton	26.57	26.46			16.50	18.50	16.00	24.61	19.29	22.64
Steel bars	Ton	26.57	24.80			21.00	18.00		29.53	18.95	22.64
Copper cable	Ton		66.14			27.50	24.50	15.00[d]	59.05		
Newsprint	Ton	64.96	32.52			26.30	19.00	19.00	26.57	29.62	24.11
Wood pulp	Ton		35.27[e]			22.00	16.35		26.08[f]		
Plate glass	Ton					32.00	29.00	27.50	35.43		
Wheat in bags	Ton		44.09			26.00	23.00	16.50	33.46		
Canned fruit	Ton		77.16			31.00	28.00	22.00	64.96		
Merchandise n.o.s.	C.M.			70.90	73.67	40.00	29.00	25.00			
	Ton			87.98	91.18	40.00	29.00	25.00			

Source: See text.

[a] Rates do not include port surcharges. "p" indicates distance via Panama Canal.

[b] KD or SU.

[c] Household goods.

[d] Bare wire any metal.

[e] Not more than 80 cubic feet per 2,000 pounds.

[f] Not more than 55 cubic feet per 2,000 pounds.

TABLE C-6. *Port Surcharges Applied in Selected Ports*

(Percent of freight rate or U. S. dollars per ton)

Ports of Origin	Ports of Destination				
	Callao	Valparaiso	Buenos Aires	Montevideo	Rio de Janeiro
U. S. Pacific	3.50–6.00	1.00–3.00 plus 15% of frt. rate	2.00	10% of frt. rate	8.00–14.00
U. S. Atlantic and Gulf			2.00	10% of frt. rate	8.00–10.50
Callao, Peru					1.00
Valparaiso, Chile					1.00
Buenos Aires					5.50

Source: See text.

made regarding each of the products selected as to whether the rate would in fact be based on weight or on volume. For most products there was no necessity to make this choice, because the tariff states explicitly whether the base is weight or volume. The problem arose only when the rate was based on ship's option, and even in this case this option frequently occurred only on a few routes and not on others, in which case the specific base was applied to all routes.

7. Care was taken to assure that the rates included cover identical operations on each route. In general, the rate given is for transport from the end of ship's gear in port of origin to end of ship's gear at port of destination, and hence does not include handling charges on land.

The Selection of an Efficient
Pattern of Shipping Routes

The maritime transport policy, recommended in Chapter IX for application by the Latin American Free Trade Association, focuses on the importance of the establishment of regular liner services among the LAFTA members. In order to permit freight rates as low as is possible, it is essential that the liner ships operate with a high use of their cargo capacity, that is, that a minimum of capacity be operated consistent with the amount of cargo to be transported. An important prerequisite for the attainment of this objective is the selection of an efficient pattern of shipping routes over which liner ships would maintain regular service.

In this appendix, a linear programming model is developed and applied to show one way in which an efficient pattern of shipping routes can be selected. Although the model has been solved using LAFTA data, the results are not directly applicable because of important limiting assumptions. First, annual data for one year (1962) are used and as a result, seasonal fluctuations in cargo are not considered. Second, only eight ports are considered and a realistic application should include many more ports. Third, average costs have been used, which should be refined in later applications of the model. Fourth, the cargo to be transported has been taken as fixed rather than as varying with freight rates. These limiting assumptions can be relaxed when better data are available.

Statement of the Problem and
Assumptions of the Model

Assuming that the 1962 intra-South American commerce had been transported by ships dedicated exclusively to this service and assuming that there were no bilateral reserve restraints, what pattern of shipping routes would have permitted this transport to be carried out at a minimum cost? The three basic ingredients of the model are thus (1) what was transported in 1962, (2) the concept of a shipping route, and (3), what is considered to be a cost.

252

Intra-South American Transport in 1962. The point of departure to determine intercountry maritime transport flows was Table 3-6, which presents the estimates of the Economic Commission for Latin America of 1962 intra-South American transport flows. In this table, ocean cargo is broken down into bulk liquid cargo, bulk dry cargo (iron ore and grains), general dry cargo, and refrigerated cargo. It is assumed that bulk liquid cargo, refrigerated cargo, and dry cargo do not compete with one another for shipping capacity. It is also assumed that bulk minerals could economically be transported by specialized carriers, so this cargo is also excluded from consideration. The model, therefore, deals solely with dry general cargo and bulk grain transport.

Within this category of transport, four alternatives are used. The first includes all the 1962 transport of general dry cargo and bulk grains. The second assumes that one of the objectives of LAFTA is to provide a minimum of cargo capacity between each pair of member nations so as to encourage the development of new commerce. An arbitrary minimum of 5,000 tons was selected, and in each case where transport in 1962 between two nations was less than this minimum, the actual figure has been increased to 5,000 tons.

The third alternative recognizes that because of the sporadic nature of bulk grain shipments, there will be a tendency to use tramp ships for this cargo. At the same time, it is believed that regular liner service can be maintained throughout the LAFTA area only if at least part of the grain transport is reserved for liners. For these reasons, the grain transport between Argentina and Brazil (689,000 tons) and between Argentina and Peru (308,000 tons) was reduced by one-half before being added to the transport of general dry cargo. The fourth alternative is identical to the third, but, as in the second alternative, an arbitrary minimum of 5,000 tons is set between each pair of LAFTA countries (plus Venezuela).

As can be seen in Table 3-6, nearly all of Paraguay's commerce with the other LAFTA nations is with Argentina, where it is reasonable to believe that in the future, as now, this commerce will be transported by specialized river vessels. Paraguay's limited commerce with Uruguay will probably be transported in the same fashion. The model is thus based on four alternative transport flows among eight countries, seven of the LAFTA nations plus Venezuela. Paraguay is excluded in order to simplify the model and Mexico is not included because data were not available. Table D-1 presents the transport flow alternatives that are used.

Shipping Routes. A shipping route is the path which is followed

TABLE D-1. *Intra-South American Transport, 1962*[a]

(Thousands of metric tons)

Exporting Country	Importing Country	1 Brazil	2 Uru- guay	3 Argen- tina	4 Chile	5 Peru	6 Ecua- dor	7 Colom- bia	8 Vene- zuela
Brazil									
Alternative	1	—	82	497	22	2	0	0	1
Alternative	2	—	82	497	22	5	5	5	5
Alternative	3	—	82	497	22	2	0	0	1
Alternative	4	—	82	497	22	5	5	5	5
Uruguay									
Alternative	1	10	—	239	1	0	0	0	0
Alternative	2	10	—	239	5	5	5	5	5
Alternative	3	10	—	239	1	0	0	0	0
Alternative	4	10	—	239	5	5	5	5	5
Argentina									
Alternative	1	707	68	—	122	309	0	4	24
Alternative	2	707	68	—	122	309	5	5	24
Alternative	3	363	68	—	122	155	0	4	24
Alternative	4	363	68	—	122	155	5	5	24
Chile									
Alternative	1	82	6	112	—	26	3	2	8
Alternative	2	82	6	112	—	26	5	5	8
Alternative	3	82	6	112	—	26	3	2	8
Alternative	4	82	6	112	—	26	5	5	8
Peru									
Alternative	1	38	7	19	146	—	5	5	9
Alternative	2	38	7	19	146	—	5	5	9
Alternative	3	38	7	19	146	—	5	5	9
Alternative	4	38	7	19	146	—	5	5	9
Ecuador									
Alternative	1	0	0	24	0	5	—	5	0
Alternative	2	5	5	24	5	5	—	5	5
Alternative	3	0	0	24	0	5	—	5	0
Alternative	4	5	5	24	5	5	—	5	5
Colombia									
Alternative	1	0	0	3	6	81	2	—	15
Alternative	2	5	5	5	6	81	5	—	15
Alternative	3	0	0	3	6	81	2	—	15
Alternative	4	5	5	5	6	81	5	—	15
Venezuela									
Alternative	1	28	0	72	5	5	0	6	—
Alternative	2	28	5	72	5	5	5	6	—
Alternative	3	28	0	72	5	5	0	6	—
Alternative	4	28	5	72	5	5	5	6	—

[a] Alternative 1, Actual 1962 general cargo plus bulk wheat. Excludes petroleum, refrigerated cargo, and minerals. Alternative 2, The same, but with minimum of 5,000 tons among all countries. Alternative 3, same as 1, but with one-half bulk wheat. Alternative 4, same as 2, but with one-half bulk wheat.

by a ship and is defined by the ports which it touches. Hence it is necessary to introduce the ports which will be used in the model and through which the cargo shown in Table D-1 will move. In order to simplify the model, one port is used for each country:

1. Brazil   Rio de Janeiro
2. Uruguay   Montevideo
3. Argentina   Buenos Aires
4. Chile   Valparaiso
5. Peru   Callao
6. Ecuador   Guayaquil
7. Colombia   Barranquilla
8. Venezuela   La Guaira

The use of only one port for each country introduces a serious distortion in only two cases, Brazil and Colombia. A more serious application of the model should at least introduce a northern port in Brazil and the port of Buenaventura in Colombia. This extension of the model is especially important if it is to take into consideration not only the programming of shipping routes for vessels dedicated exclusively to intra-LAFTA commerce but also the combination of intra-LAFTA service with service to other continents.

Two important assumptions are introduced in order to simplify the model. First, each shipping route is defined so as to permit a vessel operating over that route to make a round-trip, that is, to return eventually to the port from which it originally sailed. The introduction of this assumption excludes the possibility of considering a service which combines intra-LAFTA transport with transport to other continents when the vessel enters the LAFTA area via one port and leaves via another. In other words, if a ship sails from London to Rio de Janeiro, Montevideo, Buenos Aires, Valparaiso, and then proceeds to Japan to return finally to London without again touching South America, it is not considered within the model. If, however, after leaving Japan, it should return to Valparaiso and again touch Buenos Aires, Montevideo, and Rio de Janeiro before returning to London, its route would be included within the model. Second, it is assumed that a vessel operating between two ports also provides cargo capacity for each of the intermediate ports along its route. It may be that in fact this capacity will not be used, and the ship will not stop at intermediate ports, but the model assumes that the ship will stop if there is cargo available.

Using these two assumptions, it is possible to enumerate all possible routes among eight ports. There are 128 such routes, but only 58 of these are independent, that is, not repeated. Were either of the two previous assumptions relaxed, the number of routes would increase, as they would if the number of ports were increased.

In order to clarify the concept of route, as it is used here, consider a more simplified case in which there are only three ports. In Table D-2, the 18 routes that exist among these three ports are enumerated. Of these 18 routes, however, only 8 are independent. The other 10 are duplicates as can be seen from the number in parentheses after each route. Thus 121 represents the route of a ship which

TABLE D-2. *Shipping Routes Generated by Three Ports*

Routes Which Start and End With		
Port 1	Port 2	Port 3
121 (1)	232 (7)	313 (4)
1231 (2)	2312 (2)	3123 (2)
12321 (3)	23132 (6)	31213 (8)
131 (4)	212 (1)	323 (7)
1321 (5)	2132 (5)	3213 (5)
13231 (6)	21312 (8)	32123 (3)

departs from port 1, sails to port 2, and then returns to port 1. Once a ship begins operating on a continuing basis over this route, however, it is indistinguishable from 212, as on both routes a ship simply plies back and forth between ports 1 and 2.

The fact that three ports generate 8 independent shipping routes while eight ports generate 58 different routes suggests that perhaps the formula which relates ports and routes under the two assumptions given above is:

Number of Routes = Number of Ports (Number of ports — 1) + 2. If this formula is correct, then nine ports would generate 74 routes and the addition of the ninth port would add 16 routes to the problem.

Table D-3 lists the 58 routes which are used in the present model. The map on the following page will assist in visualizing these routes.

Cost of Transport. Two cost categories are used in the model, the navigation costs, which are incurred by the carrier in providing shipping capacity over a given route, and the inventory costs, which are

FIGURE D-1. *Distance in Nautical Miles between Ports Used in Model*

TABLE D-3. *Routes Used and Corresponding Cost*[a]
(Cost in U. S. dollars)

Route	Ports of Call	Carrier Cost per 1000 Tons of Capacity	Route	Ports of Call	Carrier Cost per 1000 Tons of Capacity
1	121	$1,057	30	34543	$4,086
2	12321	1,180	31	3456543	4,807
3	1234321	3,949	32	345676543	6,814
4	123454321	5,258	33	34567876543	7,343
5	12345654321	5,979	34	3218123	4,779
6	123456765432l	7,986	35	321878123	5,308
7	12345678765432l	8,515	36	32187678123	7,315
8	123456781	6,057	37	3218765678123	8,036
9	181	3,607	38	321876545678123	9,345
10	18781	4,136	39	454	1,317
11	1876781	6,143	40	45654	2,038
12	187656781	6,864	41	4567654	4,045
13	18765456781	8,173	42	456787654	4,574
14	1876543456781	10,942	43	432181234	7,548
15	187654323456781	11,065	44	43218781234	8,077
16	187654321	6,057	45	4321876781234	10,084
17	232	131	46	432187656781234	10,805
18	23432	2,900	47	565	729
19	2345432	4,209	48	56765	2,736
20	234565432	4,930	49	5678765	3,265
21	23456765432	6,937	50	54321812345	8,857
22	2345678765432	7,466	51	5432187812345	9,386
23	21812	4,656	52	543218767812345	11,393
24	2187812	5,185	53	676	2,015
25	218767812	7,192	54	67876	2,544
26	21876567812	7,913	55	6543218123456	9,578
27	2187654567812	9,222	56	654321878123456	10,107
28	218765434567812	11,991	57	787	537
29	343	2,777	58	765432181234567	11,585

[a] Ports of Call: (1) Rio de Janeiro, Brazil; (2) Montevideo, Uruguay; (3) Buenos Aires, Argentina; (4) Valparaiso, Chile; (5) Callao, Peru; (6) Guayaquil, Ecuador; (7) Barranquilla, Colombia; (8) La Guaira, Venezuela

incurred by the shipper. Since the entire model is based on the assumption that the cargo shown in Table D-1 must be transported, so that the only problem is one of deciding the most efficient pattern of shipping routes and the capacity that should be offered over each route, the cost of handling cargo in the ports is not considered. The cost of loading and unloading cargo in a port should not be greatly affected by the route the vessel is following, that is, by the ports the ship has touched before reaching this port or by the ports which the ship will later touch. For at least two reasons, this assumption is not entirely valid. First, ships of different characteristics may be used on different routes, and cargo handling costs are affected by the type of ship. Second, average handling costs in a particular port vary somewhat in relation to the total tonnage picked up or left in that port, and total tonnage handled from a particular vessel is influenced by the ports that ship has called at previously and will call at later. An application of the model at a more detailed level should examine this aspect more thoroughly.

The navigation cost to the carrier of providing 1,000 tons of capacity over each route is calculated in several stages. Table D-4 shows

TABLE D-4. *Distances Between Selected Ports*
(Nautical miles)

From \ To	2 Uruguay Montevideo	3 Argentina Buenos Aires	4 Chile Valparaiso	5 Peru Callao	6 Ecuador Guayaquil	7 Colombia Barranquilla	8 Venezuela La Guaira
Brazil							
Clockwise	1050	1175	3944	5254	5975	7125	7656
Counterclockwise	10206	10081	7312	6002	5281	4131	3600
Uruguay							
Clockwise	—	125	2894	4204	4925	6075	6606
Counterclockwise	—	11131	8362	7052	6331	5181	4650
Argentina							
Clockwise		—	2769	4079	4800	5950	6481
Counterclockwise		—	8487	7177	6456	5306	4775
Chile							
Clockwise			—	1310	2031	3181	3712
Counterclockwise			—	9946	9225	8075	7544
Peru							
Clockwise				—	721	1871	2402
Counterclockwise				—	10535	9385	8854
Ecuador							
Clockwise					—	1150	1681
Counterclockwise					—	10106	9575
Colombia							
Clockwise						—	531
Counterclockwise						—	10725

TABLE D-5. *Navigation Time Between Selected Ports*
(Hours)

From \ To	2 Uru- guay	3 Argen- tina	4 Chile	5 Peru	6 Ecua- dor	7 Colom- bia	8 Vene- zuela
Brazil							
Clockwise	75.0	83.9	281.7	375.2	426.7	513.9	551.8
Counterclockwise	733.9	725.0	527.2	433.7	382.2	295.0	257.1
Uruguay							
Clockwise	—	8.9	206.7	300.2	351.7	438.9	476.8
Counterclockwise	—	800.0	602.2	508.7	457.2	370.0	332.1
Argentina							
Clockwise		—	197.8	291.3	342.8	429.9	467.9
Counterclockwise		—	611.1	517.6	466.1	379.0	341.0
Chile							
Clockwise			—	93.6	145.1	232.2	270.1
Counterclockwise			—	715.3	663.8	576.7	538.8
Peru							
Clockwise				—	51.5	138.6	176.6
Counterclockwise				—	757.4	670.3	632.3
Ecuador							
Clockwise					—	87.1	125.1
Counterclockwise					—	721.8	683.8
Colombia							
Clockwise						—	37.9
Counterclockwise						—	771.0

Source: Table D-4. An average speed of 14 knots is assumed with an additional 5 hours for passage through the Panama Canal.

the distance between the eight ports used in the model. As it is assumed that a ship can stop at each of the ports along its route, the distances are built up as the sum of the distances between adjoining ports. Distances in both a clockwise and counterclockwise direction are shown as most routes include legs in each direction. In Table D-5, the distance between pairs of ports is transformed into navigation time on the basis of the assumption that average ship speed is 14 knots and that five additional hours are required for passage through the Panama Canal.

Navigation time is then transformed into an average cost of providing 1,000 tons of capacity over each route in Table D-3. This table is based on the assumption that a typical ship of 8,000 deadweight tons capacity has an average cost per 1,000 tons of capacity of $7 per hour, that is, $1,344 per day for the ship. This average cost includes both operating costs and depreciation. An additional cost of $394 per 1,000 tons of capacity is added for tolls to each route which includes a passage through the Panama Canal. The cost for each route was also adjusted to assure that the route cost is exactly equal to the sum of the cost corresponding to each of the segments which make up the route. This step was necessary because rounding off in prior steps could introduce slight cost deviations which, although apparently insignificant, might affect the solution given by the electronic computer.

The route costs shown in Table D-3 also include another and important adjustment. As will be explained below, the model used assures only that sufficient capacity is provided between each pair of adjoining ports to permit the transport of the given cargo volumes. No restrictions are included to assure that when a particular shipment leaves on one ship, it will stay on that same ship until it reaches its destination. In other words, the restrictions of the model do not exclude the possibility of transshipment from one ship to another during the course of transport from the port of origin to the port of destination. This transshipment should either be excluded entirely or should be assigned a specific cost. Unfortunately, no way was found to incorporate either of these alternatives into the model without increasing excessively the number of equations. Although the existence of transshipment in the solution is not so serious as might appear, because it can be eliminated manually, it certainly is preferable to have a solution with as little transshipment as possible.

The method adopted to reduce transshipment[1] is to adjust systematically the route costs, increasing slightly the cost of routes that touch only a few ports. Specifically, the rule that has been followed is the following: on routes that include two different ports, the route cost per 1,000 tons of capacity has been increased by seven dollars; on those which include three different ports, six dollars is added, and so on, so that on routes which include eight different ports, one dollar was added. Two exceptions to this rule are made in the cases of routes

---

[1] The analysis of the problem of transshipment was carried out by Robert M. Steinberg, who recommended the adjustment of the route costs and showed how transshipment can be eliminated manually after a solution has been given by the computer.

8 and 16, which are routes that circumvent all of South America in a clockwise and counterclockwise direction, respectively, where no adjustment is made in the original route cost.

The way in which the route costs have been calculated can perhaps be clarified by taking a specific example. Route 1 represents a voyage from Rio de Janeiro to Montevideo to Rio de Janeiro. From Table D-5, it can be seen that the total time required for navigation only on the round trip is 150 hours. At a cost of seven dollars per 1,000 tons of capacity per hour, the unadjusted cost to the carrier of providing 1,000 tons of capacity over route 1 is $1,050. Since route 1 includes only two separate ports, seven dollars is added to the unadjusted cost, giving $1,057, which is the cost shown in Table D-3.

Clearly enough, these crude average navigation costs are only useful as a first approximation to a complex problem. A more serious application of the model should analyze in detail more exact costs for each route. It should also be remembered that these navigation costs do not include the cost to the carrier of ship costs while in port nor cargo handling costs.

Shippers' costs must be introduced to take into account the fact that shippers are not indifferent to the route over which their goods are shipped. A shipper in Buenos Aires with cargo destined to Montevideo, for example, would much rather embark his goods on a ship operating over route 17 (232) than on a ship serving route 28 (218765434567812), as the second routing would require considerably more time. Again there are many alternative ways of calculating the cost to the shipper of sending his goods by one route instead of via another. In this simplified model, the cost to the shipper is based on the time his goods are in transit, and an inventory cost is calculated. A more realistic application of the model could also consider the time spent waiting for shipment.

In this model, it is assumed that all ships operating over the different routes have the same average speed and that all ships may stop at all intermediate ports along their route. Thus the only routing alternatives open to shippers are to send their goods clockwise to the port of destination or counterclockwise. Although these may be real alternatives in some instances, as between Brazil and Peru, they are obviously not real alternatives in others, as in the case of shipments from Uruguay to Argentina.

The total transit time required for a shipment to reach its port of destination by alternative routings has two components: the time spent navigating between ports and the time spent in ports. The time spent at sea has been estimated on the basis of Table D-5. The time spent in ports is based on the assumption that one day is spent in the port of origin, two days are spent at each intermediate port along the route, and one day is spent in the port of destination. To take a specific example, a shipment from Brazil to Peru would pass three intermediate ports whether it follows a clockwise routing or a counterclockwise routing, so that in both cases eight days should be added to the navigation time. From Table D-5, the clockwise navigation time from Brazil to Peru is 375 hours, and adding eight days in ports gives a total of 567 hours. Similarly, the total transit time following a counterclockwise routing is 625 hours.

Total transit time is converted into an inventory or shippers' cost per 1,000 tons of cargo shipped by using two additional assumptions. First, it is assumed that the average value of goods presently traded within the LAFTA area is $250 per ton. Although this figure is less than the average value per ton of goods imported into and exported from the United States, $436 and $339, respectively, the lower LAFTA figure is based on the importance of grain and lumber transport. Second, to this assumed average value per ton of LAFTA cargo is applied a rate of interest of 6 percent a year. The shippers' cost per thousand tons of cargo transported is thus $1.71 per hour. This figure, applied to the total transit time required by alternative clockwise or counterclockwise routings, gives the total shippers' cost per thousand tons of goods shipped. Where the shippers' cost via one routing differed so greatly from that via the opposite routing that all goods would always use the shorter routing, only the shorter routing was used in the model. The shippers' cost per 1,000 tons of goods shipped for each routing is shown in Table D-6.

The Model[2]

The model is designed to determine simultaneously (1) what combination of the 58 possible routes among the eight ports should be used; (2) what tonnage capacity should be provided over each of the routes used; and (3) what should be the routing of each port-to-port movement so as to carry out the transport requirements shown in Table D-1 while minimizing the sum of carrier and shipper costs. The model consists of two sets of equations in addition to the cost function which is to be minimized. The first set of equations concerns

[2] Gary Fromm, Clell Harral, and other staff members of the Brookings Institution assisted in elaborating the model.

Shipments		Clockwise Routing		Counterclockwise Routing	
From Port	To Port	Variable	Cost per 1,000 Tons Shipped	Variable	Cost per 1,000 Tons Shipped
1	2	59	$ 210	—	
1	3	60	308	—	
1	4	61	728	62	$1,312
1	5	63	970	64	1,069
1	6	65	1,141	66	900
1	7	67	1,371	68	669
1	8	69	1,518	70	522
2	3	71	97	—	
2	4	72	518	—	
2	5	73	759	74	1,279
2	6	75	930	76	1,110
2	7	77	1,161	78	879
2	8	79	1,308	80	732
2	1	—		81	210
3	4	82	421	—	
3	5	83	662	84	1,377
3	6	85	833	86	1,208
3	7	87	1,064	88	975
3	8	89	1,211	90	830
3	1	—		91	308
3	2	—		92	97
4	5	93	243	—	
4	6	94	412	—	
4	7	95	643	96	1,396
4	8	97	790	98	1,249
4	1	99	1,312	100	728
4	2	10		101	518
4	3	—		102	421
5	6	103	171	—	
5	7	104	402	—	
5	8	105	549	—	
5	1	106	1,069	107	970
5	2	108	1,279	109	759
5	3	110	1,377	111	662
5	4	—		112	243
6	7	113	231	—	
6	8	114	378	—	
6	1	115	900	116	1,141
6	2	117	1,110	118	930
6	3	119	1,208	120	833
6	4	—		121	412
6	5	—		122	171
7	8	123	147	—	
7	1	124	669	125	1,371
7	2	126	879	127	1,161
7	3	128	975	129	1,064
7	4	130	1,396	131	643
7	5	—		132	402
7	6	—		133	231
8	1	134	522	135	1,518
8	2	136	732	137	1,308
8	3	138	830	139	1,211
8	4	140	1,249	141	790
8	5	—		142	549
8	6	—		143	378
8	7	—		144	147

the creation and use of transport capacity and the second stipulates that the required transport movements shown in Table D-1 must be carried out.

Each of the 16 equations of the first set of equations corresponds to a directed arc between two adjoining ports; the first eight equations refer to clockwise arcs and the second eight to counterclockwise arcs. Each equation stipulates that the capacity provided over the corresponding arc by the different routes which include that arc must be equal to or exceed the use of capacity over that arc by shipments. Thus the first part of the first equation is the sum of all the routes which, if service were provided over them, would create capacity between port 1 and port 2. The second part of the same equation, which is subtracted from the first part, is the sum of all the shipment routings which, if they were followed, would absorb capacity between port 1 and port 2. So that this difference may be placed equal to zero, a slack variable is also subtracted from the left-hand side of the equation that represents capacity created over the arc between port 1 and port 2 which is not used.

Each of the 56 equations of the second set corresponds to the cargo shipments that must be transported from each port to each of the other ports. Each equation states that the sum of the cargo transported between a particular pair of ports in a clockwise direction plus that transported in a counterclockwise direction must be equal to the total cargo to be transported between those two ports. In the instances where only one routing is considered (see Table D-6), the movement variable is set equal to the transport which must be carried out. Several examples of each set of equations are shown on the following page.

The cost equation which is to be minimized is easily derived from Tables D-3 and D-6. Table D-3 shows the cost associated with providing 1,000 tons of capacity over each of the 58 routes (variable x_1 through x_{58}) while Table D-6 shows the shippers' cost of sending 1,000 tons of cargo via the alternative routings (variables x_{59} through x_{144}).

Since all the entries in the data matrix are either plus one, minus one, or zero, it is probable that an algorithm can be derived which takes into account this characteristic. It is even possible that the algorithm is simple enough to permit its application without the use of a computer. Here, however, an electronic computer was used, and the problem was treated as a traditional linear programming problem. Two separate computer runs were made. The first used a cost function that included both carrier and shipper costs, while the second included only carrier costs. In both runs the four alternative transport requirements shown in Table D-1 were included, so that a total of eight solutions were obtained. Each run required slightly more than three minutes of computer time.

Arc Equations

Arc 12: $x_1 + x_2 + x_3 + x_4 + x_5 + x_6 + x_7 + x_8 + x_{23} + x_{24} + x_{25} + x_{26} + x_{27} + x_{28} + x_{34} + x_{35} + x_{36} + x_{37}$
$+ x_{38} + x_{43} + x_{44} + x_{45} + x_{46} + x_{50} + x_{51} + x_{52} + x_{55} + x_{56} + x_{58} - x_{59} - x_{60} - x_{61} - x_{63} - x_{65}$
$- x_{67} - x_{69} - x_{108} - x_{110} - x_{117} - x_{119} - x_{126} - x_{128} - x_{130} - x_{136} - x_{138} - x_{140} - x_{145} = 0$
$\cdots\cdots$
$\cdots\cdots$
$\cdots\cdots$

Arc 87: $x_7 + x_{10} + x_{11} + x_{12} + x_{13} + x_{14} + x_{15} + x_{16} + x_{22} + x_{24} + x_{25} + x_{26} + x_{27} + x_{28} + x_{33} + x_{35} + x_{36}$
$+ x_{37} + x_{38} + x_{42} + x_{44} + x_{45} + x_{46} + x_{49} + x_{51} + x_{52} + x_{54} + x_{56} + x_{57} - x_{62} - x_{64} - x_{66} - x_{68}$
$- x_{74} - x_{76} - x_{78} - x_{84} - x_{86} - x_{88} - x_{96} - x_{135} - x_{137} - x_{139} - x_{141} - x_{142} - x_{143} - x_{144}$
$- x_{154} = 0$
$\cdots\cdots$
$\cdots\cdots$
$\cdots\cdots$

Shipment Equations

$x_{59} = 82$
$x_{60} = 497$
$x_{61} + x_{62} = 22$
$\cdots\cdots$
$\cdots\cdots$
$\cdots\cdots$

The Results

The computer solution shows for each of the eight alternatives used the routes that should be used, the capacity to be provided over each route, the direction each shipment should take, and the total cost of transport. In addition the solution also indicates where excess capacity exists over particular routes.

Table D-7 presents the routes selected under each of the eight alternatives, the capacity provided over each, and the corresponding total cost. As can be seen, under each alternative nine routes are used. Table D-8 shows the unused capacity on particular arcs which is produced under each of the eight alternatives. In each instance, excess capacity occurs on seven arcs.

Under the first four alternatives, those which consider both carrier

TABLE D-7. *Capacity Provided over Selected Routes—Unadjusted Solutions under Eight Alternatives*
(Thousands of metric tons)

Routes Utilized	Considering Shipper and Carrier Costs				Considering Only Carrier Costs			
	Actual Transport 1962 (1)	Actual with 5,000 Tons Minimum (2)	One-Half Bulk Wheat (3)	One-Half Wheat with 5,000 Tons Minimum (4)	Actual Transport 1962 (5)	Actual with 5,000 Tons Minimum (6)	One-Half Bulk Wheat (7)	One-Half Wheat with 5,000 Tons Minimum (8)
2	510	493	382	365	483	469	376	369
3	77	51	—	—	97	92	—	—
4	150	166	119	119	130	130	73	68
5	—	—	—	—	27	34	27	34
6	79	71	74	71	99	107	99	107
7	20	41	—	13	—	—	—	—
8	74	71	14	31	74	71	14	31
17	44	42	131	138	71	66	158	162
20	27	24	27	24	—	—	—	—
38	—	—	21	28	—	—	—	—
43	29	54	64	66	9	13	43	38
50	—	—	—	—	—	—	25	15
51	—	—	—	—	20	36	21	36
58	—	—	4	—	—	—	—	—
Total Cost ($)	4,389,536	4,689,675	3,508,037	3,766,922	3,301,751	3,532,769	2,628,152	2,817,316

TABLE D-8. *Slack on Arcs*

(Thousands of metric tons)

Alter-native	12	23	34	45	56	67	78	81	18	87	76	65	54	43	32	21
1	261	174			168	144	59						31	94		
5	261	174			168	144	59						31	94		
2	254	158			160	141	55						47	114		
6	254	158			160	141	55						47	114		
3				63	108	84			60	1					230	143
7				63	108	84			60	1					230	143
4				67	120	101	15		40						226	130
8				67	120	101	15		40						226	130

and shipper costs, individual shipments *always* are transported in the direction which minimizes shipper costs. In no instance is a shipment moved in the direction of greater shipper cost, as shown in Table D-6. Under the second four alternatives, those which consider only carrier costs and ignore shipper inventory costs, again all shipments move in the direction of lesser shipper costs with only two exceptions. Under both the sixth and eighth alternatives, the shipments from Brazil to Ecuador move in a clockwise direction, while the cost to shippers would be lower in a counterclockwise direction, and the shipments from Ecuador to Brazil move in a counterclockwise direction, although the cost to shippers would be lower using the clockwise direction. In both instances, the total tonnage to be moved from Brazil to Ecuador and from Ecuador to Brazil is 5,000 tons, that is, the traffic is exactly balanced. In both instances, the service through the Panama Canal, which is more costly to the carrier because of the canal tolls, has been avoided.

Because of these two exceptions, it is understandable that the routes selected in the solution of alternative number six should differ from those of alternative number two, despite the fact that the total port-to-port transport is identical under the two alternatives. A similar difference should exist logically between alternative number eight and alternative number four. When just the carrier cost is calculated for alternative number two and is compared with the carrier cost under alternative number six, the former exceeds the latter by $780. This same difference of $780 exists between the carrier costs corresponding to alternatives numbers four and eight.

The difference in the routes selected under alternatives one and five, where both the total port-to-port transport and the direction of individual shipments are identical, is at first glance more difficult to explain. The answer lies in the fact that because of the way in which route costs have been determined, different combinations of routes can have an identical cost. For this reason, the carrier cost of the pattern of routes selected under alternative one is exactly equal to the carrier cost under alternative five. Similarly, the carrier cost under alternative three is exactly equal to the cost under alternative seven, despite the fact that a different pattern of routes has been selected. Because of the way in which carrier costs have been defined in the model as the mere sum of costs between pairs of ports, there is no unique solution to the problem. Had real costs been introduced, which reflect more accurately variations in carrier cost over different routes, the routes selected should have been identical when the transport to be carried out is identical.

The solution given to the linear programming problem does not relate individual shipments to particular routes, and hence does not exclude the possibility of transshipment from a ship operating over one route to a ship operating over a different route. To determine whether transshipment has in fact occurred in the solution to one of the alternatives, it is necessary to assign the individual shipments to appropriate routes. This was carried through manually only for alternatives one and five. In the case of alternative one, it was found that no route had been included in the solution which would permit direct shipments from Buenos Aires to Barranquilla. The solution implicitly assumed that these goods would be transshipped between routes 7 and 43. In order to permit direct shipments, a new route, route 35, was introduced in the solution, with capacity just sufficient to permit the required transport. So as not to increase the total capacity provided, a reduction was made in the capacity provided over routes 7 and 43. Finally, to complete the balance, it was necessary to introduce another new route, number 29, and also to increase capacity over route 6. With these modifications, it was possible to carry out all the required transport using only direct shipments. The changes introduced increased the total cost of alternative number one by $32. Table D-9 shows the adjusted solution for alternative one, where each shipment has been assigned to a particular route. It should be noted that considerable flexibility exists for this assignment, as particular shipments can often be assigned to any of a number of alternative routes.

Figure D-2 shows graphically the routes selected after these ad-

Movement	Tons	Routes										
		2	3	4	6	7	8	17	20	29	35	43
59	82		55								4	23
60	497	497										
61	22		22									
63	2			2								
66	0											
68	0											
70	1											1
71	239		47	148				44				
72	1											1
73	0											
75	0											
78	0											
80	0											
81	10			7		3						
82	122		55		2	8	26		3	4		24
83	309			148	81	8	48		24			
85	0											
88	4										4	
90	24											24
91	707	510		105	79	13						
92	68							44	24			
93	26						26					
94	3								3			
95	2				2							
97	8					8						
100	82		77		4							1
101	6					3			3			
102	112			86	26							
103	5								5			
104	5				5							
105	9					5	4					
107	38			38								
109	7			7								
111	19			19								
112	146			86	60							
113	5				5							
114	0											
115	0											
118	0											
120	24								24			
121	0											
122	5					2			3			
123	15						15					
124	0											
126	0											
128	3						3					
131	6				4	2						
132	81				79	2						
133	2					2						
134	28										4	24
136	0											
138	72						71					1
141	5					5						
142	5					5						
143	0											
144	6					6						
Tons	2813	1007	256	646	347	72	193	88	89	4	12	99

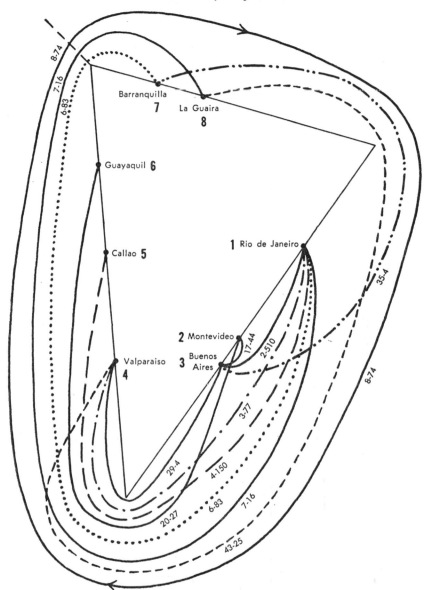

Number before dash shows route; Number after dash shows capacity provided over that route.

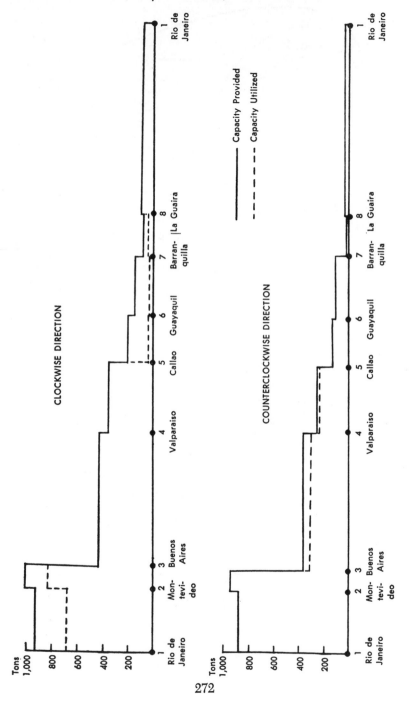

justments have been made and the capacity provided over each route. As can be seen, the routes are concentrated around the southern half of the continent. Figure D-3 shows the capacity provided and used under alternative number one. In a clockwise direction, there is excess capacity between Rio de Janeiro and Buenos Aires and between Callao and La Guaira. In a counterclockwise direction, there is excess capacity between Callao and Buenos Aires. Despite the fact that trade flows are unbalanced between La Guaira and Rio de Janeiro, there is no excess capacity over this arc in either direction. The use of route 8, which provides capacity in a clockwise direction around the entire continent, absorbs the surplus flow.

In the case of alternative number five, the solution provided by the computer implicitly assumed transshipment for three shipments. Again these were removed manually by introducing new routes and reducing capacity on other routes. As a result, the total cost was increased by $200. Figure D-4 presents graphically the routes selected. Although this pattern of routes differs from that presented in Figure D-2, the capacity provided between each pair of ports is identical in each solution. Presumably, it would have been possible to adjust the computer solution in the case of alternative five in a way which would increase the total cost by less than $200. Table D-10 shows the adjusted solution for alternative five, where each shipment has been assigned to a particular route.

At the end of Table D-10, the cost per ton carried over each route has been calculated. Although the average cost is $1.17 per ton, the cost on different routes varies from $0.065 to $4.09 per ton, depending on the distance shipments are transported and on how well the capacity provided over the route is used. Again, it should be noted that the arbitrary assignment of individual shipments to particular routes affects the resulting cost per ton transported.

It is also of interest to note to what extent the cost per ton transported varies among the four alternatives selected, that is, according to whether all bulk wheat is included or only half the bulk wheat, and whether a minimum of 5,000 tons capacity is provided between each pair of ports. This variation can be seen in the table on page 275.

It is immediately clear from this table that the average cost per ton of cargo transported is higher if all the wheat is assigned to liner ships, as the cost drops from $1.17 to $1.14 if half the bulk wheat is given to tramp ships. Presumably, other alternatives could be found to distribute the wheat in such a way as to reduce this average cost even further. It is also interesting to note that the provision of a

FIGURE D-4. *Routes Selected and Capacity Provided Under Alternative 5*

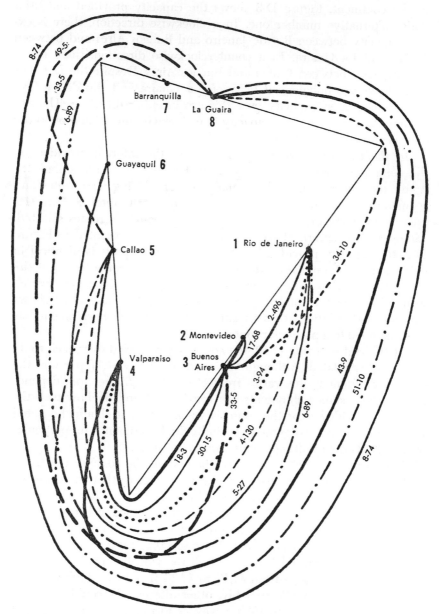

Number before dash shows route; Number after dash shows capacity provided over that route.

274

Alternatives	Carrier Cost per Ton Transported
5. Actual tonnage transported—1962	$1.17
6. Actual tonnage, with a minimum of 5,000 tons between each pair of ports	1.21
7. Actual tonnage with only one-half of bulk wheat	1.14
8. One-half of bulk wheat with a minimum of 5,000 tons between each pair of ports	1.17

minimum of capacity between each pair of ports does not increase the carrier cost unduly. Although the table above is based on the original computer solutions, which includes some transshipment, it has been seen that this transshipment can be eliminated with only a slight increase in total cost.

By comparing the average cost per ton transported under the first four alternatives, where both carrier and shipper costs are included, with the cost under the second four alternatives, where only the carrier cost is included, it can be seen that the inclusion of the shipper cost increases the total average cost per ton by $0.38 to $0.40, that is, by roughly one-third of the carrier cost as defined here.

The average carrier cost per ton of cargo transported within the LAFTA area shown in the table above will undoubtedly seem incredibly low when compared with the freight rates presented in Tables C-1–C-5. There it was seen that present rates vary from a low of around $15 per ton to well over $80, depending on the particular product and route, while the computer solution gives an average cost of $1.14 to $1.21 per ton. Part of the difference can be explained on the basis of the narrow definition of carrier cost which has been used in the model, where carrier cost includes solely the navigation cost to the carrier between ports. In the course of a year, a liner ship operating within the LAFTA area spends only 35 to 40 percent of its time navigating, and the rest of its time is spent in port. Thus the total carrier cost per ton, without including cargo handling charges and port charges, is perhaps around $3.35, assuming nearly complete use of cargo capacity as is implicit in the computer solution. Handling charges and port charges per ton of cargo handled are perhaps at least $8 to $10 when both loading and unloading are included, so that the total cost per ton incurred by the carrier with efficient ship utilization is around $12 to $14. This, however, is an average cost for the entire LAFTA area based on actual transport in 1962, so that the

TABLE D-10. Alternative 5—Adjusted Solution

Movement	Tons	Routes														
		2	3	4	5	6	8	17	18	30	33	34	43	48	49	51
59	82			10		72										
60	497	483				14										
61	22		22													
63	2			2												
65	0															
68	0															
70	1															1
71	239	3	40	128				68								
72	1		1													
73	0															
75	0															
78	0															
80	0															
81	10						10									
82	122		3	7	27	2	64						9			10
83	309		71	128		87			3	15	5					
85	0															
88	4															4
90	24											10	9			5
91	707	496	9	85	27	89										1
92	68							68								
93	26				24		2									
94	3				3											
95	2					2										
97	8						8									
100	82		82													
101	6										8					
102	112		3		1	89							9			10

276

Item														
103	5													
104	5													
105		9												
107			38											
109			7											
111			19											
112	146	80	66											
113		5												
114	0													
116	0													
118	0													
120	24			2½										
121	0													
122	5			3										
123	15								15					
124	0													
126	0													
128	3							3						
131	6				6									
132	81				81									
133	2				2									
134	28					2								
136	0													
138	72					72								
141	5									5				
142	5												5	
143	0													
144	6													
Tons carried (000)	2,813	982	231	490	114	536	182	136	6	15	13	20	36	5	47
Adjusted Cost Thousands of dollars	3,302	585	371	684	161	711	448	9	9	61	37	48	68	16	94
Cost/Ton Carried ($)	1.17	0.60	1.61	1.39	1.42	1.33	2.46	0.065	1.45	4.09	2.82	2.39	1.89	3.27	2.00
Cost/Ton of Capacity Provided ($)		1.18	3.95	5.26	5.98	7.99	6.06	0.13	2.90	4.09	7.34	4.78	7.55	3.27	9.39
Tons of Capacity Provided (000)	496	94	130	27	89	74	68	3	15	5	10	9	5	10

cost per ton on specific routes will be higher or lower than this average.

The fact that rates are considerably higher than this average on nearly all routes at the present time is an indication of the potential benefits which are possible from a more efficient use of ship cargo capacity. The application of programming techniques such as those outlined in this appendix to select shipping routes and to adjust the capacity offered over those routes to transport requirements can make an important contribution to improving ship utilization and to lowering transport costs.

Index

Index*

Accessibility of countries within the South American continent: as a determinant of trade patterns, 35-36; good and poor access between pairs of countries, 37-39

Agricultural products: increase of through economic integration, 63; marketing of, 63; intra-South American trade in, *64*

—trade in products of animal origin: meat and live animals, 66-68; hides and hair, 68; dairy products and animal fat, 68

—trade in products of plant origin: grains and milled grains, 68-69; raw and baled fibers, 69; fresh fruits, legumes, vegetables, 69, 70; coffee, cocoa, tea, yerba mate, 70; canned and processed food, 70; vegetable oils, 70

Air transport in South America: importance of for mountain regions, 23, 211; use of for perishable products, 69; suitability of for sparsely populated regions, 72; in colonization programs, 76; passengers carried by, *202, 203, 204;* factors in the growth of, 203, 205, 207; role of in international transport, 203-9; freight carried by, *206,* 207, *208,* 209; operating costs and freight rates, 208; efficiency of for economic integration, 209-10; defects of, 210-11

ALAMAR. *See* Latin American Shipowners Association

Amazon Basin region: geographic description of, 27-29; transport served

by navigable rivers of, 28, 225; effect of sparse population on choice of transport modes for, 201, 225

Amazon River: travel on by river vessels and ocean steamers, 23, 28, 201; navigation difficulties in, 23, 29; transport priorities for, 215, 216

Andes (Eastern slope) region: geographic description of, 22-23; strategy for future development of, 23; height of as impediment to railroad construction, 169-71; transport planning for, 216

Anesi, Carlos P., 196, 199

Angulo, Enrique H., 148

Argentina: signatory of the Montevideo Treaty, 5; part of in the industrial heartland region, 11, 12; part of in the hinterland region, 14-17; mentioned *passim*

Asociación Latinoamericana de Armadores (ALAMAR), 111*n*, 127*n*. *See also* Latin American Shipowners Association

Asociación Latinoamericana de Libre Comercio, 110*n*, 112*n*

Avendaño Fuenzalida, Andrés, 127, 128

Babson, Roger, 11

Baerresen, Donald W., 31*n*, 32*n*, 34*n*, *36n*

Balance of payments of Latin American countries: foreign exchange earned or saved by national merchant fleets, 96-102, 106; transportation credits and debits in (by country), 97, *98, 99;* expenditures in domestic and foreign exchange by transport carriers, 100, *101*

281

Living standards: divergence of between rural and urban communities, 1; improvement of through establishing new industries, 6; effects of increased population on, 71

Lloyd Brasileiro: a shipping service opened to Japan and Africa, 103

McNeil, Wilfred J., 99n

Magariños de Mello, Mateo J., 96, 97n

Marín Vicuña, Santiago, 169n

Maritime shipping industry: characteristics of, 115-17

Maritime transport in South America: distances between ports, 24; intracontinental commerce dependent on, 39, 44-47, 88; in trade with other continents, 44; types of cargo moved by, 44, 45, 114; tonnage carried by (1962), 45, 46, 128; potentials of for economic integration, 95, 216-24; costs associated with, 114, 116-17; categories of freight vessels used in, 115; not conducive to creating new industrial centers, 116, 226; "pooling agreements" among carriers, 120-21; appropriate and inappropriate products for, 121-22; variables in service of, 122, 124-28; improving service of vs. protecting LAFTA ships, 217-18; international regulatory commission suggested for, 220-23; lack of statistics on, 221

Martirena de Mantel, Ana M., 54n

Marx, Daniel, Jr., 159n

Mexico: signatory of the Montevideo Treaty, 5; mentioned passim

Meyer, John R., 159n

Montevideo Treaty: designed for cooperation in the increase of trade, 5, 121; position assigned to agriculture by, 63; emphasis of on industrial products, 71; transport principles of, 107-8; bilateral cargo reserves incompatible with purpose of, 156; formulas of on intrazonal trade barriers, 212

Motor vehicles. See Highways

National defense: consideration of in formulating transport policies, 2; importance of national merchant fleets for, 94, 95-96

National economy: in relation to the continental economy, 4; merchant fleets serving as protection for, 106

National merchant fleets: growth of in selected countries, 91, 93; tonnage of in selected countries, 92; arguments in support of, 94; "trade follows the flag," 94, 102-7; a factor in national defense, 95-96; a means of assuring ocean transport in world crises, 95, 106; as contributors to the balance of payments, 99; high cost of vs. benefits, 107; cargo reserves for vessels of, 108-12

Nemec, Frank A., 96n

Northeast Brazil region: geographic description of, 29-30; poverty and overpopulation of, 29, 77; need of improved land transport in, 216

Ocean transport. See Maritime transport

Organization of American States: Economic Conference of on transportation in the La Plata River System, 15n, 200n; Meeting of Governmental Experts in Civil Aviation, 76n, 210n; report of the Ad Hoc Committee of Experts of the American Republics for the Study of the System of Freight and Insurance Rates, 135-36, 146; port conferences sponsored by, 219

Pan American Conference on the Regulation of Automotive Traffic (1930), 195

Pan American Highway Congress, 195, 196

Pan American Highway Education Confederation, 195, 196

Pan American Highway idea (early 1920's), 194, 196, 203

Pan American Highway System, 196, 197, 198, 199, 203, 228

Pan American Railway idea (proposed